This Is Our Freedom

This Is Our Freedom

Motherhood in the Shadow of the
American Prison System

Geniece Crawford Mondé

UNIVERSITY OF CALIFORNIA PRESS

University of California Press
Oakland, California

© 2022 by Geniece Crawford Mondé

Library of Congress Cataloging-in-Publication Data

Names: Mondé, Geniece Crawford, 1983- author.
Title: This is our freedom : motherhood in the shadow of
  the American prison system / Geniece Crawford
  Mondé.
Description: Oakland, California : University of
  California Press, [2022] | Includes bibliographical
  references and index.
Identifiers: LCCN 2021050536 (print) | LCCN 2021050537
  (ebook) | ISBN 9780520380714 (hardcover) |
  ISBN 9780520380738 (paperback) |
  ISBN 9780520380745 (ebook)
Subjects: LCSH: Mothers—United States—Interviews. |
  Women ex-convicts—United States—21st century.
Classification: LCC HQ759 .M849 2022 (print) |
  LCC HQ759 (ebook) | DDC 306.874/30973—dc23/
  eng/20211109
LC record available at https://lccn.loc.gov/2021050536
LC ebook record available at https://lccn.loc
  .gov/2021050537

Manufactured in the United States of America

28 27 26 25 24 23 22
10 9 8 7 6 5 4 3 2 1

To my parents
Orlene and Glenroy Crawford

Contents

Contents

Acknowledgments

Writing one's first book is a daunting undertaking at any time. To begin the endeavor in a year like 2020 felt, at many times, nigh impossible. As I wrote in the midst of looming uncertainty, fueled by a global pandemic and the palpable heartache and passion of protests for justice, I meditated on motherhood. I thought of the women who candidly shared their stories with me, their joys and their tears. I thought of how motherhood drove many of these women forward and how, for some, it was a role fraught with ambivalence and pain. Had I embarked on this project solely driven by intellectual curiosity, I do not doubt that the tsunami that was 2020 would have drowned out any ability to write or think. But after a day or two of tears or rage, or whatever emotion the day's news elicited, I thought of a woman sitting across from me, smiling at the thought of a new chapter in her life or grimacing at the recollection of all that life had stolen. It was in those moments that I stilled myself, muttered a prayer, and began this work anew. To each woman who gave of her time and a portion of her story, I thank you from a place where words do not suffice. And, to the staff and organizations who generously opened their doors to me, my gratitude runs deep.

I am deeply indebted to the scholars who shaped my formative years. From my undergraduate advisors, Michael West and William Martin, to my graduate advisors and dissertation committee members, Kathryn Edin, Bruce Western, and Chris Winship. There is a tender place in my heart for the scholars who provided me with a glimpse of what was possible for a Black girl from Queens, whose world felt a long way from Cambridge. Thank you, Marla Frederick, Alice Brown Collins, and Audrey Ellerbee Bowden, for modeling excellence for this generation and for the next. To Dr. Bowden: I have never forgotten the act of kindness and generosity which you extended toward me when I was doubtful I could complete graduate school. You may be world-renowned as an engineer and innovator, but your lived-out faith and mentorship is intimately known to those who have been blessed to cross your path. To the friends and mentors who brought laughter and joy during my graduate studies, Temi Ogunbodede, Dr. Tiffany Jackson, and Tammi Ruley, Pastors Brian and Carmen Greene and Deacon Vera Alleyne, thank you for making my life in Cambridge full and balanced. I will always be grateful for the decades-long friendships I have had with Ysmaelle Pierre-Louis, Roman Hailu and Florence Akinyemi that have seen me through life's vicissitudes. During the writing of this book, I was grateful that I could share updates, no matter how small, with fellow New Yorker–turned–Charlottean Gina Antilus.

In the very early days of this project, when I was unsure if I should even submit a proposal, I spoke to two women who encouraged me that the book had merit and generously shared their own experiences in writing their first monographs. Great thanks to Christy Cobb and Magdalena Krajewska for being wonderful colleagues. The book also greatly benefited from the feedback of Anna Curtis and anonymous reviewers. It was so refreshing to read comments that were detailed, constructive and kind. This work would not have been possible without the sabbatical leave that afforded me uninterrupted time to write during the fall of 2020. To the 2019 faculty development committee and the provost's office at Wingate University, many, many thanks.

One of the unexpected sources of support that encouraged me as I wrote was the Black Women's Studies Association's writing group, led by Dr. Nneka Dennie. No matter how my week was going, I knew that there were two hours on a Wednesday afternoon in which I would sit with other sister scholars (via video conference) and commit myself to the task at hand. It was through that writing group that I had the wonderful fortune of connecting with Dr. Janet Garcia-Hallett, who became a writing accountability partner during the fall of 2020. Sometimes my only motivation to write during a given week was my commitment to keep our appointment.

To my editor, Maura Roessner, thank you for believing in this work and supporting me throughout this process. I did not know what to expect in an academic editor, yet I can say that you have exceeded my expectations in every way. I honestly cannot say enough about how grateful I am for your support, particularly in the moments when self-doubt reared its head. A special thanks to everyone at the University of California Press who has worked to make this the best book possible. Thank you, Madison Wetzell, Cindy Fulton, and Teresa Iafolla.

When I began interviewing women for this project as a twenty-something-year-old graduate student, motherhood felt abstract. By the time I began writing this book, however, I had come to feel the weight of motherhood in a personal and intimate way. I thought of my two boys, Jonathan and Jude, often as I wrote and empathized with the women featured in this book in unexpected and palpable ways. Many of us desire nothing but the best for our children, irrespective of life's arrows or gifts. So, to you, my dear hearts, be all of who you are. You are more than this world can hold. To my husband, Jean-Mérès, I love you deeply and can say that the man that you are and the father that you are has helped me to fulfill this goal. *Mwen renmen ou.*

To my parents, Orlene and Glenroy Crawford, thank you for instilling in your girls the importance of education and hard work. I could not imagine what it was like leaving Jamaica and arriving in Queens, NY, with a small child in tow. Mom, I know that perhaps no one feels the weight of this work more than you do, since you witnessed the tears and frustrations of my intellectual insecurities from grade school onward. I am grateful to have a smart and gifted younger sister, Adriana, who I do not doubt will impact the world with her words. I know that my grandmother, Lottie Wilson, would have been so incredibly proud to hold this book in her hands and I feel her joy and pride, though for now we are separated by this earthly plane. In so many ways, through family and friends, I have been deeply blessed. And when those blessings have felt a long way off, I have been upheld by and leaned upon the Everlasting Arms.

Introduction

The scene in downtown Columbia, South Carolina, was a raucous one. Unified chants of "No more years!" and "Impeachment now!" were interspersed with declarations of approval for the president of the United States. Against the backdrop of protest signs and red "Make America Great Again" baseball caps, a very different gathering was being held at nearby Benedict College.[1] On his first visit to a historically Black college, President Donald Trump was scheduled to receive the Bipartisan Justice Award at the 2019 Second Step Presidential Justice Forum. While the protesters outside decried the president's record on social justice and immigration policy, inside he received a warm reception as he touted the impact of his administration's signature criminal justice reform measure.[2]

The Formerly Incarcerated Reenter Society Transformed Safely Transitioning Every Person Act or the First Step Act, was passed by Congress the previous year and by the summer of 2019 was responsible for the early release of over three thousand nonviolent drug offenders in federal custody.[3] According to the president, the First Step Act had done more to benefit the African-American community than any recent criminal justice reform legislation. His remarks, no doubt, were a thinly veiled jab at his predecessor, the first African-American president of the United States. While critics would dismiss Donald Trump's words as nothing more than political bluster, it was difficult to dismiss the words of one of the event's attendees, Tanesha Bannister.

In many ways Tanesha embodied everything that was wrong with the War on Drugs.[4] In response to the rising drug epidemic of the 1980s, the United States' criminal justice system implemented policies and laws that led to militarized policing and mass incarceration.[5] By the time Tanesha was arrested in 2002 her sentence, though harsh, was hardly surprising.[6] At twenty-seven years old, Tanesha along with fifteen other defendants, was arrested and charged with conspiracy to sell five kilos of cocaine and fifty grams of crack cocaine. Upon her conviction she was given a sentence of life imprisonment, which was later reduced to twenty-three years. Because the First Step Act included a provision to retroactively apply the 2010 Fair Sentencing Act, nonviolent drug offenders like Tanesha were eligible for early release. Signed into law by President Barack Obama, the 2010 law was intended to reduce the sentencing disparity between crack and powdered cocaine possession, which was largely responsible for lengthy sentences of minority nonviolent drug offenders.[7]

Standing on a stage in the same city where she was sentenced sixteen years prior, Tanesha was unambiguous in declaring her feelings about the First Step Act and the politicians who supported the legislation. Turning to face the president, she smiled and declared: "I want to thank the president for giving me another lease on life. If it wasn't for you Mr. President I'd still be serving five [more] years in prison." The audience erupted in applause.[8] Advocates of prison reform want nothing more than for nonviolent offenders like Tanesha Bannister to be released from lengthy prison sentences.[9] But what happens after the applause? What happens to the majority of women who don't gain national attention or meet politicians or celebrities? More often than not they and the lives impacted by their incarceration are easily forgotten. While leaving prison is an important step a woman takes toward starting a new chapter in life, it is far from the end of her relationship with the criminal justice system. The seventy women I interviewed for this study provide insight into the challenges of navigating life after prison and the factors that shaped their lives before, during and after incarceration.[10]

Central to understanding the challenges a woman faces after incarceration is realizing that imprisonment is not an event that begins and ends at a definitive moment in time. Rather, it can be thought of as a life experience that brings into sharp relief the lived experiences of the past, while framing one's prospects for the future.[11] Each year, when approximately two million women are released from prisons and jails across the United States, they are faced with the daunting task of rebuilding their lives.[12] The encompassing nature of the prison system is such that carcerality impacts almost every aspect of a formerly incarcerated woman's life. Her relationships, employment opportunities, and even her very body is policed based on the assumption that criminality is the default worldview through which she must define herself and be judged by others. Even the parts of her identity that might be more readily viewed as socially acceptable are often ignored or delegitimized as a result of her ex-offender status. This is key to understanding how and why formerly incarcerated women frame and reframe their identities as women and as mothers.[13]

This book is as much about women like Tanesha Bannister as it is about the broader factors that create and sustain a system bent toward punitiveness rather than restoration. You see, the harrowing images of overcrowded prisons and jails exists alongside the silence of the empty seat at the holiday dinner. The scale and frequency of both scenes are woven into the fabric of so-called American exceptionalism, and without interrogating how the structural shapes the individual, it is difficult to understand the relationship between the experiences of formerly incarcerated women and the living legacy of mass imprisonment. The women I met in Massachusetts, New York City, and New England City may not have articulated their challenges using the language of social science but they knew those experiences intimately.[14]

Upon leaving prison, women return home, or finding no home to return to, grapple with a sense of placelessness in the literal and figurative senses.[15] Most women are mothers when they enter prison, and so for many women motherhood provides a type of grounding, giving them a sense of purpose as they secure their footing in the world. But being a mother with a criminal record is an identity fraught with tension because it presents women with competing messages about their social value. In one sense motherhood is perceived as an identity that holds the rare place as an almost impenetrable moral benchmark when performed in a way that meets mainstream norms.[16] But that framing of motherhood did not apply to the women I met, and they knew it. Because the women I spoke with were morally compromised in the eyes of society, the ability to approximate a version of motherhood which met the expectations of state actors and rehabilitation organizations competed with their own beliefs about who they were as mothers and as women. In this book I address the question presented by women's competing narratives about motherhood and criminalization: *How do formerly incarcerated mothers reframe their marginalized identity, while presenting a version of motherhood acceptable to state actors that wield influence over their postincarceration lives?*

What I found in speaking to women is that they don't reject normative expectations of motherhood, even though they know that they are viewed by broader society as undeserving or unworthy of motherhood. Moreover, the period of incarceration was not the first time women found themselves outside normative definitions of who they should be, so they were well aware that they were outsiders before their involvement in carceral institutions. As a result, women spent much of their lives carving out a space for themselves by deploying, in both informal and strategic ways, definitions of criminality, marginality, and motherhood that centered their lived experience. Recognizing the tenuousness of their place in the world, these women's experiences show how they in engage in agency-driven acts of resistance.[17] *This is Our Freedom* follows the nuanced journeys of women, as they upend notions about marginalized motherhood, the effectiveness of rehabilitative efforts and ideals about justice in the United States.

When I began interviewing formerly incarcerated mothers in 2010, the national conversation around criminal justice reform was in a different place than it is today. While the Fair Sentencing Act had just been signed into law, on a national level little had been accomplished in the way of countering the devastating consequences of mass incarceration. At the time there was a burgeoning "Ban the Box" movement, which sought to eliminate questions that required job applicants to disclose their criminal history. Still, in 2010 there were only a handful of states which had adopted such practices.[18] That same year also saw the publication of Michelle Alexander's *The New Jim Crow*.[19] While previous scholars had examined the impact of aggressive criminal justice policies on marginalized groups, Alexander's book struck a chord both within and outside of academic circles by detailing how judicial, legislative and public policy measures upheld systemic race-based injustice. Now, over a decade since its publication, some have begun to question whether the causes and consequences of mass incarceration were exaggerated to fit a liberal narrative that emphasizes racism within the criminal justice system.[20] Moreover, some pundits argue that the continued emphasis on mass incarceration is nothing more than a political boogeyman unsupported by recent data. After all, incarceration rates have declined over the past decade and there appears to be political will on both sides of the aisle to reform some aspects of the criminal justice system. Rather than drumming the beat of systematic injustice, they argue that the country should just move on and treat the War on Drugs like an unfortunate footnote of U.S. history.[21]

If mass incarceration is understood solely as the rise and fall of statistical trend lines, it stands to reason that once numbers decline to meet some arbitrary threshold, society has entered a post–mass incarceration period. However, the truth is that the impact of mass incarceration isn't solely reflected in a snapshot of data points but is the result of decades-long policies that have transformed communities and lives long after a sentence has been served. For a country whose nationalistic rhetoric invokes notions of being "the greatest country in the world," yet also has one-third of the world's imprisoned female population, there is a clear disconnect between ideals and realities.[22] In fact, for the last four decades, women have been the fastest-growing population in U.S. prisons and jails.[23]

Between 1978 and 2015 the number of women incarcerated skyrocketed, increasing by 823 percent.[24] Drug offenses accounted for 800 percent of that figure.[25] For minority populations trends are even more discouraging: Black women are incarcerated at twice the rate of their white counterparts and Latina women are incarcerated at 1.3 times the rate of white women.[26] Currently, white women have a 1/111 chance of being incarcerated and Latina and Black women have 1/45 and 1/18 chance of incarceration respectively. Not only does race impact who is most likely to occupy this nation's prisons, but physical differences within racial groups further exacerbate inequities. The phenotypical presentation of Blackness that influences other aspects of social life, such as employment and health, also impact incarceration.[27] While Black people on the whole have a roughly 36 percent chance of incarceration, being Black and having dark skin increases that chance by 30 percent. For women this means that dark-skinned Black women serve sentences that are 12 percent longer than Black women with lighter complexion. These statistics further underscore how criminalization is gendered and racialized, leaving the already marginalized most susceptible to this country's carceral system.[28]

DUALITY AT THE MARGINS

On average incarcerated women have 2.5 children. Incarcerated mothers are also more likely to be the custodial parent for children under the age of eighteen when compared to incarcerated fathers, which means that each year approximately two hundred thousand children experience the absence of their primary caretaker.[29] Studying mothers involved in the criminal justice system thus requires understanding the unique circumstances that shape how they enter into and are subsequently labeled by that system. The commission of crime and the social responses to crime are not only informed by the laws that regulate behavior, but also the social context in which the offense occurs and is adjudicated. Like so many others labeled as moral outsiders, formerly incarcerated women understand the challenges associated with an identity that relegates them to the social margins of life. In this book the concept *duality at the margins* is used to describe the ongoing emotional labor and reframing of social circumstances that shape the decision-making processes of marginalized women before, during, and after incarceration. Duality at the margins describes the metaphorical splitting of oneself into identities acceptable to mainstream society, while remaining authentic to one's personal experiences. It is the undefined space between powerlessness, appealing to those in power and exerting one's agency through counternarrative and critique.

Duality at the margins draws upon sociologist W. E. B. Du Bois's concept of double consciousness. Double consciousness describes the internal conflict of being a marginalized citizen, yet deeply desiring social inclusion in a space to which one holds a legitimate claim.[30] While double consciousness describes how one thinks of herself through the lens of others and self-defined personhood, duality at the margins focuses on how an individual balances agency and acquiescence when the challenge to existing social norms can result in real and lasting social consequences. In framing women's narratives, I primarily focus on actions and rhetoric that women harness to assert an identity separate from their criminal records, even as they strategically defer to the expectations of authority figures.

To be clear, duality at the margins is not a cavalier shedding of one persona for another in an appeal for fleeting acceptance. Rather, it is a framework used to understand how women respond to the headwinds of social exclusion in their daily lives as they adapt to their surroundings. Furthermore, duality at the margins is not a rigid dichotomous framing of marginalized people's interpretation of the social world. What the framework captures is the complex process whereby marginalization is experienced differently, depending on the context, and thus may elicit a variety of responses. In other words, how marginality takes shape will vary from woman to woman. Moreover, the reframing that women engage in as a means to resist or challenge their otherized position exists in relation to risks to their safety, the possibility of further criminalization, and their roles as mothers. Thus, duality at the margins acknowledges the complex, messy, and even contradictory ways that women make decisions as a result of their marginal status.

In using an approach that builds upon Du Bois's concept of double consciousness as embodied in the everyday lives of marginalized women, I want to be clear: Du Boisian analysis is not and should not be thought of as isolated from other theoretical interrogations. In particular, writing about marginalized women means considering how their intersecting identities shape their lives as formerly incarcerated mothers.[31] As Morris notes, Du Bois's work recognized the distinct experiences of women and how race and gender informed social status.[32] Likewise, Rabaka and Gilkes illustrate how Du Boisian sociology helps to foreground early intersectional analyses of marginalized women, with Gilkes noting: "early in the history of sociology, W.E.B. Du Bois emphasized that gender, race, and class intersected in the lives of Black women to foster an important critical perspective or standpoint."[33] Even while recognizing Du Bois's contributions to intersectional studies, it is important to recognize that his framing of women's place within society sometimes fell short of centering their contributions. Therefore, in describing the lived-out application of conflicting identities, I offer a framework for understanding marginalized women in the fullness and complexity of their lives.[34]

Relying upon a Du Boisian framework is also significant for ongoing discussions about how the lived realities of marginalized people are written about and analyzed in social science. In recent years, a critical interrogation of the sociological canon has called into question why Du Bois, whose study of Black life illuminated the experiences of Black folk and American society writ large, had been discounted as a pivotal figure in shaping American sociology. What might at first seem like an insular academic debate, the glossing over of Du Bois's contribution in shaping early sociological analyses of U.S. society speaks to broader issues of inclusion, exclusion, and centeredness. These are issues central to studying formerly incarcerated women. Who is studied and how studies are conducted are influenced by one's intellectual and personal positionality relative to power and agency. Thus, a Du Boisian framework which centers the intersectional experiences of justice involved women provides a lens to understand women's framing of their social experiences, while expanding the conceptual frameworks used to write about those experiences.

CRIME AND MOTHERHOOD IN THE LIFE COURSE

One of the analytical strengths of duality at the margins is that it can complement and strengthen existing frameworks that have been used to examine criminal involvement. In particular, the use of life course theory, a developmental perspective used to study criminality, can be more effectively applied to the study of marginalized populations when expanded to include Du Boisian analysis.

Glen Elder, a sociologist of life course development, defines the life course perspective as an examination of the intersection and relationship between individual developmental pathways and social institutions structured by broader societal forces.[35] Pathways shaped by one's family background or career, for example, are believed to impact patterns and behaviors over an individual's lifetime. By contrast, transitions refer to short-term events, such as graduation or retirement, that are embedded within one's life trajectory.[36] The interplay between events that evolve over the long term (trajectories) and those that evolve over shorter periods of time (transitions) can produce what sociologists Laub and Sampson call turning points. Turning points are significant in that they mark a moment in an individual's life that impinge on decision making in ways that can alter their criminal trajectory.[37]

While each of these developmental categories is relevant for understanding the relationship between motherhood and criminalization, it is turning points that address most directly the possible impact of motherhood on a woman's entry into or exit from criminal involvement. It might be tempting to assume that becoming a mother is a uniformly positive turning point for women, at least as it relates to their participation in criminal activity. Research on young fathers, for example, shows that fatherhood motivates young crime-involved men to become more present in the lives of their children and change their behavior.[38] By contrast, pregnancy and mothering can add to the already stressful reintegration process for women.[39] There are other reasons for the divergence of experiences between men and women. A criminal past does not negate the fact that like the majority of mothers in this country, child care is gendered, with women more likely to be single heads of households. So, while fathers returning from prison are grappling with the challenges of housing and employment, the majority of women are grappling with these same issues, while also trying to reunify with their children and shouldering the burden of childcare.[40]

Nearly 80 percent of mothers are the custodial parents at the time of their arrest.[41] As a result, when women are arrested they must often scramble to identify suitable caretakers for their children or face the prospect that their children will be placed in foster care.[42] Because children are more likely to already be in the custodial care of their mother, they are all the more vulnerable to the risk of intergenerational criminal involvement when their mother is incarcerated. So, while paternal criminal involvement and incarceration has historically been the focus of most criminological research, the impact of maternal incarceration is likely more detrimental to the development of children.[43]

Recent work in life course theory shows how centering the experiences of often ignored populations provides rich insight into their understanding of the world around them.[44] A Du Boisian framework extends this scholarship by showing how society's moral outsiders view their own turning points relative to the expectations of mainstream norms.[45] This is particularly relevant for women I interviewed, since many of them were apart of what might be called the War on Drugs cohort. Some were like LaToya, who was a teenager in the late 1980s and early 1990s and saw her mother's decline into drug addiction. Some were younger, like Aaliyah, who witnessed her community ravaged by addiction and recalls drug raids in her own home. Their lives were shaped by experiences at the individual level, but those individual level life events occurred within the context of aggressive drug policies, militarized policing, and broad systemic inequities.[46]

SPEAKING TO MARGINALIZED WOMEN

When I met with women they were grappling with the challenges of motherhood, while navigating their postincarceration lives. The ability to walk around a neighborhood, grab a meal at the local bodega, and drop their children off at daycare provided women with a moment of respite from performing an acceptable version of motherhood. Yet, the daily reminders that they were viewed as outsiders to be managed, regulated, and judged came in the form of curfews, probation officers' check-ins and denials for jobs and housing. Because women were trying to make sense of their own precarity, they were actively interrogating the normative representations of motherhood and womanhood that they were expected to attain in order to demonstrate rehabilitation.

I made the decision to interview women in New York, Massachusetts, and New England City because I was able to interview women
with diverse rehabilitative experiences within transitional organizations. There were relatively few organizations that solely focused on
formerly incarcerated mothers and children in the New England sites,
so in order to identify an organization that served a large number of
women within a residential setting, it was necessary to identify a setting
with significantly more transitional organizations. New York City
proved to be one of the nearest cities meeting that criteria. Furthermore,
the accessibility of the settings factored into my decision to select each
site. Because I wanted to be able to reinterview available women, it was
important that I identify sites relatively close to my residential location
at the time, Cambridge, Massachusetts.

While in-depth interviews formed the basis of much of my research,
I also spent time observing activities at two of the sites. I spent approximately three hundred hours at Mother's Love and a hundred hours at
Helping Hands, Inc. observing daily operations or assisting staff in
administrative tasks. Given the combination of interviews and focused
observations that formed the methodological basis of this study, I would
characterize it as an interview based short-term ethnography.[47] To be
clear, this study is distinct from long-term ethnographic studies which
often evolve over the course of one year or more. Nevertheless, the time
I spent observing and participating in activities at research sites shaped
how I describe participant conversations and interactions that would
otherwise not be possible.

The decision to interview women involved in transitional organizations was based on two reasons. First, the institutional context of transitional organizations made it more likely that the clients who chose to
participate in the study were recently released from jail or prison.
Because so much of the interview relied on women's recounting of their
postimprisonment experiences, it was important to hear from women
who were actively engaged in the process of reacclimating to society.
Second, there is relatively little scholarship about the role of nonprofit
reentry transitional organizations as intermediaries for carceral institutions. While the organizations themselves are not the focus of the book,
they provide a context for understanding how women navigate society
vis-à-vis these institutional liaisons. To date, there are relatively few
reentry organizations for women, so most women who are released
from prison or jail are unable to gain entrée into such organizations.[48]
As a result, the women I interviewed held an advantage that many

formerly incarcerated women did not. Still, that advantage was not without its limits and addressing the strengths and weaknesses of the institutional context offers insight into how women must manage their marginal status across diverse spaces.[49]

HELPING HANDS, INC.

Early in 2010, when I approached Ms. Brown, the director of Helping Hands Inc., about the possibility of interviewing formerly incarcerated women she was initially reluctant. Although Helping Hands was a fixture in the Massachusetts neighborhood where it was located, Ms. Brown confided that the small nonprofit organization was struggling. Burdened by the volume of clients she and her small staff served and the fundraising needed to keep her organization financially viable, the last thing she wanted was to manage a graduate student. Upon meeting, I explained to Ms. Brown that an important part of my research would entail learning about the daily operations of the organization and I would best be able to do so through weekly volunteer work. Soon after, I was given the task of organizing and updating information about one of their programs for children of incarcerated mothers. It was during this time that I conducted my first interviews.

Some days at Helping Hands I spent more time creating flyers for upcoming events or updating contact information for clients than interviewing women. On those days, the staff and I conversed informally about the social matters of the season—the temperamental Massachusetts spring weather, my experiences as a graduate student, and so on—and light-hearted topics like the upcoming nuptials of Prince William and Kate Middleton. Over time the offices at Helping Hands became a familiar part of my life. As my level of rapport with staff and clients increased, so too did my awareness that the theories, facts, and figures I had so diligently examined prior to beginning interviews, did not fully capture the heaviness of women's stories, relationships, and lived experiences.

In Massachusetts the majority of crimes for which women were incarcerated were nonviolent offenses, with drug offenses comprising the largest share of those crimes.[50] Because I conducted my first interviews in Massachusetts, it soon became clear that it would be difficult for me to examine the intersection between motherhood and carcerality without discussing the underlying traumatic experiences that led to substance abuse and other law-violating behavior. Moreover, it would be difficult to discuss those underlying experiences without drawing connections to the broader social structures that disproportionately impacted women of color and those from poor communities. The concerns Ms. Brown expressed during our early conversations were largely due to the organization's limited resources and high client volume. In Massachusetts the majority of newly released ex-offenders returned to poorer sections of the state, further illustrating that the individuals in their social networks may not have the resources to financially help them when they returned from prison. The highest number of recently released individuals were concentrated in blocking groups with the highest levels of poverty and highest percentages of female-headed households. In the twenty-block area in which the majority of households were headed by single mothers, thirteen of those blocks were home to five or more ex-offenders.[51] While data show the relationship between poverty and incarceration in some of Massachusetts' poorest neighborhoods, they still fail to capture the experience of women returning home. The majority of returning ex-offenders reflected in data are male and are often returning to areas and homes with higher concentrations of single mothers.

MOTHER'S LOVE

Following my initial interviews in Massachusetts during the early spring of 2010, I traveled to New York after the director of Mother's Love, Ms. Flynn, expressed interest in my study after our initial conversation. The women I met in New York provided a snapshot of the broader issues facing incarcerated women at the time. Between 1982 to 2006 the New York State female incarcerated population increased at a rate that far outpaced that of their male counterparts (245 percent versus 118 percent). Roughly 60 percent of women were incarcerated for nonviolent offenses, with drug offenses comprising a third of those crimes. While women of color comprised 30 percent of New York's female population at the time, they made of 68 percent of the prison population, with African-American and Latina women making up 46 percent and 22 percent of the inmate population respectively.[52]

During June and July 2010 and the following summer in 2011, I spent approximately six hours a day, five days a week observing activities at the organizations' headquarters, attending workshops, training sessions and visiting local businesses operated by Mother's Love. I typically arrived in the mornings and spent the day either at the organizational headquarters engaged in conversations with staff and clients or conducting interviews.

RESTORATION HOUSE

When I conducted interviews in New England City the state was grappling with staggering drug addiction statistics. The National Survey on Drug and Use Health (NSDUH) found that New England City had one of the highest number of drug use categories in the nation.[53] At the time, national data showed that roughly 8 percent of individuals over the age of twelve reported using drugs within the last month. In New England City that figure was several percentage points higher.[54] The state where New England City was located also had a higher rate of drug-related deaths than the national rate. Only two of the formerly incarcerated mothers interviewed for this book were apart of Restoration House. There were organizational restrictions that limited my participation in daily activities and women's participation in the study. Unlike the other two organizations, I did not conduct fieldwork at Restoration House, but speaking to the manager gave me insight into the differences between their multi-step addiction treatment model and the methods used at the two other organizations featured in the book.

At the outset of the study I wanted to explore how women's views on postincarceration life evolved over time. To do so required follow-up interviews. However, because many of the women I spoke to were transient due to unstable housing arrangements, follow-up interviews proved to be challenging. I was able to reinterview seven respondents and discuss how their views of transitional organizations evolved in chapter 5.

An important part of my role as a researcher was to be reflexive about my position and identity and how that would inform my analysis. On a regular basis I found myself reflecting on a reality that I had seldom contemplated during graduate school, even as doctoral student at an Ivy League institution: my privilege. As a readily identifiable Black woman, the invisible privilege of my educational background only marginally influenced my daily interactions outside of campus life. However, spending hours with women whose life histories were significantly different from my own, required interrogating how my positionality shaped my relationship with women, so that what I wrote and how I wrote would be analytically rigorous, while centering the humanity of women.

TABLE 1 RESPONDENT RACE, EDUCATION, CRIME, AND ORGANIZATIONAL BACKGROUND

	Number of Respondents
Race	
African American	33
Caucasian	22
Hispanic/Latina	9
Mixed Race	6
Transitional Organization	
Helping Hands, Inc.	29
Mother's Love	39
Restoration House	2
Average Age of Respondents	36.4
Total Exoffender Respondents	70
Education	
Less than High School Degree or GED	18
High School Degree or GED	36
Some College	13
College Degree	2
Graduate Degree	1
*Crime Participation**	
Drug Related	49
Assault	17
Murder Related (actions indirectly led to death)	2
Property	13
Fraud/Identity Theft	3
Prostitution	7
Child Neglect/Kidnapping	3

*Some respondents were convicted of multiple crimes.

Rarely did the women I interview mention how my status influenced their responses but in subtle ways class and race were discussed. For example, in one preinterview explanation of the study, a respondent inquired about my job. Although I had mentioned that I was a student, it seemed odd to her that I was interviewing women rather than sitting in a classroom. When I explained that I was pursuing a doctorate degree in sociology from Harvard, she explained that she was proud of the work I was doing, especially as a fellow Black woman. Other women shared that they wanted to participate in the study, not solely to help other formerly incarcerated women, but to help me, a young Black woman pursuing a doctorate. In another instance Bridgette, a Hispanic interviewee, in describing what she admired about the disciplinary practices of African-American mothers stated: "You stick to your words, African-American mothers," implying that I understood, from personal experience, what it meant to be a Black woman and mother.[55] Even in these interactions it is difficult to assess the extent to which my race, age, social class, and gender influenced my conversations with women.[56] Given my visibility at two of the research sites, some women saw me as occupying a pseudo-clinician role. Even when I indicated that I was not connected to correctional entities or the organizations some women saw me as an informal therapist and described interviews as cathartic. As a result, some women felt comfortable sharing information with me that they had not disclosed to other program participants or staff members.

ABOUT THIS BOOK

During an interview, one of the women with whom I spoke recounted how she felt ignored by her own legal team. While in prison, she immersed herself in the law books available to her and spent her days in the library contemplating her legal options. As far as she was concerned the criminal justice system had failed her and if she ever wanted her case to be retried she would have to advocate for herself. "They not thinking about us," she told me in frustration. "This is our freedom we talking about. They already free. We trying to get free."[57] *This Is Our Freedom* is not only the title of this book, but it is also emblematic of a recurring theme embedded in women's responses to their outsider status. At its core, this book documents how marginalized motherhood that results from both incarceration and the factors contributing to incarceration informs how women interact with and are treated by the world around them.

Women experience the formal and informal consequences of a criminal record but they also frame incarceration as one event in a series of experiences that places them on the margins of moral society. The stories of formerly incarcerated mothers are not only stories about their parenting experiences following imprisonment. Their stories reveal that social exclusion and marginality predates incarceration and reverberates beyond their date of release. In chapter 1, I share the experiences of women like twenty-year-old Aaliyah. When we met, Aaliyah was a new mother, excited to share her dreams for her two-week-old daughter. During the course of our conversation I learned that her daughter was not her first child. Her first child, she clarified wasn't really *her* child. Too embarrassed to divulge this part of her life to other women in the program, she confided that she abandoned a child that was a product of the dysfunctional and abusive experiences that shaped her childhood. Her "brother's child," as she described, was not a product of consent or love. It was the result of family members, schools, and social workers failing a 13-year-old girl. When she was incarcerated years later, she framed imprisonment as a source of frustration, rather than a personal and social nadir. For Aaliyah, her worst days occurred during childhood, not in jail.

Chapter 1 explores how formerly incarcerated women like Aaliyah exist on the moral periphery of their families and communities and how that informs their interpretation of and response to criminality and motherhood. While they recognize the social consequences that result from a criminal record, they also acknowledge that their marginalization began long before they set foot inside a courtroom or jail cell. Their interactions with the criminal justice system, though publicly recorded and socially consequential, were framed as less traumatizing than the private experiences of exclusion and abuse.

In chapter 2 women like Kishana illustrate how one's perception of their moral standing vis-à-vis family and intimate partner relationships can shape reactions to pregnancy. Women's relationships prior to pregnancy were unstable to varying degrees, ranging from casual partnerships to volatile relationships. Moreover, some of the men with whom women were involved were either engaged in criminal activity, coerced women to commit crime, or created situations that led some women to resort to actions that later resulted in arrest. For example, if a woman believed that her partner's affair with another woman drew economic resources away from her and her children, she framed violent retaliation against the other woman not as an act of personal jealousy but of motherly protectiveness. Or, if law enforcement repeatedly failed to arrest an abusive partner, then responding with violence wasn't indiscriminate or callous, but a form of protection toward a woman and her children. Becoming pregnant and having a child were pivotal moments in the lives of the women with whom I spoke. Pivotal both because they no longer wanted to engage in risky or illegal activities and because they *were* willing to engage is criminal activity if the perceived benefit to their child outweighed the risk of incarceration. Their intimate relationships with family members and partners figured prominently in how and why they ultimately made their choices.

One might assume that because the ex-offender label negatively impacts employment and housing, those with a criminal record would be more likely to regret the public and formal consequences of their actions than the private intangible repercussions of their crime. For example, a violent crime conviction for armed robbery or battery might ostensibly be more stigmatizing than drug possession or petty theft. However, women illustrate that the kind of crime for which they were convicted was not as important in how they perceived their own moral status. In chapter 3, women like Kiana illustrate the extent to which women depart from the legal and moral distinctions made by the criminal justice system when defining their own moral status. Charged with several crimes after a failed carjacking that resulted in the death of an innocent bystander, Kiana contested her criminal charge not solely because she believed it was wrong but because of the moral implications of the charge. This interpretation of criminality presents a puzzle: why do women like Kiana uphold the morally laden narratives about motherhood but use an alternative metric when evaluating their own criminal record? In this way duality at the margins illustrates how women deploy a multipronged approach to evaluating criminality and morality, rather than universal codes of morality.

In chapter 4, I introduce Cadence and Sage, who use morally coded language to outline an informal moral hierarchy between themselves and other mothers with criminal histories. What they reveal expands on prior research on mothers who exist outside of mainstream norms that dictate "good" motherhood. Previous work on marginalized motherhood shows that women define their roles and the decision to have children in ways that counter mainstream societal norms and expectations. In *Promises I Can Keep* Kathryn Edin and Maria Kefalas upend the notion that unwed mothers are symbols of a broader pathology of poverty and that they lack agency over the timing of their children. Contrary to the assumption that young women were haphazard in their family planning decisions, Edin and Kefalas found that women made strategic choices about when and why to become mothers.[58] The women in *This Is Our Freedom* depart from mainstream norms about motherhood but they also offer reasons that in some cases depart from the explanations detailed in *Promises I Can Keep*. What the women in *This*

Is Our Freedom reveal is that where one falls along the spectrum of marginality and societal morality shapes how closely they align themselves to mainstream expectations for mothers.

Young single mothers, like those Edin and Kefalas interviewed, described the choice to have children as intentional and timed. However, criminally involved women, socially marked primarily by their criminal record and not their economic or marital status, frame motherhood in markedly different ways. My conversations with women show that not only do they draw distinctions between themselves and normative ideas about motherhood in order to justify their decisions, but they also embrace the very ideals that seem to conflict with their ex-offender status. Drawing upon images like Betty Crocker or aspiring to be like Michelle Obama, demonstrated that women not only wanted to be better mothers, but that they wanted to exceed even conventional expectations.

Chapter 5 focuses on the methods of postincarceration rehabilitation used both by women and transitional institutions. In discussing women's methods of navigating the challenges of reentry, I focus on how women use the language of critique and acceptance to cope with the deficiencies of the social institutions around them. The overlap and distinction between personal responsibility framing and how women describe their own methods of achieving success illustrates that women value the role of institutional support, even while relying on the strengths of their own worldviews. Moreover, women adopt and adapt the messaging of personal responsibility selectively. Women accept messages that position them to receive support and recognition in institutional settings, while relying on a personal framing of success when institutional contexts fail to affirm their experiences.

Rehabilitative success, women explain, wasn't solely about meeting curfews or abstaining from illegal activity. The ability to establish oneself as an exemplar of motherhood was rewarded by organizations in both tangible and intangible ways. Moreover, some women were surprised that participation in organizations like Mother's Love came with the informal labor of securing welfare benefits, that sometimes exacerbated the stress associated with meeting postincarceration expectations. To explain this tension, I introduce the term *rehabilitative paradox* to describe the competing expectations of transitional organizations to meet the needs of women, while also meeting the requirements of the correctional institutions with which they partner. Their dual roles are often competing and, as a result, provide a context for critique among women who feel that their needs are secondary to the financial and organizational demands of the organization.

The book's conclusion examines the connection between women's experiences and broader political and public policy concerns. I explore the programmatic goals and policies aimed at addressing mass incarceration, while offering a critique of how those policies fall short and fail women. I offer recommendations for transformative ways to ameliorate existing problems within the criminal justice system, while calling into question the legitimacy of the existing model of punishment.

CHAPTER I

Marginalized from the Beginning

As I watched Pablo walk toward me, I quickly turned my gaze downward. Hoping that my newfound interest in the pavement below might temporarily render me invisible, I pretended to be too busy to engage in conversation. When we met a few weeks earlier, he was loading furniture onto a delivery truck. A few times a month Mother's Love would deliver recently purchased secondhand furniture to local customers. Because the furniture was donated, Mother's Love was able to put the proceeds from sales toward their fundraising efforts. Even though one of the staff members at Mother's Love had introduced me as a researcher, by that point in the summer Pablo and some of the residents at Mother's Love thought of me as a pseudo-clinician.[1] On this day Pablo wanted an update on our relationship status. "I told you, I'm not interested in a relationship," I replied, trying to balance the seriousness of my answer with a smile. He didn't press the issue any further but if our previous conversations were any indication, this would not be the last time we had such an exchange.[2]

In the weeks since I had been at Mother's Love I had experienced a few moments like this. I wanted to build rapport with women, staff members, and neighborhood residents like Pablo, yet I was keenly aware of the importance of maintaining my objectivity and establishing boundaries. *Boundaries.* Boundaries are those unwieldly divides that researchers assume shield against subjective overreach and preserve the critical gaze. In many ways they're important, even necessary, to protect the people and communities that are studied. In others ways, however, boundaries can create a researcher versus "subject" relationship that is extractive rather than participatory. I thought often about what it meant to establish boundaries and how for the women I spoke to, boundaries like those created by class and inequality had shaped much of their lives. For my part, I soon learned that establishing boundaries did not mean that my role was to "give voice" to women's lived experiences; women had voiced their challenges long before they met me, despite the unwillingness of institutions to listen or respond to their concerns. Rather, I tried to listen to women's experiences in a manner worthy of their words. This meant that I needed to be reflexive about my position as a researcher and how boundaries of class, race, and gender connected and separated women's narratives from my own.

On one hand, I was an outsider: A researcher interviewing mothers as part of study examining the challenges of being a formerly incarcerated parent. On the other hand, the neighborhood where Mother's Love was located reminded me in some ways of the one in which I was raised.[3] I grew up in the South Hollis/St. Albans section of Queens, a New York City neighborhood comprised of a mix of mostly working-class and middle-class Black families. Families like my own, immigrants from Jamaica, were not uncommon in the neighborhood that was once the bedroom community for some of the country's most notable figures, like Ella Fitzgerald, Jackie Robinson, Lena Horne, and W.E.B. Du Bois.[4] Like my neighborhood, most of the businesses near Mother's Love were mom and pop enterprises like car repair shops, the neighborhood bodega, and eateries that reflected the ethnic composition of the residents. In the early 2010s neither neighborhood had been swept up in the wave of gentrification seen in other Queens neighborhoods. Most residents in the area where Mother's Love was located were Black and Brown just like the faces in the murals of jazz musicians and civil rights leaders I admired on walks and drives through my own community.[5]

When I got off the train each morning and made the walk to Mother's Love, the sights and sounds were not unlike those that shaped my childhood and adolescence. When I spoke to Pablo and other local men who tried to gauge my level of non-Platonic interest, it was not unlike the kind of back-and-forth repartees I'd engaged in while waiting for the Q2 bus or F train on my way to a high school summer job in Jackson Heights or waiting at the Jamaica Avenue bus stop after an afternoon of shopping. I felt at ease in the neighborhood where I spent the summer of 2010 and 2011, yet I knew that there were ways social class and education shaped the questions I asked and way that I listened to women's responses.

As children, the families into which we are born and other factors beyond our control shape the quiet and loud parts of our lives. For me, this meant that my world revolved around school, church, and immersing myself in all things Whitney, Mariah, Michael, and mid-1990s R&B.[6] For some of the women with whom I spoke, this meant balancing the levity of youth with the gravity of victimization, unacknowledged trauma, and arrests. Our beginnings do not necessarily determine our endings, but we can often look at our endings and find glimmers of the past. This is where I began my conversations with women, and for women this is often where their understanding of marginality and how to negotiate their marginal identities first took shape.

AALIYAH'S STORY

I knew that the woman I was meeting in the small living room in Mother's Love's shared housing building had recently given birth, yet I was still taken aback at the sight of the tiny pink newborn she was holding. As I settled into the chair across from the couch where Aaliyah sat, cradling her two-week-old daughter, I congratulated her on first-time motherhood and thanked her for agreeing to meet with me despite adjusting to parenthood. It wasn't until well into our interview that Aaliyah would reveal that her daughter, Destiny, was not her only child. She didn't know where her first daughter was or if she was even alive.

To describe twenty-year-old Aaliyah's childhood as difficult would be an understatement. Before incarceration, before motherhood, and before entering Mother's Love, she had grown accustomed to being abandoned by the people entrusted to care for her. As a child, she grew up in one of the Midwest's most economically depressed cities. The poverty that gave way to rising crime and violence in her community would eventually find its way into her home. Her mother was never around and her father was more likely to be in the company of a girlfriend or selling drugs than meeting the needs of Aaliyah and her sixteen brothers and sisters. When her father was around, he would remind her that she was inferior to her sisters, who met his standard of physical beauty. Full-figured with smooth, deep brown skin, Aaliyah didn't look like her sisters, who were lighter shades of brown. For reasons beyond her control Aaliyah was labeled an outsider in her own family, a fact that struck a painful chord during our interview.

Aaliyah: I was like the one that was different . . . because my sisters were lighter than me. Because I'm darker I was the ugly one. . . . I was always the ugly one and they was always the much prettier, smarter and most likely to succeed ones. So, I was discriminated against in my own family. . . . The main reason I always fought when I was younger because it was a way for me to fit in, a way for me to feel like I had a place.

I remember when I was younger I had joined our school orchestra and I was playing the cello. And I'm telling you, my daddy went to all my sisters' graduations, cheerleading competitions. I told him about the cello thing. I was really proud of myself because I was playing the cello. So, it was just like he didn't even come. Nobody showed up. But I remember my stepmother, my aunties, my grandfather, my grandmother, they would show up to her competitions and all types of stuff. . . . I didn't even go to my own fifth-grade graduation, my eighth-grade graduation, my twelfth-grade graduation, none of that. I was left out. I watched my sister dress up and go to prom, go to homecoming. I never got to be the one to like dress up to go anywhere. I was messed up for no reason, for no reason at all.

For Aaliyah, fighting at school was born out of her desire to compensate for the attention she lacked from her father and family members. Receiving negative attention in the form of school discipline or reprimands from family members was, for her, better than no attention at all.

But Aaliyah was only a child and could not foresee just how unwilling the adults in her life were to guard her against abuse if it meant risking their own status in the community. Aaliyah was thirteen when she discovered that she was pregnant. Given her age a social worker was required to ask her about the circumstances of her pregnancy. Under strict orders from her father, she was told to say that the baby's father was "a boy in the neighborhood." The truth was she had undergone years of sexual abuse at the hands of her older brother and he was the father of the baby she was carrying. If she lied about who her unborn child's father was, she would appease her own father, a man she desperately wanted to please. But if she told the truth, she thought, she might be able to end the ongoing abuse that had robbed her of childhood. She chose the latter option and was immediately rejected by her family.

Aaliyah: I remember once upon a time I couldn't even look in a mirror and think I was pretty. I couldn't even look in the mirror and say I was somebody [*crying*]. My whole family turned against me. . . . I didn't look at this baby and see love. I didn't feel love nowhere for this baby. I hated her. It wasn't her fault. It really wasn't my fault either. The baby never asked to be here. But I didn't ask for her to be here either. That was my thing. And just to please my family I had tried to keep her and tried to keep going with her just to please them and show them that I can do this. But it didn't work. I found myself neglecting her, abandoning her. I would let her sit up a long period of time with her diapers on, pissy and wet, and I didn't care. I just did not care about her. I had so much animosity towards that child.

Most of her life Aaliyah felt like the proverbial black sheep within her family. As a young adult Aaliyah continued to struggle with her family's refusal to acknowledge the abuse she experienced.

> Aaliyah: People don't understand. Nobody here [Mother's Love] knows what happened to me. Nobody knows, because it's just like I'm ashamed. I've seen how my whole family turned against me. My whole family shunned me like I was a nobody. That's why it's hard for me to trust people because it's like if your own family, your own father and your mother can just turn you away, why not the whole world? . . . It was like everybody wanted to push—like even today, everybody pushes it under the rug.
>
> Geniece: Because they know how it happened?
>
> Aaliyah: It's crazy! It's like they bring him around and treated him like nothing ever happened. I'm supposed to walk around the same way to them. That's how they want me to be, like a robot or something. But I can't be like that. It hurts. I can't even look him in the face. While it was happening, because he lived in the same household as me, I accepted him. He was still my brother. But after I got pregnant, after what happened to me, it was like I can't even look him in the face.

Unable to discuss the abuse with her own family, Aaliyah was left to face her painful past alone. At the age of fifteen, two years after giving birth to her first daughter, Aaliyah enrolled in a children and mothers program in her city. One day, still struggling with her family's rejection and overwhelmed with the responsibilities of raising a child while still a child herself, she placed the toddler in a closet and walked out the door. At the time of our interview she didn't know where her first daughter was and admitted feeling haunted by her decision to leave.

Soon after leaving her first daughter Aaliyah moved to New York City, where she was later arrested for petty theft. While in jail, she learned that she was pregnant and viewed the news as a second chance at motherhood. She left jail determined to create the life for her daughter that she never received. While she knew that the ex-offender label would limit her opportunities, she also felt that she had already overcome her greatest challenge: the constant feelings of worthlessness and rejection that marked much of her life. To Aaliyah, her most significant accomplishment was accepting herself and not acquiescing to her family's wishes that she ignore the sexual abuse and other dysfunctional aspects of her childhood. Sharing her outlook Aaliyah says:

> Yo, the person I am today makes me proud of myself, and that's what gives me confidence. Yo, you could be the baddest chick walking the street, nice butt, nice skinny waist. I'd be like, girl, you're not badder than me because I know who I am now. You can't tell me nothing because I know who I am today. It took me a long time. Yo, I remember I used to cry when I would tell this story because it took me a long time to get me to look in the mirror and say, "I am somebody."

Compared to her feelings of shame about childhood abuse Aaliyah saw her ex-offender label as a conquerable obstacle, not an indication of her broader moral status. She knew the label held negative consequences but there was a key difference: agency. Defining who she was at the hands of her abuser was beyond her control. Getting pregnant and having her first child were also outside of her control. However, even with a criminal record, Aaliyah felt that she was now in a position to define morality and motherhood on her own terms. Just as marginalized motherhood is nuanced, influenced by intersections of race, gender and criminalization, so too are women's own framing of their marginality. The addition of a criminal record might seem like an obvious enhancement of Aaliyah's marginal status and, at a structural level, it is. But in terms of how she saw her social status as a mother and as a woman, a criminal record was understood within the context of her other experiences.

Although I met Aaliyah shortly after she was released from jail, it was her experiences from childhood, not her time incarcerated that weighed most heavily on her mind and shaped her postrelease plans. In this way, understanding marginality is not about identifying the aspects of a person's past that seem to directly impact what appears to be their most stigmatizing status. The totality of a woman's identity is not bound up in their ex-offender status and therefore women do not view their marginal status solely through the lens of that part of their lives.[7] So, when formerly incarcerated mothers like Aaliyah negotiate marginal identity it is not only in relation to a criminal record, but also the experiences that sustained and reinforced an outsider status over the course of their lives. By framing their experiences this way, women like Aaliyah show that being a formerly incarcerated person should not be defined as a self-inflicted marginal status. Yes, women have violated the law but that event was an extension of a process preceded by other events, some occurring at the most vulnerable times in their lives.

Child sexual abuse, like other forms of abuse and traumatic events, is sometimes framed as a signature experience that shapes life course development in ways similar to marriage, employment, or imprisonment.[8] There are, however, important differences with these forms of trauma. Marriage and employment can be positive experiences and the beneficial aspects of each can contribute to the desistance of criminal activity.[9] The uniformly negative nature of abuse means that it creates disadvantages repeatedly throughout the life of a victim. So, when a seemingly significant life event like incarceration occurs, it isn't necessarily framed as a nadir in the life of victim who has already traversed other negative life defining events.

What women like Aaliyah reveal is that abuse and the accompanying moments that can retraumatize victims are ongoing processes, rather than events marked by a date on a calendar. One of the first steps taken by child victims of sexual abuse is disclosure. Brazelton, in analyzing the disclosure process among African-American women, finds that the act of disclosing abuse occurs multiple times over the course of a victim's life.[10] For the women she interviewed, disclosure was often met with silencing, a response that meant that the abuser was not held accountable for their actions and, most painfully, the victim was either revictimized by continued sexual abuse or by having to interact with the abuser in social settings.[11] When Aaliyah was admonished not to tell a social worker that her brother was the father of her first daughter, her family feared his punishment and their shame. This reasoning is not uncommon across families of various backgrounds. In particular, for some African-American families, the distrust of police, the criminal justice system and social services can further exacerbate the justifications used for withholding information from authorities.[12]

A key consideration often overlooked when trauma-laden experiences of formerly incarcerated women are studied is the impact that revealing past sources of stigma have on present and future life experiences.[13] While the ex-offender identity isn't one that can be readily identified in informal social spaces, modern technology has placed such information at the public's fingertips.[14] Knowledge of child victimization, by contrast, primarily relies on disclosure from the victim and that disclosure can expose the victim to ostracization, blame, and even abuse from intimate partners. It is therefore incomplete to study the stigma of imprisonment without considering how women were, in many cases, already socially excluded and stigmatized by their communities and family members. And to appreciate the full extent of community-level marginalization it is important to acknowledge how structural disadvantage, inadequate social services, and suspicion of the criminal justice system, reinforces the silencing of Black girls and women. Therefore, the continued marginalization of already marginalized women underscores the depth of structural-level factors that shape the lives of the majority of crime-involved women.

THE PAIN OF SILENCE

After having her sons, Kiana longed for a little girl. By the time she decided to have another child, however, so much in her life had changed. She had severed ties her ex-boyfriend, the father of her sons and was now in an exclusive relationship with a woman. She had also recently returned from prison after serving time for armed robbery and a kidnapping that left an innocent bystander dead. Still, a new baby might be a chance to mark a new beginning. After discussing their options, she and her partner came to a decision: Kiana would contact a friend via social media and ask him to father their child. After seeing all the images that he posted on social media of his daughters, Kiana and her girlfriend concluded that he could "make girls." Initially he was reluctant to help Kiana. Even though Kiana had no romantic interest in him, he was worried how his wife would react if she learned that he had sex with another woman. Upon the promise that Kiana would never seek child support or inform his wife about their arrangement, he eventually agreed to father her third child.[15] After carefully timing their meetings around her ovulation, Kiana conceived quickly and nine months later gave birth to a girl. As she recounted the circumstances of her daughter's birth she beamed with pride. After the tumultuous years of her twenties and early thirties, having her daughter provided the fresh start she craved.

As a child, Kiana knew what it was like to be the only girl in a house full of boys. She was confident, however, that her daughter would not suffer the same fate she had. Growing up in a high crime area of New York's inner city, violence and drug activity were ever present and introduced Kiana to criminal activity. Despite witnessing crime firsthand and constantly seeing news stories about her neighborhood on the evening news, she didn't feel afraid when she stepped outside of her home:

Kiana: So I really was never afraid unless I seen somebody get shot, which I've seen somebody get shot before and people stabbed and stuff. I mean, that touches me, definitely I was afraid of that. Not afraid of seeing somebody killed right before your eyes. But other than that, like just the activities that were going on, I really was never afraid.

The connection between what she learned about crime on the streets and her level of fear were not one in the same, however. What she feared more than the street violence outside of her home was the dysfunction within it.

Kiana was the middle child in her family. Her mother and father raised her and her two brothers, providing for them to the best of their ability. She describes her relationship with her father positively but she had ongoing problems with her mother. Much of the tension between her and her mother was a result of her mother's reaction to a traumatic incident involving Kiana and her eldest brother. Echoing Aaliyah's encounter with heartbreaking similarity, at the age of thirteen Kiana's older brother raped her. Almost instantly, her demeanor changed after the assault. She would sometimes gaze at herself in the mirror for long periods of time criticizing her physical appearance. Perhaps if she could identify what about her body, her face, or personality led to her brother's actions, she could hide it or change it so that she would never again be victimized. Like other victims of child sexual abuse, Kiana blamed herself for the violence committed against her.[16] When she informed her mother about the incident, the response was devastating.

Kiana: She attacked me, actually. She's like, "You better stop getting fresh with your brother." And I looked at her like, "Are you serious? I'm your only daughter!"

When silencing is the response to childhood abuse it not only discourages the victim from seeking help for that particular instance of abuse, but it also discourages disclosing future instances of abuse. As a result of the rape and her mother's response to it, Kiana grew withdrawn and distant from her family. Day in and day out Kiana had to interact with her brother, all the while living with the memory of his assault and the fear that it could happen again. It was only in adulthood that her abuse was finally acknowledged. Years later at a family New Year's Eve gathering her older brother approached her, hugged her, and wept. With no words exchanged between them, Kiana viewed his actions as the apology she waited years to receive. Still, by that point irreparable damage had occurred. She continued to harbor resentment toward her brother for assaulting her and her mother for turning the other way.

In a similar way Juanita, a forty-four-year-old Puerto Rican mother of two from New York, recounts how silencing functioned in her household.

Geniece: You said your household was abusive. What do you mean by that?

Juanita: Well, my grandfather was in World War II, so who know what he went through, that World War II. I can remember to the—Well, I remember him working and bringing bags of peanuts. Not regular peanuts like pistachios. He would also bring a bottle of Johnny Walker every Friday. And every Friday we knew what that was. That was like try to run away as far as you can because he becomes abusive. He would drink. He would hit us with the buckle belts. He would molest us. I was one of them who was molested as a little girl by my grandfather. And my grandmother would condone what he did because she was afraid. She was afraid of him.

Childhood abuse and the silencing that sometimes follows is largely ignored by the adult criminal justice system.[17] While there are therapeutic programs that encourage incarcerated and formerly incarcerated persons to identify the root causes of risky behaviors and criminal activity, at a practical level criminalization, rather than treatment, characterizes the model care.[18] Kiana, like most respondents, drew few direct connections between difficult childhood experiences and adult actions. To her mind, her sexual assault was just that, *her* sexual assault. Kiana may not have been responsible for her brother's actions, but to her it was a result of problems within her home and a private family matter. Years later, when a judge sentenced her to prison, she saw the crime as detached from untreated trauma that may have influenced harmful relationship choices that led to criminal involvement.[19]

Women's individual framing of abuse does not occur within a vacuum. When formerly incarcerated women discuss their criminal involvement within the broader context of early abusive experiences, it can sometimes be interpreted as a denial of responsibility. This is not without consequence. A prerequisite to early release from prison or receiving alternatives to incapacitation is the ownership of full responsibility.[20] Thus, there are institutional incentives for women to decontextualize criminal involvement from their abuse and trauma. The suppressing of trauma at the microlevel as seen in Kiana's story is reinforced by the requirement to disconnect past pain from present actions in the courtroom or before a parole board. Women are therefore provided little

TABLE 2   CHILDHOOD ENVIRONMENT AND CHILDHOOD
ABUSE EXPERIENCES

Home/Community Environment	Number of Respondents
Guardianship Experiences (some respondents experienced more than one home structure)	
Two-Parent Household	19
Single-Parent Household	48
Adopted	3
Foster Care	5
Group Home	4
Familial Dysfunction	
Parent Incarcerated	6
Parent Addicted to Drugs/Alcohol	23
Witnessed Abuse as a Child	6
Poverty at Home/Community	7
Types of Abuse	
Sexual	13
Physical	17
Emotional	8
Psychological	4
Neglect	3
Total Women Abused as Children	27

room to expose brokenness because to do so would mean that they are refusing to be accountable or demonstrate the capacity to be reformed.

I argue that given the overrepresentation of victims of child abuse in our nation's prisons, early life events should be a stronger consideration in the adjudication and sentencing process. However, acknowledging that a disproportionate number of female inmates are also victims of child abuse means the criminal justice system must also face an uncomfortable truth: the American prison system retraumatizes society's most victimized, warehouses our nation's most socially and economically disadvantaged, and places those historically excluded from the right to life and liberty in spaces designed to deprive them of those very rights.

Of the seventy women I interviewed there were a total of forty-five instances of childhood abuse, including physical abuse, sexual abuse, neglect, emotional abuse, and verbal abuse. These accounts of abuse were limited to twenty-seven of the women who participated in the study. The summary of the types of abuse respondents' experienced is reflected in table 2, along with descriptions of their home and community context.

The reason this chapter focuses on sexual and physical abuse, rather than other forms of abuse, is that some interactions that I identified as verbal abuse or neglect, were not explicitly described as such by respondents. For example, when describing relatives who would visit her parents' home, Kiana recalls the derogatory statements they would make to her and her brothers, such as: "'Shut the fuck up" [they would say], calling us all kinds of names like crack babies." However, she didn't categorize these exchanges as verbally abusive. By contrast, when speaking about sexual abuse or physical abuse, women were unambiguous in describing those experiences as abusive.[21] While respondents might characterize some instances of verbal abuse as harsh or an ordinary and expected aspect of childrearing, they were clearer that instances of molestation and physical abuse during their childhood were law-violating behavior.[22]

"I LOOKED UP TO THEM"

When I met twenty-eight-year-old Trisha, it was clear that she had spent much of her time in prison processing the childhood abuse that marred her youth. In prison she called her mother regularly, as they began to mend the fractured relationship that resulted from her mother's neglect. Trisha was also angry. She was angry with the adults who had failed her, a criminal justice system whose institutionalized racism and homophobia had scapegoated her, and a society that viewed her as a perpetrator of crime rather than as a victim of injustice. Unlike some of the other women I interviewed, Trisha's contention wasn't that she received an unfairly lengthy sentence. No. Trisha knew that she should never have been arrested or convicted in the first place.[23] Compared to women like Aaliyah and Kiana, who framed their childhood experiences as the most salient aspects of their life when juxtaposed against incarceration, Trisha's story departed in important ways. Trisha had an abusive childhood, but she also had adults who valued her, saw her potential, and provided a refuge from the turmoil she experienced at home. The influence of positive social bonds is widely believed to be one important mitigating factor in criminal behavior, especially for young adults.[24] Trisha identified several positive relationships during childhood that would prove lifesaving at her darkest moments.

Trisha grew up in an environment she described as the "opposite of comfortable." Unlike Kiana, the prevalence of drugs and violence in her community made her feel unsafe as a child. Despite her surroundings, she had an attentive mother who cared for her and her younger brother. This changed, however, when her family moved when she was around nine years of age.

> *Trisha:* I always admired my mother, I guess because I was the only girl and before I knew that she was doing drugs she would like pay special attention to me. Like I always had barrettes in my hair. I always had bows and earrings on and little dresses. Like I never wore jeans or anything like that. And then once we moved uptown and I started seeing her getting more into the drugs, she abandoned all responsibility.

Soon after they relocated Trisha noticed strange men entering and exiting their home at odd hours of the evening. Then, her mother stopped working, combing Trisha's hair, and caring for the household. It wasn't long before Trisha learned that her mother, like so many mothers and fathers in her community, was engulfed in drug addiction. Trying to regain normalcy, Trisha looked to school as a haven but there she found more rejection and her first encounter with sexual abuse:

> *Geniece:* What was it like, your experience in school?
>
> *Trisha:* School? In third grade I had a teacher who used to make me sit on his lap. And I hit him with a bottle. School was the worst. I think it was worst for me because of what I was going through at home. I felt like school should have been a safe haven for me where I go and pretend that nothing is wrong. Because my mom abandoned us and not making sure we was clean, we got picked on a lot. We was outcasts. I didn't have any friends growing up. They used to pick on me and fight me and chase me after school.

If you have never witnessed the taunting and heartbreaking rejection a child experiences because of their parent's drug addiction, it might be difficult to fully understand the impact of the ridicule Trisha describes. As I listened to Trisha and tried to visualize her childhood interactions in school, it brought to mind a classmate of mine in elementary school. We were both among the quieter students in our fifth-grade class, usually keeping to our small group of friends. During recess he would hang his head as his mother called to him from outside the fence which separated the playground from the adjacent street. Rail-thin and often speaking both quickly and incoherently, his mother was a recognizable member of our neighborhood. I soon learned from the whispers of other children that she was addicted to drugs. This woman, though ill, was ever present at the same time each day to see her son despite of her own struggles. Having to answer questions about one's parent and decide whether to ignore or respond to the torrent of insults from peers is a burden for anyone, let alone a child.[25] I certainly didn't know, nor could I imagine what Trisha felt, but the taunts and teasing she recounted brought to mind the ones I heard directed at my childhood classmate: devastating and painful.

In the midst of witnessing her mother succumb to addiction, Trisha was also hiding a secret. Not long after relocating, Trisha's mother married a man who pulled her deeper into drug addiction. He was also molesting nine-year-old Trisha. Years later, when Trisha's mother was released from prison after serving a sentence for drug possession, she reunited with her estranged husband causing Trisha to fear that the abuse would resume.[26] Beside herself with fear and grief, Trisha tried to end her life. Recounting her attempt to die by suicide Trisha says,

> And it was like when she started dealing with that guy that she was dealing with she got married to him and I felt that she didn't know enough about him and she didn't have enough family approval to marry the guy. So many people were saying "no." All she knew was that he was her provider with the drugs and that's all that meant anything to her. At the age of nine he started molesting me, raping me and sodomizing me and I didn't say anything to anybody until I got to fifteen and tried to kill myself. That's when it all came out. But he's still in jail. He was in a half-way house and he was coming to see her and I was afraid that he was going to be a part of her life again so I tried to kill myself and that's when everything came out. She left him alone, pressed charges.

The suicide note detailing her plans was discovered by a friend who promptly relayed the information to Trisha's mother. Her mother's swift response proved to be a critical moment for Trisha. For all of her mother's challenges, Trisha saw her mother's willingness to immediately sever ties with her husband as an important and necessary step in preserving her well-being.

Other relationships in Trisha's life proved to be vital when her mother was incarcerated. A few of the Black teachers in her school took on motherlike roles that provided Trisha with a sense of community and support. Describing those relationships, she states:

> When I got in junior high school that's when I started to develop my own sense of what I want my family to be like so I had this picture. And [these teachers], Ms. Wilson and Ms. Rollins which was like . . . my mom and this

one was my aunt. It was more like a mentor thing. So I looked up to them and I used to go to their house and eat with their family and everything. . . . And I used to bring my little brother with me and Ms. Bryans was like an aunt too and they inspired me in a lot of ways. They used to read my poetry and they used to call me the next Maya Angelou. They made me feel good about myself. Regardless of what was going on at home. When I graduated middle school Ms. Bryans brought me two things of roses 'cause I wasn't going to go to graduation because my mom was clean at that time but she just started a new job and she said she couldn't take off. And I felt that everything that you done missed already let them fire you. You missed my sixth-grade graduation, you missed my first menstrual cycle, everything. Let them fire you. . . . Ms. Bryans bought me some roses and they bought me a dress and some shoes and they got my hair done, my nails done.

One of the key mitigating factors in criminal desistance, particularly among juveniles, is the presence of positive social bonds. These bonds are often fostered within the context of extracurricular activities like sports participation and religious involvement. More than activities, the strong personal relationships that develop within these settings can serve as a buffer against negative influences in the lives of high-risk youth.[27] Still, as important as these buffers are, they did not make young girls like Trisha impervious to the risk of abuse or shield the woman Trisha would become from the consequences of childhood trauma.

Trisha's experience captures the nuance of existing on the margins. Victimization is part of her story, yes, but so too is love and support. To separate those conflicting narratives is to fail to capture the multidimensionality that informs how other events, namely motherhood and criminalization, come to hold meaning in the lives of justice-involved women later on in life. Furthermore, the support that women receive early in life cannot replace the broader collapse of community, institutional and structural level support. In the midst of chaotic community contexts, the impact of positive social bonds can be stymied by the pervasive dysfunction engulfing a young person's life, allowing the negative consequences of abuse to overwhelm the potentially positive aspects of those relationships. Supporting this, Jessica Craig and her colleagues found that when examining the extent to which positive social bonds decreased the negative consequences of adverse childhood experiences (ACEs), "stronger bonds did not reduce the deleterious effects of exposure to more types of ACEs on recidivism."[28]

This finding paints what seems to be an almost hopeless picture for victims of childhood abuse. If positive role models can't "save" women from the consequences of abuse, one might ask, are they fated to be victims of circumstance? I posit that this question makes the misguided assumption that individual and personal interventions can or should bear the exclusive burden of ameliorating issues rooted in much broader systemic factors. When solutions are limited to individual-level actions, so too are the causes. This framing exonerates economic, political, and criminal justice systems from their role in perpetuating broad-scale inequality at the community level. As an analogy, imagine an old decrepit apartment complex in your community. With peeling paint and exposed insulation, the state health board finds that residents are likely to be exposed to asbestos toxins. If a disproportionate number of cancer cases are linked to that complex, what would be a reasonable response? Perhaps those residents should improve their diet, exercise more, or spend more time outside? Of course not! Such a response does not address the root cause of those health issues but places the onus of responsibility on those most harmed. For victims of childhood abuse the answer to breaking the chain that links their trauma to later criminality requires a response bigger than relationships and more complex than personal responsibility. When a social worker accepts a thirteen-year-old mother's explanation, without further investigation, that her child's father was a local boy (Aaliyah), or an elementary-school-aged child's daily unkempt appearance is ignored or unaddressed (Trisha), it can be difficult for occasional interactions or sporadic encounters to remedy ongoing issues.

FACING THE PAIN

One of the reasons that incarceration is such a significant life event for women is that it is, by definition, forced separation from the world around them. The deprivation of rights and liberty is exchanged for surveillance and something often in rare supply: time. The rehabilitation logic of incarceration is that it forces women to assess the reality of their situation and ostensibly use that time to decide to change. I argue that for women with abusive histories the prison environment isn't necessarily a space of revelatory reflection that inspires radical change.[29] Given that the majority of crimes for which women are convicted are rooted in addiction, mental illness, poverty, or a combination of the three, social support rather than prison provides women with the greatest chance at desistance.[30] Nevertheless, for better or worse, it is within the prison environment that some women begin to examine previously unexplored aspects of their lives.

When Trisha was incarcerated for assault, she felt that her struggles with anger management were partially responsible for her wrongful conviction. Finding no better alternatives for therapy within prison, she enrolled in the prison's drug education program, even though she felt her occasional use of ecstasy pills differentiated her from most of the program's participants who battled ongoing addiction. She hoped that at least within that setting she could come to terms with her troubled childhood and her complicated relationship with her mother. Recalling the day that she requested to watch a video on addiction, she described the subsequent conversation that she had with her mother:

> When I started doing my drug program, I was locked up in October, I told them I wanted to watch a video on heroin. And they was like "Why? Your drug of choice was E pills." I said my mom used to use all that, I want to understand. I watched it and they talked about reconciliation. . . . So I called her and asked her if there was anything—I didn't want her to think that I was focusing on her because I didn't want her to relapse and that's why I was always scared to talk to her about things that I was holding in. So when I talked to her I was like, "Was there anything that I did that made you not proud of me, that disappointed you?" She said, "No, when you got pregnant I was disappointed but you got pregnant your last year of high school and you completed, you graduated, you're still working and you're a good mother. So no you never really disappointed me." . . . And then I was like, "I need to tell you what you did that disappointed me." And I told her, "When you found out that Mark had raped me and sodomized me you just took me shopping and that was it. You never talked to me about it." She was like she cried and she was like, "I never talked to you about it because I didn't want you to re-live it again. I was waiting for you to come talk to me about it." And I was like you was waiting for me and I was waiting for you to talk about it, so it was like miscommunication or whatever. . . . But the only thing is I was holding that inside. It was the resentment I held against her. And once I told her that I forgive her she passed away two months later. So it was a burden lifted because if my mother had passed away and I had never got a chance to talk to her she would have passed away and I still would have had resentment in my heart not knowing that she was waiting for me to talk to her about it the whole time.

One might read Trisha's description and view it as an example of what all women who faced abuse should do: Seek out the appropriate therapeutic resources and take ownership of their own psychological and emotional well-being. But how did Trisha come in contact with the resources that led her to address her childhood abuse? Is it only possible for victimized women to be imprisoned before they have access to resources that might only marginally address elements of their trauma?

Trisha didn't begin the process of healing because of the circumstances that led her to an addiction support group. She began the process of recovery in spite of those circumstances.

Devah Pager details how the stigma or mark of having a criminal record and being a racial minority excludes formerly incarcerated individuals from employment.[31] For these women, the mark of a criminal record is preceded by the stigmatizing mark of childhood abuse that placed them on a path toward unstable living conditions, unplanned pregnancies, and abusive intimate-partner relationships that in many cases contributed to criminal involvement. The stories of Aaliyah, Kiana, and Trisha illustrate that long before their criminal records, they bore the invisible stigma of abuse and structural disadvantage. After an arrest and a criminal conviction, a woman is labeled by the criminal justice system and often family, friends, and future employers view her in terms of that label. Upon completing her jail, prison, or probation obligations there are other mediating factors that shape how formerly incarcerated women begin their postrelease life. The stigma of the ex-offender status in the public sphere is compounded by other life experiences, often traumatic events that took place long before the individual committed any crime. To understand this is to understand that for some ex-offenders incarceration was not so much of a sharp turning point but a culmination of negative life experiences.

Some women were arrested for criminal activity years after leaving their childhood home. This was true of Aaliyah, Kiana, and Trisha. For other women, the turmoil they experience at home expedited their participation in illegal activity. In the face of alcoholic fathers and abusive mothers, some of the women I spoke with ran away from home and began engaging in risky and illicit behaviors early in their teens. What they share in common with women who were convicted as adults is that there wasn't necessarily a distinct moment that triggered their turn toward crime. Childhood abuse sets the backdrop for decisions, relationships, and crime that would influence later life decisions.

"I DIDN'T WANT TO DEAL WITH THE FAMILY ISSUES"

Thirty minutes from the hustle and bustle of Boston, the neatly appointed Cape Cods on tree lined streets capture the quintessential New England ethos of Ariana's childhood hometown. Unlike most of the women I interviewed, Ariana grew up in a middle-class neighborhood with both parents. Describing the large backyard where she and her siblings played, she also recalls feeling alone and excluded. Adopted as a baby, she felt different from her peers. As one of the few Latina girls in her school, she was subject to teasing by her white classmates because of her physical characteristics and her name. Her home life was also challenging. While her household seemed stable from the outside, she describes it as dysfunctional. A self-employed businessman, her father was abusive to her sister. Witnessing this abuse, she says, led to her delinquent behavior.

> *Ariana:* And then after, when I was fourteen, I just started like drinking. And my father was abusive to my sister. He would hit her, he would verbally abuse her, so I just became a runaway. I just didn't want to deal with the family issues, you know, like with my dad. And they were like never home, so it was like I was by myself. And my friends could come to the house, and my father would tell them to leave. So I just took off pretty much, just took off. And when I was sixteen, I was living with a thirty-seven-year-old guy.

Early onset of alcohol consumption, a response associated with other forms of childhood abuse, was one way that Ariana coped with her difficult home environment.[32] Running away from home and having no one to support her, Ariana entered into a relationship that she later realized was unhealthy. Not only can witnessing domestic violence have negative psychosocial effects on children, such as depression, anxiety, and aggressive behavior, but it can also increase the risk of behaviors, such as drug abuse and running away, that often lead to more serious acts of delinquency or crime.[33]

Felicia, a white thirty-eight-year-old mother from New England, recalls a similar experience from her childhood:

> *Geniece:* Okay. And so, how would you describe your upbringing, up to the point at twelve, and then afterward?
>
> *Felicia:* My dad was a violent, abusive alcoholic. Very unpredictable and I was very fearful, very scared, like, all the time. And then, my mom left, and she came back and got us, and like, it was kind of a normal childhood. You know, she worked, she went to school. Like, he wasn't part of our lives after that.

For some women the presence of an unstable parent in the household was intermittent and unpredictable. Their exposure to the volatility of an abusive parent was therefore interspersed between periods of relative calm. Still, even when not living with the abusive parent the fear of those future interactions took a psychological toll.[34]

Twenty-six-year-old Summer, a white mother of two boys from Upstate New York, witnessed her mother's addiction occasionally. Because she saw her mother sporadically she felt that she was shielded from her mother's drug abuse. Moreover, the relationship she developed with her father's ex-wife provided her with a motherlike figure that helped to fill the void created by her mother's absence.

> *Summer:* I speak to her [biological mother] but I have. . . .my father's ex-wife, like I call [her] my mother. She's my mother. I like to this day call her mom and talk to her all the time even though she's not married to my father anymore so.
>
> *Geniece:* Oh, okay and so did you ever meet your biological mom?
>
> *Summer:* Oh yeah. I talk to her still but like we don't have a close relationship like she's still my mother. She was just never there. She was in and out of our life our whole lives so.
>
> *Geniece:* Okay and so do you know why she didn't stay around?
>
> *Summer:* Because she had a drug habit. She was smoking crack all her life so.

Twenty-two-year-old Trina, an African-American mother from the Bronx, also experienced the absence of her mother growing up due to drug addiction. However, unlike Summer there was no one available to fill the maternal void left by her mother once she was incarcerated. As a result, Trina spent much of her formative years resenting her mother.

> *Geniece:* How did he feel about the fact that your mom wasn't the person raising you?
>
> *Trina:* Now that I've been to jail and I've done a lot of soul-searching and I learned about her addiction through the drug program that I did when I was incarcerated at kinds of don't blame her nothing because the drug to the best of her. But at first I couldn't really stand her. My mother is a good mother. . . . She was strict about school in certain areas of our lives but . . . I felt comfortable talking to her about anything, doing anything. So at one point I was very mad. And I'm still kind of mad to a point. Not that my grandmother raised me any different but my grandmother was harder. . . . Now, I do wish she would've raised us. Like sometimes I think like if I was with mommy I would have been better. And it's not even like my grandmother raised us bad it was just she was a little too extra.[35]

Despite knowing that her mother's addiction would have created an unstable home for her and her siblings, Trina felt that being raised by her mother would have provided her with the guidance her grandmother could not.

There is wide consensus among clinicians that childhood physical and sexual abuse have severe long-term effects on victims who don't receive appropriate intervention.[36] Exposure to abuse, such as witnessing domestic violence and crime within one's community, can also negatively influence a child's behavior in ways that may indirectly affect adult outcomes.[37] For example, witnessing illicit methods of earning money made participation in crime easier according to some respondents. Those who lived in communities where access to drugs was readily available described drug dealing as an avenue for financial security. Little of this seems to matter, however, as a woman awaits trial in a jail cell or serves a prison sentence. As far as the judicial system is concerned, her story began the day that she was arrested. From that day onward, her responsibility has been to redeem herself in the eyes of a society that has pronounced her morally compromised.

THE OTHER WORLD

When you think about a boundary, you likely call to mind something that represents a division, a separation, or a border. Moving past a boundary takes one into a new space that brings with it the possibility of opportunity or peril. When I thought of the boundaries that shaped the lives of women like Trisha and Aaliyah, it seemed that their boundaries shifted constantly, pushing them further from where they wanted to be. And these shifts did not begin in adulthood, they began before they were ever cognizant of what it meant to be an outsider in one's own world. Being marginalized means always having to think about boundaries because what one does or says can mean the difference between security and insecurity. Indeed, marginality is not like crossing a boundary that brings you from one side of a street to another. Instead, it is standing on a precipice, one side representing housing, freedom, and holding one's child, and the other, unbearable loss.

These boundaries become clearer as adults, but they are present early in life. They hearken to the distinction Du Bois makes between his marginal identity and the society from which he was excluded: "Between me and the other world . . . " he notes, as he describes the separation between life as an African-American and white American society.[38] This "other world" represents the promise of full citizenship and inclusion but is also a reminder of what is being denied. For young Trisha and Aaliyah, there was a place beyond their bounded worlds, another world, in which they were safe at home. For twenty-eight-year-old Trisha and twenty-year-old Aaliyah there was another world in which healing rather than punishment was at the center.

The childhood experiences of the women I interviewed are unfortunately not uncommon for formerly incarcerated women. Research shows that incarcerated individuals are more likely to be victims of traumatic childhood events than people in the general population. The impact of those childhood experiences lasts well into adulthood and creates a vulnerable population that is more likely to be criminalized rather than offered treatment.[39] Moreover, Horwitz et al. find that all other variables being equal the relationship between childhood victimization and adult mental health points to the impact of a "matrix of disadvantage" that includes factors beyond childhood abuse.[40]

The stories that women tell about their childhoods reveal that their awareness of their marginal identity began long before their incarceration. The details of their early lives provide insight into what it means to be born on the margins and how that later shapes relationships and decisions. It was those earlier experiences, for example, that shaped women's understanding that institutions and social services did not save girls like them and likely would not advocate for the women they would one day become. The negotiation of criminal identity, then, must be seen as an extension of how women negotiated other marginal statuses. What they learned in those early years would inform how they engaged with correctional entities and their ability to read the unwritten codes required of them to navigate life after incarceration.

CHAPTER 2

Love, Baby, and Chaos

"Have you ever seen the show *Snapped*?" Kishana asked me, as she recalled the day that she was arrested for aggravated assault. Before I could respond that I was familiar with the show, which centered around crimes of passion committed by women, Kishana described the events of the day.[1] Kishana remembered seeing her boyfriend's car parked outside of their apartment building and she remembered holding the box cutter. She even remembered calling first responders. However, the time in between lunging at her boyfriend and the blood pouring out of his neck, was a hazy fog of fear and adrenaline. What she did recall was believing that the man she loved was going to kill her. The very thing she wanted from her boyfriend Gary was the same thing she wanted from her own father: love. And it was that longing for love that seemed to upend her life. For Kishana, finding what she thought was love led to pain, and having a baby, which for some might offer a temporary respite from the turbulence of criminal activity, seemed to further drive the instability in her life. A two-parent household, long-term relationships, childbirth: all these might be markers that indicate positive social bonds. However, for Kishana and other women I spoke to, they were catalysts for heartbreak and a prison sentence.

Crime occurs for any number of reasons: It may be a seemingly rational, albeit law-violating response to a perceived need, a result of a sudden, survival-based reaction. Or it may be the consequence of an intentional decision to cause harm to another person. Many of this country's laws and policies center on the latter of these reasons, even if it means defining crime in ways that benefit some at the expense of others.[2] Women like Kishana were aware that their actions violated the law, but they were also aware that pregnancy, motherhood, and relationships could exacerbate existing sources of trauma and influence future criminal activity. In this chapter I attend to this issue by examining an often-overlooked element of justice involving women's marginal status: the intersection between pregnancy and intimate-partner relationships. When women remain in unstable relationships it can be easy to dismiss their actions as the result of poor decision making. I argue that there is more at play in these situations, particularly as it relates to how women negotiate their status as expectant mothers who have been stigmatized in formal and informal ways. When women enter into a relationship that might seem unwise or stay with a partner who has proven to be harmful, they are often adjudicating between their pregnancies, their roles as mothers, and what that relationship means for their status vis-à-vis the criminal justice system.

Pregnancy and motherhood, while closely related, are not one in the same, and it is important to consider how the context in which pregnancy occurs influences women's later decisions about motherhood. Motherhood is a life-long journey but pregnancy is a finite period, bringing with it hope, fear, and for some women, interpersonal upheaval. At the moment a woman learns that she is pregnant, she and her partner are thrust into navigating questions and challenges that come with parenting.[3] In this way, the impact that a pregnancy has on a relationship is not solely a result of the pregnancy itself but what the pregnancy will mean for the future of the relationship once a child is born. This can draw a couple closer as they plan for their life as parents or it can expose fault lines within the relationship.[4] In concert with other destabilizing aspects of life, pregnancy can function almost like a flashpoint moment, a sudden and often unexpected time of high stress that places women further outside the margins of society.

Kishana's story illustrates the complex interplay between pregnancy and marginality, as do the stories of other women who shared their journey to motherhood with me. The beginnings are similar: Growing up, life at home was troubled, so they sought love from a boy or a man who seemed to offer a tangible escape from the worst parts of life. Whether it was love or the promise of love, those relationships were often a whirlwind of emotions, with a pregnancy occurring early in the courtship. Faced with the prospect of staying in a volatile relationship or bearing the economic burden of being a single mother, women found themselves deciding between one version of marginality over another. In this context, duality at the margins means making seemingly counterintuitive decisions that appear to be risky at one level, yet intended to protect mother and child at another. Recognizing this means also acknowledging that decisions are rarely as straightforward as choosing the objective best option. Rather, women are deciding how to avoid one type of harm, even when those decisions may expose them to another.

KISHANA'S FIRST BABY

For as long as Kishana could remember, she was a protector. After she was given up for adoption, Kishana and her younger sister were soon placed in a permanent home, avoiding the prolonged stay in foster care not uncommon for Black children.[5] Avoiding the instability of the foster care system was not a guarantee of domestic tranquility, however. A child herself, Kishana was quickly thrust into the role of guardian, as she did all she could to make her younger sister feel safe. When her adoptive father's drunken rages escalated from verbal assaults to physical violence she tried her best to shield her sister from his blows, even if it meant that her small body would be covered in bruises. When she realized that her mother wouldn't or couldn't fight back, she became her mother's protector as well. Embittered by her father's abuse and resentful of her mother's perceived weaknesses, Kishana decided early on in life that she would never allow anyone to mistake her for anything but strong. By the time Kishana and I met, she was a twenty-five-year-old woman who had already lived a lifetime's worth of protecting and fighting, heartache and disappointment. While her protective nature had helped her sister, mother, and her own children, she believes it also contributed to her arrest and incarceration.

By all accounts, Kishana was raised with advantages that should have insulated her from delinquency, teen pregnancy, and incarceration. Her parents were in their forties when they adopted her and her sister and were economically stable. Raised in a two-parent household, with parents who valued their daughters' academic success, many on the outside might assume that she and her sister enjoyed the security of a middle-class upbringing. Beneath the veneer of stability was what Kishana describes as the authoritarian-like posture of her father. Sleepovers, skating, and going to the movies were all strictly forbidden, while failing to earn perfect grades was met with corporal punishment.

The constant pressure Kishana felt to meet her father's expectations and the fear of verbal and physical abuse soon became untenable. By the time she was in middle school the simmering rage she felt toward her father boiled over. It was well known throughout their neighborhood that Kishana's father was not one to be trifled with, leading many of the neighborhood boys to steer clear of his young daughters. There was one exception, however. A seventeen-year-old boy caught Kishana's attention because he seemed unbothered by neighborhood lore surrounding her father. It wasn't long before Kishana's admiration of his irreverent posture toward her father turned into romantic attraction. Once they began dating, the two devised a plan whereby she would spend the night at his grandmother's home and they would sneak out once his grandmother fell asleep. No sooner had Kishana and her boyfriend begun their late-night rendezvous than Kishana's mother noticed the changes in her daughter's body.

Shortly before Kishana was to begin ninth grade her mother brought her to a doctor to confirm her suspicions: her fourteen-year-old daughter was pregnant. Not only that, but Kishana had managed to hide her pregnancy from the adults in her life for five and half months. When I asked Kishana to describe how her parents responded to the pregnancy she described two very different reactions. Her mother was upset because Kishana went without proper prenatal care for over half of her pregnancy. Her father, on the other hand, was less concerned with his daughter's health or the health of the baby and more angered by the fact that his daughter was sexually active. Unable to come to terms with her pregnancy and the disrespect to his authority he felt it represented, Kishana describes how his treatment toward her went from cold to cruel:

> After the pregnancy I would talk [back]. Because I already had so much animosity towards him anyway. So once he started doing more evil things that just gave me an excuse not to speak to him. I just didn't care what he felt about anything.

Up until her pregnancy the one area in their relationship in which she and her father shared common ground was the importance of academic success. Once a perennial honor roll student, Kishana's grades plummeted as she lost interest in school and no longer cared about meeting her father's expectations. When she dropped out of school and began running away from home, her father retaliated by seeking to press charges against her boyfriend for statutory rape. For Kishana, this was the tipping point in their relationship. Packing a few of her possessions, she fled to her boyfriend's home. Leaving home meant that she no longer had to comply with her father's rules or experience the verbal and physical abuse that followed when she fell short of his demands. Leaving home also meant that her mother and younger sister now had to fend for themselves. Kishana was used to feeling unprotected, but for the first time in her young life fourteen-year-old Kishana had no one to protect.

The relief Kishana felt after leaving the volatility and violence of her parents' home was short-lived. Two weeks after her daughter was born her boyfriend was sentenced to ten years in prison for murder. When I asked Kishana to explain her feelings about her daughter's father, she was circumspect:

> The only communication he had with her was when his mother brought us or when I got older I went myself. Or if I didn't take my daughter his mother took her. So my daughter know her daddy. She's very close with him. She loves him and they have a good relationship to this day.

Despite the fact that he was incarcerated during his daughter's early childhood, Kishana described him as a good father. For some, his inability to be present with his daughter and the reason for his absence might exclude him from the label "good father." But Kishana knew what it was like to have a father present within the home, and for her that simply was not enough.

KISHANA AND GARY

After her daughter's father went to prison Kishana returned to her parents' home, only to soon realize that she needed to leave. Her father never failed to remind her that he viewed her as a failure and her mother, though she supported Kishana, would ultimately acquiesce to her husband's wishes. By her early twenties Kishana made the decision to relocate to Upstate New York. She and her daughter had been living there for only a few months when she met Gary. At this time she was at a vulnerable place in her life, trying to make ends meet on a retail job's wages, while balancing the responsibilities of being a single mother. The toll of keeping herself financially afloat each month in a new city left her feeling isolated and alone. It was no wonder, then, that when Gary walked into her life, she was drawn to the security he could provide for she and her young child. Gary was charismatic, financially stable, and, at twenty years her senior, seemingly more mature than other men she had dated in the past. So relieved was she to no longer have to worry about providing for her daughter that she recalls overlooking an early red flag in their relationship. At the time they met Gary was attending domestic violence classes as part of a requirement from a previous court ruling.

As much as she wanted their relationship to work, Kishana had a difficult time accepting Gary's history of domestic abuse in light of her own experiences with her father. To put her mind at ease, she contacted all four of his ex-wives to inquire about his abusive past. In each conversation they confirmed her worst fears: Gary had a short temper that erupted in physical violence. Still, Kishana wondered, was it possible that he had changed? Gary tried to allay her fears by telling her his ex-wives were lying and, at the time, Kishana felt no reason not to trust him. After all, by the time Kishana spoke to his ex-wives she and Gary had been dating for seven months and during that time he hadn't so much as raised his voice at her.[6] Perhaps he *had* dealt with his demons in the court-mandated classes he regularly attended. At least this is what Kishana told herself. As their relationship continued to progress without incident Kishana started to believe that perhaps Gary was indeed a victim of character assassination and that his ex-wives conspired to destroy their relationship. She simply could not reconcile the man she loved with the monster his ex-wives described. Just as Kishana began to settle into her relationship with Gary, however, he began to display the very behaviors his ex-wives described in their conversations with Kishana.

Because she had her daughter at fourteen, Kishana often felt that she missed out on the carefree joys of adolescence and young adulthood. So, when she finally found stability with Gary she was eager to go to clubs and parties on weekends. Gary, however, was in his forties and no longer interested in the party scene. Her place was not at the club, he told her, but at home. Taking his words as merely a difference of opinion, Kishana didn't think that her decision to go out on weekends would create a problem within their relationship. However, after one night of partying, Kishana returned home to find Gary enraged. Soon, physical abuse began to permeate every aspect of their relationship and Kishana could do nothing to appease Gary.

After each violent episode Gary would engage in what psychologists call "love bombing," showering her with attention and gifts to ensure that their relationship remained intact.[7] Realizing that her situation was unlikely to improve, Kishana decided to use his attempts at winning her forgiveness to her advantage. Gary would often give her access to his debit card so that she could go shopping. Rather than shop, however, Kishana would withdraw cash and put it into a personal account. Knowing that she eventually wanted to start a new life for her and her daughter, she hoped that the money she saved would make her break up with Gary easier. Initially her plan worked. She was able to save up enough money for a deposit on an apartment in another area of their city. However, it wasn't long before a mutual acquaintance informed Gary about the apartment. According to Kishana, this happened repeatedly in the course of their relationship. She would try to leave and he would find her new residence, often reacting violently when he did. When she sought help from law enforcement, she felt she was either ignored or his social connections worked to his advantage. Over the course of their relationship Kishana stated that she filed thirty-five police reports, none of which resulted in his arrest.

An important detail that Gary used as leverage over Kishana was not unlike the experiences of other women who found themselves in vulnerable legal predicaments.[8] Shortly before meeting Gary, Kishana had been in a fight at a local bar. She was sentenced to jail for six months and on probation for another four. Although the punishment for this crime was far less serious than the crime she would be convicted of years later, there were still serious consequences. For example, because she was still on probation when she dated Gary, he was able to strike fear into her by merely threatening to call law enforcement. He knew that if she had police contact at any point during her probation she might have to return to jail. So, while she was not afraid to file police reports against Gary, she also knew that if he called law enforcement to their home under the auspices of a domestic dispute, a judge might require her to return to jail. Kishana explained to me how he would use her probation as a means of control:

Geniece: You said that he held it [probation] over you?

Kishana: Yeah, he used it a lot. He used it a lot. Like if [I] didn't do something he wanted me to do he would say, he would threaten that he was going to call the police. So if the police came to the house that's police contact, especially if he called them and made a report.

Geniece: He could call at any time and that automatically that was proof of contact?

Kishana: Yeah. And I would go back to jail.

While a judge or a prosecutor might exercise discretion and not require her to return to jail, the mere possibility was enough to fill her with fear. Tired of the rollercoaster nature of their relationship, Kishana decided that it was time that she and her daughter leave town. The very stability that had drawn her to Gary had become golden handcuffs, keeping her in an abusive relationship and exposing her daughter to the same environment she witnessed as a child.[9] In addition to wanting to start a new life without Gary, there was another reason Kishana wanted to leave: she was pregnant with her second child.

When Kishana learned that Gary had an upcoming business trip, she made plans to quickly pack her belongings and move out. Because he was well connected and a number of his close friends were in law enforcement, she resolved that a move to another part of their city would be pointless. Her only option was to leave the region entirely and return to her parents' city down south. Her plans to leave were going well until Gary unexpectedly returned home. His trip had been cut short and he arrived home to find most of her belongings missing and other items packed away in moving boxes. She wasn't at home when he returned but she knew he was there when she saw his car parked outside. By that point, however, she was so determined to leave that the fear of what might happen when she stepped inside the apartment wasn't enough to keep her from walking in. When I asked her to explain what happened next, she described the events of that day as a blur:

> To be honest with you I don't know what was going through my head. But I knew that when I came home I was going to walk into a fight with him because you know you just don't leave somebody overnight. . . . I had already packed most of my things and had removed them from the house because he was on like a retreat in Florida and he wasn't supposed to come home that week and he was there. When I came in, I let myself in and I had a box cutter in my hand for the boxes. He went to reach back to do one of these numbers [she gestures, raising her hand over her head] and I swung the box cutter.

As Gary's neck bled, Kishana called first responders who arrived on the scene to take him to the hospital. She was taken into police custody the same day.

When examining the role of pregnancy in the life of single mothers, criminal involvement is an added and significant variable that influences what happens in the days and weeks that follow.[10] Kishana's experience illustrates that there are varying degrees of marginality for expectant mothers and those differences matter. Being a young couple, burdened by the financial concerns of taking care of a baby, is a type of instability that may be mitigated, even if briefly, by a child's birth. But in Kishana's case, when her family was unsupportive, one child's father was incarcerated for murder, and her unborn child's father was abusing her, pregnancy had the opposite effect. She was vulnerable and her partner exploited this. With that reality at the forefront of her mind, Kishana made decisions that she might not have made otherwise. On the day she assaulted Gary with a box cutter, an act she describes as self-defense, Kishana desperately wanted to start her life over with her children. When Kishana decided to leave New York it was because she could not imagine going through pregnancy while bearing the physical and emotional blows of Gary's fists and words. Instead, she found herself pregnant and in prison, wondering if at twenty-two years of age she would ever be able to raise her children without the fear or threat of danger.

THE ELUSIVE MAGIC MOMENT

Mainstream representations of pregnancy are filled with images of couples scrambling to find suitable childcare, assembling baby furniture, and searching for a pediatrician. For Kishana, the heightened state of urgency created by the need to leave an abusive partner made that vision of expectant motherhood feel incredibly distant. She wanted stability and had hoped that she and Gary might experience what researchers describe as a "magic moment."[11] Facing the uncertainty of impending parenthood, the magic moment describes how a new baby provides a type of relational anchoring for a couple. Relationships are restored, fathers want to become family men, and women are willing to forgive past grievances with their child's father.[12] This magic moment, however, would remain elusive for Kishana.

At the time we spoke, Kishana had only been out of prison for two and a half weeks. Early in her three-year prison sentence for aggravated assault, she gave birth to a son and had to decide whether to place him in foster care or place him in the custody of the very man she held responsible for her criminal conviction. Ultimately, Gary assumed custody of their son for the duration of her sentence. In an unexpected turn of events Gary regularly sent her care packages and met all of her material needs. To Kishana this was his attempt to make penance for his role in her incarceration. His attentiveness did little to compensate for the years of abuse she experienced at his hands and for the years in prison she would have to spend away from her children.

After the birth of her second child, Kishana made a promise to God: from then on she would carefully consider her choices in a partner. No man, she concluded, was worth the heartache that she had experienced up to that point. Before going to prison Kishana warned her young daughter to avoid her pitfalls. Recounting the experiences that led her incarceration she admonished her then nine-year-old daughter that "men are not worth this." Indeed, for Kishana, it was her volatile and unstable relationships with men—her father, her daughter's father, and her son's father—that created the contexts for her most difficult life experiences. While she had no choice in who her father was, she also felt that she made choices that placed her and her children in vulnerable positions. In her life, the pregnancies that resulted from her relationships weren't the kind of turning points that positively impacted her trajectory. Rather, they exacerbated the challenges of already fraught relationships and contentious domestic environments.

In examining Kishana's and other women's experiences it is important to distinguish the stigma of criminal involvement from other stigmatizing characteristics often used in analyses of marginalized mothers. The stigma of poverty, for example, while significant in shaping life chances for low-income single mothers, holds different implications for women who are societally marked by a criminal record.[13] Family support, for example, may be less available if an individual's criminal activity caused a rift in existing relationships.[14] Moreover, a criminal record is often one factor that excludes individuals from the very things couples prioritize before having a child, such as housing and employment.

When the challenges that shape the life of women extend beyond that of a relationship and are rooted in early life experiences, having a baby may arrive at a moment so volatile that there is little space for even the temporary optimism that a new life might bring. Within the first half of Kishana's life she experienced varying degrees of love and chaos. In a place where she might have experienced stability, a two-parent middle-class home, she yearned for the love of her father. From her criminally involved boyfriend she found love and a sense of protection from her father's rules, but there too she encountered turmoil and heartache when he was incarcerated. By the time Kishana was fifteen she was raising a daughter, who would spend the first years of her young life getting to know her father during visits to prison. Years later, that same daughter would visit Kishana when she too was incarcerated.

DECIDING TO HAVE A BABY

In analyzing how women I interviewed described their reactions to pregnancy, I found that there were twenty-seven instances in which women stated that happiness was the primary emotion they felt when they learned that they were pregnant. By contrast, there were fifty-four instances in which women expressed feelings of unhappiness, fear, or worry about the prospect of being parents. In considering the factors surrounding pregnancy it is important to understand how women view both their pregnancy and their decision to have a child. Amid a stressful home environment and the lack of social support, women can simultaneously acknowledge the impact of circumstances beyond their control, while also exerting their agency in the choice to have a child.

It can be tempting to view the decision to have a child as dichotomous: Either a woman has the ability to freely make a choice to carry her child to term or she does not. Either she wants to be a mother or she does not. This view is incomplete and overlooks the broader issues at play. The agency that women exert when making decisions about pregnancy and motherhood do not exist in a vacuum. Rather, the decision is framed within the context of a number of other vulnerabilities that impact how women view their options.[15] Aaliyah's experience, for example, illustrates what happens when a young girl's agency is stripped from her through sexual assault. For some women the experience of pregnancy may be more nuanced. For example, a pregnancy may be unplanned but welcome news. For other women it may be both unplanned and unwelcomed, yet termination may not be an option due to a woman's limited access or her personal views about abortion.[16]

Kishana, for example, considered abortion to avoid the ire of her father, but at fourteen years old didn't believe that was a viable option.[17] Distraught and overwhelmed with fear, she also considered self-harm. Explaining her early reaction to pregnancy, she stated:

> I was actually thinking about cutting the baby out of me, I was so scared. Like I didn't know what to do. I was still a child myself. I just didn't know what to do.

Similar to Kishana, forty-eight-year-old Jane, a white mother from Massachusetts, recalls her reaction to learning that she was pregnant with her first child:

> I wasn't really ready to have a baby, and I didn't want to have a baby. And I remember going to my mom and telling my mom I didn't want to have a

baby. I'd really rather have an abortion because I wasn't ready for kids. And my parents didn't believe in that. You know, Catholic, and so my mom was like, "I don't think that's an option for you." She said, "If you don't want to have the baby, give it up for adoption, or whatever." And I was like, you know—I was not discussing this with him [boyfriend], I was just talking to my mom about it. So. . .I had the baby. I wasn't prepared to have a baby because I had a lot of dreams, a lot of things I wanted to do. And I'm very smart, but I ended up having him and I had to really deal with it, you know? And I always felt like I held onto resentment because of that, because I didn't want to have a baby.

Like Kishana, the most influential people in shaping Jane's feelings about her pregnancy were her parents. Neither mentioned their boy-friend's reactions playing a role in their decision to continue with their pregnancies because in both cases they were living at home and depend-ent upon their families for economic support. This illustrates how preg-nancy provides one of the starkest examples of the limitedness of young women's agency. Because the decision to have a baby was decided for them by the adults in their lives, their entrée into motherhood was more influenced by others' views about their pregnancy rather than their own.[18] In this way, the inability to express fears or apprehension about one of the most life-shifting roles a person can inhabit, underscores the intersection between agency and marginality. Women can come to embrace motherhood, as both Kishana and Jane eventually did, but that does not negate what that early experience told them about their place the world: that as young women, their place was marginal.

Even when there are not obvious outside forces pressuring women to keep an unwanted pregnancy, there may still be significant factors that impinge on a woman's decision to carry a pregnancy to term. Drug offenses, a leading reason for arrest and conviction among women since the mid-1990s, also shaped the experience of pregnancy and the deci-sions women made about having children.[19] Valerie, a 41-year-old white mother from Manhattan, was shocked to learn that she was pregnant. When I asked her to share her initial reaction she stated:

The first thing I said was . . . how could this have happened? Because I was really carefully with condoms, I mean, I was going to have an abortion, but I was too busy getting high, every time I went for an appointment, the drugs I wanted to get high, so I wouldn't go and then it was too late.

Like Valerie, Brittany, a thirty-six-year-old white mother from Staten Island, was struggling with addiction when she discovered that she was pregnant.

Brittany: I was twenty-one. I didn't really want to be a mother, but I just went ahead and went through with it. When I found out I was pregnant it wasn't a great time to have an abortion.

Geniece: What do you mean by that?

Brittany: When the baby grows it's not good to have an abortion; like twelve weeks or something like that. When I found out I was like three or four months. I was really small, I was smaller than I am now and you couldn't even tell. I got my period for the first three months, so I didn't even really know. I was drinking a lot too. I didn't want to, but I felt like I had to have him. Then when I had him, I loved him. If you're not a mother then you don't know.

Elise, a Black twenty-eight-year-old mother born in Pennsylvania, also shared how addiction shaped her reaction to an unplanned pregnancy.

Elise: During the pregnancy I didn't spend anytime with the baby because when I gave birth to the baby in prison they took the baby. . . . I have a really long history of drug abuse so I was trying to fight to get my kids back and I just kind of got discourage and then I started using again and that was when I found out that I was pregnant with the fourth baby. And um that's when things really got bad.

Geniece: With the second father?

Elise: Mmhm. And then with the [domestic] abuse and the using [of drugs] it was just too much and my sister took the baby too.

Rose, a fifty-one-year-old Black mother who moved to Massachusetts in the 1970s, also describes how she felt when she learned that she was expecting her fourth child:

Fourth child, that wasn't like such a good one . . . because I had started drinking, at that time, and I saw myself kind of spiraling down with the alcohol. So that was a kind of scary experience. And plus, the father, he was drinking, also.

Both Valerie's and Brittany's decision to carry their pregnancies to term were not intentional in the way in which we typically understand decision making. Addiction and the passage of time seemed to decide for them, and they framed pregnancy as yet another unplanned life event. Although Elise and Rose never mentioned contemplating abortion, both of their pregnancies occurred during drug addiction, alcoholism, and intimate-partner victimization. Eventually, they expressed coming to terms with pregnancy. Elise, for example, stated, "I kind of got used to the fact that I was going to be a mother and I became happy about it." These examples of pregnancy suggest a view of unplanned pregnancy that doesn't conform to theories that pathologize single motherhood but also diverges from perspectives that describe how low-income single mothers choose single parenthood.[20] Somewhere along the spectrum of marginalized motherhood are the women who didn't choose motherhood but arrived there through circumstances they identify as tumultuous. And, when facing the prospect of motherhood, women like Valerie did what some of the other women I spoke with did: they adapted and they moved forward.

The manner in which women discuss their feelings about their pregnancies yet again reveals how duality at the margins functions in the lives of criminalized women. Pregnancy and motherhood can garner some women esteem, particularly when they meet socially embedded heteronormative ideas related to femininity and gender.[21] But for criminalized women, pregnancy seems to further marginalize them. More precisely, others' reactions to their pregnancy decenters their agency. Pregnancy reminds women that the ability to make decisions for themselves about their lives will be a hard-fought battle. This marginalizing aspect of pregnancy, however, is not the sum of women's experiences, and nor do women internalize that message passively. Even while experiencing the marginality that comes with pregnancy for women like them, they also reframe pregnancy as a site of agency.

This occurs even when most pregnancies are unplanned. Of the seventy women I interviewed only five stated that their pregnancies were planned. Among those with unplanned pregnancies, some welcomed the birth of a child. In important ways women who welcomed unplanned pregnancies were not significantly different from those who didn't want to be pregnant. Troubled childhoods and economic instability were not uncommon for both groups of women. In fact, some of the *same* women who described wanting an abortion for one pregnancy, saw subsequent pregnancies as positive news. As is the case with most aspects of understanding social life, context is important. Pregnancy is shaped by the events that surround it, both in the past and in the immediate future. While one pregnancy might occur during a volatile time, another might occur when a woman is in a different relationship or has secured stable employment. The two factors women most frequently viewed as shaping their positive outlook on pregnancy was the presence of consistent social support and, counterintuitively, the pregnancy arriving at a challenging point in their lives.

The first reason is not particularly surprising since existing literature shows how the influence of support systems positively impacts a mother's experiences with childrearing.[22] An involved prospective father, for example, was a key reason some women saw an otherwise unexpected challenge as a potentially positive development. The second reason—a pregnancy providing a sense of calm at an otherwise difficult time in a woman's life—not only seems counterintuitive but it also seems to substantiate the idea that women did in fact benefit from a postpregnancy magic moment. Women's positive feelings about pregnancy, however, did not necessarily overlap with positive feelings about their intimate-partner relationships. Rather, women might view their unplanned pregnancies positively, not because of what the pregnancy meant for the future of their relationships, but because of what it meant for how they could define their own identity as women.

When twenty-five-year-old Audrey learned that she was pregnant she and her boyfriend were making money by selling drugs. Still, she describes feeling optimistic about what motherhood would mean for her future.

Geniece: Now how old were you when you got pregnant with your first child?

Audrey: Twenty-one.

Geniece: So this is the pregnancy [*indiscernible*] when you . . .

Audrey: Yeah, like twenty-one going to twenty-two, yeah.

Geniece: How did you feel when you found that you're pregnant?

Audrey: Happy. Excited.

Geniece: And your child's father was supportive?

Audrey: Yeah.

Geniece: He was very supportive?

Audrey: Yeah, with our first child. Yeah, he was happy.

Geniece: So, you were selling, you said?

Audrey: Mmmhmm.

Geniece: And with you selling or were you, you had different jobs?

Audrey: We both were selling.

For Audrey, her partner's involvement in illicit activity did not preclude him from being a supportive father. In this context economic support from a partner wasn't limited to mainstream definitions of economic stability. Their shared method of economic gain meant that Audrey's definition of support was based on her partner's ability to meet her emotional needs, rather than his ability to conform to normative representations of fatherhood. Moreover, Audrey's feelings about a new baby were specific to the arrival of the child, but didn't change her views about the relationship with her partner. She didn't fear that a baby would negatively impact her life, nor did she expect that it would change their lives for the better.

At forty-nine, Marcia, a Black mother who moved to Massachusetts from Chicago, could easily pass for a woman ten years younger. Upbeat and loquacious, she was eager to describe the moment she learned that she was pregnant. Like most of the women with whom I spoke, her life lacked the stability she would have wanted for a baby, but she nevertheless welcomed the news.

> *Geniece:* So, how did you feel the first time—well, when you found out you were pregnant? You were eighteen and you were pregnant, how did you feel about the situation? Were you surprised?
>
> *Marcia:* No. No, I was happy.
>
> *Geniece:* You were happy?
>
> *Marcia:* Yeah. I was happy because I was in love with my boyfriend. But I was older that he was, but he lied. When I got pregnant, I was eighteen. He was sixteen. And he lied about his age. And I'm pregnant and I like—forget it, you know what I'm saying. But then, I was happy, I did what I needed to do.
>
> *Geniece:* Yeah. He was with you for four years?
>
> *Marcia:* Yeah. But he was kind of abusive. That's why we're not together. I made him go in the army. He became a sergeant. And we're friends and that's all it's going to be.

Marcia's experience is not unlike the tumultuous journey other women described in pregnancy. Even when they initially welcomed the news of pregnancy, the weeks and months following the news could bring about relational strife and, ultimately, the dissolution of the relationship. In Marcia's case, as was true for Kishana, the prelude to criminal involvement was intimate-partner victimization. Not every woman who is victimized eventually commits a crime, but for those who do, the trauma of past abuse is not unconnected from future experiences within the criminal justice system.[23]

The literature on turning points examines key life experiences that promote criminal desistance. On the other side of those experiences are life events that can place individuals at greater risk for criminal involvement.[24] For some of the women I interviewed the link between pregnancy and criminal activity were closely related. The combination of an abusive intimate-partner relationship, a lack of strong social networks, and financial instability created an environment of precariousness that was made all the more unstable when women became pregnant. In Kishana we see the portrait of a woman who wanted nothing more than to escape an abusive relationship. For other women, however, their criminal activity was born out to a desire to *remain* in a relationship.

"IT HURT ME TO SEE HIM WITH SOMEBODY ELSE"

As the judge read her sentence, Dani felt her legs grow numb. At that moment, the gravity of her circumstances began to register. It wasn't just the number of years in prison she would have to spend away from her children that left her physically weak. Rather, it was the judge's words, a devastating indictment about why she found herself in court that day. Paraphrasing the judge's words, Dani recalls his comments: "I want you to realize how you threw your life away for the love of beer." As the judge handed down her sentence, he described all the ways in which Dani squandered the good fortune of being raised in a two-parent home with hard-working parents. But to Dani, he like so many others was either oblivious to or uninterested in the fact that her biography on paper did not align with the reality of her story.

Wanting to shelter their daughter from becoming another statistic in their neighborhood, Dani's parents sent her to a good school. They monitored where she socialized, taking care to shield her from New York City neighborhoods with reputations for violent crime. Although well intentioned, Dani found her parents' rules burdensome and restrictive. By the time she reached adolescence, she regularly disregarded their rules and would socialize in the areas of the city forbidden by her parents. Eventually, she began skipping school and spending time with a local drug dealer named Shawn.

When Dani first learned that Shawn was cheating on her, she was living in his apartment with limited options. She had dropped out of high school, she was estranged from her family, and she was pregnant with her first child. Although she felt discouraged by her situation, she was optimistic that once the baby arrived she and Shawn would reconcile and work together to raise their child. The birth of her son, however, did little to quell her ongoing concerns. Not long after she gave birth, she learned that Shawn was also in a relationship with another young woman from their neighborhood. She ended their relationship but still found the betrayal deeply painful. Overwhelmed with the responsibilities of motherhood and loneliness, Dani begin to drink. In her words:

I didn't realize one of the girls he was sleeping with, actually lived maybe a block from me. So here I am, coming from work, you know picking the baby up from my mom, 'cause she was like my babysitter. I would see him with this girl, and her family. . . . So here I am, he's playing daddy with her kids and I'm like, "Really?" . . . I don't know what it was, but I didn't want him, but it hurt me to see him with somebody else. And I would drink and drink and drink, drink again. My mom kept questioning me about my alcoholism, and I always denied it.

Her mother's persistence eventually prompted Dani to seek help from Alcoholics Anonymous. Still, her anger toward her ex-boyfriend remained intact. She simply could not come to terms with the idea that his new girlfriend and her children were receiving the support that she and her son should have been receiving. Her anger came to a head during a routine trip to a hair salon.

On that day her ex-boyfriend's new girlfriend was also at the salon and she began to boast loudly about their relationship and sex life in an effort to upset Dani. Eventually, Dani became so enraged that her stylist had to physically restrain her from getting into a physical altercation with the other woman. Leaving the salon did little to diffuse her anger and, along with a younger relative, she arrived at her ex-boyfriend's residence. It was at that point that Dani says she blacked out. Upon seeing her ex's new girlfriend, she stabbed the woman repeatedly, leaving her face severely disfigured. She was soon arrested and eventually found guilty of first-degree assault.[25] At her sentencing she describes the moment she realized how deeply infidelity motivated her actions and contributed to her criminal conviction.

The judge was very mad. It was because he felt like I came from a good family. . . . But that didn't make a difference . . . he said something to me on my sentencing day and I'll never forget it, he said, "I want you to realize how you threw your life away for the love of beer." And that, when he said that to me, I felt my legs like, they went numb. And I almost fainted, because I mean it was like I was staring at my own face when he told me that . . . like [it] make me see truly for what it was. It did something to me.

That day in court the judge pointed to her alcoholism as the cause of her crime. To Dani, it was more complicated than that. The root of her "love of beer" as the judge put it, was the love of a man who rejected her and her child.

For women who lacked social support, news of a partner's unfaithfulness had two immediate implications: First, women felt that their partners didn't value them and might leave the relationship without warning.

Second, infidelity meant that the economic resources a woman needed to support her and her children was being diverted to the care of another woman and her children. Looking back, Dani was deeply remorseful and continued to grapple with why she reacted the way she did. Part of the reason, she believes, had to do with the recent birth of her child. Although she did not discuss receiving a clinical diagnosis, the postpartum period can be a destabilizing time for many women, and since she lacked assistance or effective coping strategies, her boyfriend's new relationship seemed like so much more than a breakup.[26] She was alone, a single mother with a new born and had no job. Those moments after leaving the salon seemed like an opportunity to reclaim some shred of agency, to prioritize her needs and to let everyone else know the depth of her pain. In the end, however, a criminal conviction would place her further at society's margins.

Reframing agency for most women can be one way to reject powerlessness. But for others like Dani it can illustrate just how complex and messy the process of challenging marginalization is when one does so in ways that harm those around them. Soon after ending her relationship with her daughter's father, Dani entered into another dysfunctional relationship. Describing her history of relationships, she states:

> I've had a lot of relationships that I was always get hurt. I get hurt a lot. I think I give people my all. I'm a very nice person, even when it comes to friends. It's like with the last person I was with, I really cared about her a lot. But she's an alcoholic, and I tried to help her. I've been a drug addict, I've been an [drug] abuser, I've been through God only knows, you know? My daughter's father, he's betrayed me. He's lied to me, he's just treated me like I'm just shit. And then my other relationship with the other girl that I was with, she hurt me a lot too. She would lie to me a lot.

Dani's relationship with her ex-boyfriend may not have directly contributed to her addiction and the assault charges for which she was eventually convicted, but it was the start of a toxic cycle, complicated further by pregnancy. Like other factors that precede criminal involvement, there isn't necessarily a linear or causal relationship between one event or moment that precipitates a crime. Rather, factors and experiences create the context in which law-violating behavior occurs.

"I THOUGHT THAT MARRIAGE WAS GOING TO MAKE ME HAPPY"

The pathway to pregnancy-related vulnerabilities shows how a number of factors can contribute to a volatile period. But what about the impact of marriage? Certainly, marriage isn't a panacea for relationship conflict, but a long-held view within sociological research is that children conceived within marriage are more likely to experience the financial and social benefits of a two-parent household.[27] Would this hold true for women in the throes of substance abuse and criminal activity? Did married women experience pregnancy in ways similar to their unmarried counterparts? I wondered this when I spoke to Sage, a forty-one-year-old Black mother of two boys. She had her first son at the age of thirty-two and her second eight years later, shortly after her wedding at age forty. Unlike some of the other women I interviewed, Sage had a stable and enjoyable childhood. She didn't use drugs or engage in the kind of risky behavior that often precedes serious criminal activity. Learning that she was pregnant was welcomed news and seemed to set the stage for her new life with her husband. Within a year, however, Sage was sitting in jail reading through divorce papers.

Early on in our conversation it was clear that Sage was different from other women I interviewed. She had completed college and, prior to her arrest, planned to complete master's and doctorate degrees. Her life felt settled, with one exception: the contentious relationship with the father of her first son. She had been granted sole custody of her older son but, according to Sage, the custody agreement changed without her knowledge. Because she didn't comply with new visitation orders, she was arrested and charged with parental kidnapping. What made matters worse was that her arrest wasn't just a result of careless administrative paperwork on the part of the courts. Her new husband had conspired with her older son's father to ensure that she would not receive the information needed to comply with court orders. According to Sage, the sudden and unexpected alliance between her husband and first son's father was born out of her husband's desire to pursue an extramarital affair. Moreover, Sage felt that the underlying tension between her and her husband's family played a role in his decision to pursue another relationship.

Sage: His family didn't care for me. I was more educated than they were. I was fairer complected than they were. I wasn't from the South. So there was three strikes against me. I didn't think like they think. And I'll never think like they think, and I pray that they're not putting that thinking on my youngest son. But I'll deal with that when I get him back. . . . When I was giving birth to my son and we were there at the hospital, she [Sage's mother-in-law] would call him just so that she could tell me, "See, I told you. Even with you being a new mother, he left you at the hospital to tend to me." She would always do things like that. His family was very control-

ling in that manner. And they were very much a source of contention. . . .
So I mean she did a lot of damage for our marriage. Now, I cannot say
that he does not take responsibility, because everyone takes responsibility
for their actions. But I will say that she was a good driving force. She was.
And then his sister and his niece.

Geniece: Did you know that [about the affair] beforehand?

Sage: Absolutely not. That came to pass when there was a woman surfacing
up that is now raising my son. My husband filed for divorce while I was
incarcerated. I was served in prison. And then he wrote the most ridiculous thing. "I didn't know my wife was a kidnapper. That's the reason for
divorce." I thought that was ridiculous.

Relationships and the birth of children impacted Sage's life in ways
markedly different from other woman I spoke to, particularly younger
single mothers. There were no parents deciding if she should or shouldn't
have another child, she was not involved in criminal activity, nor was she
embroiled in interpersonal conflict with her husband. The relationship
with her in-laws was a tense one, but even then, she didn't experience
marginality in the way that Kishana or Dani had. By all accounts, her life
was stable. For all the reasons that she might experience some level social
exclusion, such as race and gender, on the surface at least, her life was so
different from the other women she met in jail and at Helping Hands.
What her story reveals is that there is no singular version of marginality,
and the manner in which women navigate pregnancy and incarceration
will also be diverse. Yes, most women shared experiences that bore
resemblance to the stories outlined in statistical analyses: most incarcerated women are custodial parents, single mothers who don't have a college education.[28] But others are like Sage and Felicia.

Like Sage, Felicia, a white forty-eight-year-old mother of twin boys,
was college-educated and hoped to create a stable life for herself in the
middle-class New England city where she was raised. Years before fin-
ishing school, however, at age seventeen, she was introduced to cocaine.
While she was able to maintain the pretense of sobriety, those closest to
her knew she was not well. Despite her escalating substance abuse she
had one source of stability in her life: her boyfriend Tony. They were
married by the time she was eighteen, and during their ten-year marriage he helped to keep the family afloat as she continued to battle drug
addiction. A supportive spouse, however, did little to mitigate the
underlying sources of her drug addiction, and she and Tony eventually
separated.

Geniece: So later on in your marriage when you felt you were kind of being smothered . . . Did he [Tony] think that drugs may have played a role? Did he ever mention it or bring it up?

Felicia: He knows that I was using a little bit. But I think . . . I don't know if he didn't want to come home so I wouldn't leave and go use drugs or he just wanted me to grow up and say, "You have kids now. Start being responsible." He never really said anything. . . . It's like pulling teeth with him to get him to really talk. In his eyes he was doing what was responsible on his part. But when I left it was great, because he had to be there. And he's like an amazing father now. I don't know if that would have happened if I stayed.

Although Felicia was engaged in illicit activity, unlike other women I interviewed, she had a supportive partner who cared for their children. Her pre-pregnancy drug use was rooted in complex reasons that simply could not be resolved within the conventional family life that she spent her life longing to attain. The image of the "hurting little girl" that Felicia uses to describe her troubled childhood was likely an indication of psychologically traumatic experiences which were exacerbated by her pregnancy and postpartum recovery.[29]

While Felicia's drug addiction continued over the course of her children's lives, she wasn't arrested until her sons were six years old. The presence of a partner who was not criminally involved and was able to care for the children was, in Felicia's opinion, an important reason that she was able to avoid criminal prosecution for so long. By the time she was arrested she and her husband had divorced. Still, he brought the twins to visit her regularly even going so far as to conceal the fact that she had broken the law. Reflecting on later relationships with physically abusive partners, Felicia maintained that it was her relationship with her ex-husband, Tony, that partially insulated her children from her addiction.

I wasn't surprised that most of the women I interviewed had no history of marriage, since the majority of women who comprise this nation's carceral institutions are unmarried.[30] This can, however, lead to the misconception that for married formerly incarcerated women, pregnancy does not further exacerbate existing challenges. Each of the eighteen married women whom I interviewed entered into marriage optimistically, believing that the relationship would anchor their families. For Felicia, marriage was no match for her battle with drugs, though it did help to limit the exposure her young children had to her addiction. By contrast, Sage's marriage, which she initially viewed positively, derailed her ambitions for the future and resulted in the loss of her parental custody. Their experiences underscore that while marriage is correlated with economic and social stability for many women, the story can be much more complicated for justice-involved women. In other words, when discussing the impact of marriage in the lives of criminally involved women, it is important to view their experiences within the context of the events that led to their arrests and the relational dynamics between them and their partner.

OTHER SIDE OF THE GAME

In the third single from her widely acclaimed album *Baduizm,* Erykah Badu paints the picture of a woman facing a harrowing moral dilemma. The song, "Other Side of the Game," describes the experience of a woman in a relationship with a man involved in crime.[31] His illegal source of income affords them economic stability but the impending birth of their child causes her to reconsider the risks associated with the relationship. By the end of the song she poses a philosophical challenge to the listener: should an expectant mother forgo material security because of the risk of legal consequences? We the listeners can empathize with this woman but not necessarily from a place of genuine care or concern. Knowing that this hypothetical woman is facing a hypothetical problem, neatly contained to six minutes, means the situation is unreal to many and unrelatable to most. The reality, however, is that the song is one that women like Kishana could have composed, save for an ending far more tragic than Badu's lyrics. Reflecting upon the role of pregnancy in the lives of women already experiencing a storm of problems should leave little room for armchair theorizing. Unfortunately, however, punitiveness has been the default policy response to marginalized women who are pregnant, poor, and crime-involved.

Poor women, especially those who have a criminal history, are often demonized in the court of public opinion for giving birth to children that they may not be able to support. This kind of moral finger wagging was no more clearly illustrated than during the media sensationalism of the 1980s and early 1990s that plastered images of addicted mothers and "crack babies" across the evening news.[32] Women were criminalized for using drugs, characterized as irresponsible for getting pregnant, and labeled immoral for considering abortion. Yet, rather than prioritizing policy that addressed underlying issues of poverty, discrimination, and addiction, politicians and members of the media opted for the path of judgment and criminalization. What has been particularly disheartening is that while the images of frail Black and Brown babies have subsided in the media, policies that address the challenges of minority and poor women have progressed at a glacial pace. Today, minorities continue to bear the brunt of harsh drug laws even while public health–informed policies benefit the many white Americans who struggle with opioid addiction and investors openly brag about the lucrativeness of now-legal marijuana dispensaries.[33] Even in the wake of federal legislation like the First Step Act, the majority of formerly incarcerated mothers who are prosecuted at the state level remain imprisoned for nonviolent drug offenses.

At the margins of society, the women I interviewed found themselves navigating multiple challenges at once: economic insecurity, a strained or abusive relationship, and the prospect of a raising a baby alone. These challenges don't only exist at the individual level. The inability to secure economic resources or receive protection from an abusive partner are institutional-level failings that hold tangible consequences for women in their daily lives. What if, for example, the same system that placed Kishana on probation for getting into a bar fight recognized the fear and desperation that would cause a woman to file thirty-five police reports? Perhaps, the first few years of her son's life would not have been spent building a relationship with his mother within the confines of prison.

The multilayered nature of this marginalization, the individual and the institutional, parallels women's response to their own marginality. Although they have little ability to transform the way that they are treated by institutions and powerful actors, they do seek ways to center their needs. How they ultimately respond isn't always consequence-free, but for these women few options are. This includes pregnancy and motherhood. Women's discussions of pregnancy demonstrate that within the context of their marginal identities they may make decisions inimical to their personal safety for fear of an uncertain future.

Formerly incarcerated mothers are often framed as a monolithic group, leading to broad assumptions and mischaracterizations about the circumstances of their pregnancies. While research since the 2000s has offered more nuanced analyses of this group, highlighting how single mothers are not mere byproducts of inner-city pathology, there still remains a need to further understand the nuanced ways in which single mothers of varying social statuses experience pregnancy and motherhood.[34] The criminally involved women I interviewed discussed their pregnancies within the context of tumultuous relationships that included intimate-partner violence and crime-involved boyfriends. But they also addressed how their own involvement in crime shaped their experience of pregnancy and later participation in criminal activity.

What was perhaps most surprising about my conversations with women was learning how married women with a criminal record spoke about pregnancy and motherhood. It is well known that marriage is one key indicator of socioeconomic stability, educational outcomes, and other long-term factors used to forecast a child's life chances.[35] Yet, as women like Sage illustrate, marriage is, like any other social institution, only as effective as the social circumstances of the individuals involved. Marriages marred by economic instability and abuse are not inherently protective against the same pregnancy-related vulnerabilities that unmarried women I interviewed experienced. Where marriage did play a distinctive role was in the lives of women like Felicia who were involved in ongoing illegal activity prior to pregnancy. In that situation, a committed partner carried the weight of parenting and financial responsibilities in a way that didn't happen for women who were not in long-term stable relationships. This finding in and of itself isn't so much novel as it is an indictment of the dishonest treatment of poor and minority single mothers. Marriage is challenging for many couples and a source of distress for many women. Yet, when the social ills of unmarried women are enumerated, without fail their "unwillingness" to marry and provide their children with a two-parent household is the key talking point of conservative and neoliberal pundits alike.[36] Little attention is paid to the sociohistorical factors underlying low marriage rates, like systemic racism and mass incarceration that dismantles families in already vulnerable communities around the country. The women I interviewed don't view marriage as inherently negative, but neither do they view it as a cure-all, able to remedy the experiences of trauma and marginalization that have impacted them. In this way, the on-the-ground reality of women provides insight not captured by simplistic policy explanations that elevate political expediency above compassion and structural reform.

CHAPTER 3

Crime, Agency, and Postcarceral Narratives

As Kiana dressed herself in all black, she felt a sinking uneasiness unlike anything she had felt before previous robberies.[1] "You know what Kiana . . . your luck is going to run out," she recalls thinking. And, that night, it did. Just before the evening rush hour, Kiana joined her ex-boyfriend and a few other associates as they got into a New York City taxi. In what was supposed to be her last robbery, the unfolding events turned into a scene so surreal and so tragic that by the end of the night she was in handcuffs and an innocent bystander was dead.

One of the reasons Kiana even considered robbing drug spots in the first place was her ex-boyfriend's suggestion that it would be an easy way to make quick money. Recalling their first conversation, she says:

> And one day he put a gun in my hand, like, "You want to rob a weed spot?" . . . I think yeah, we need money. I said it's [drug dealing] not a legit business so I don't feel bad. I'm justifying things now. It's crazy. I said they can't call the cops on me.

The fact that her robbery victims were drug dealers, the very men she blamed for the decline of her community, lessened her guilt. After all, these were the very men and vices she warned her young sons to avoid. These were the men she feared her sons might become. Still, being a stick-up artist was dangerous and she knew that at any moment the consequences for her and her children could prove costly.

After weighing the risks, Kiana concluded that the possibility to score a few thousand dollars was too much to pass up. Her first robbery was mostly a solo job. She ambushed drug dealers while her ex-boyfriend waited in the getaway car. He knew the men at that particular location and risked almost certain retaliation if he was associated with the robbery. Following the instructions they rehearsed beforehand, Kiana pointed her gun at the men and shouted orders. Trying to embody the bravado and authority she saw in Hollywood films, she cautioned against sudden movements and attempts to retaliate. The success of that first robbery was exhilarating, but also terrifying. With each subsequent robbery came a looming sense of danger. Although her victims were themselves criminals, Kiana was under no pretense that she was a Robin Hood–like figure. The money she stole went to her own household and even though making ends meet on low-income wages was a challenge, she never felt that robbery was her only option.

The details of the night Kiana, her ex-boyfriend and associates were arrested illustrates how quickly plans can go awry. Once they were in the taxi, Kiana noticed that her ex-boyfriend was unusually tense. In what Kiana describes as an almost dreamlike sequence, her ex-boyfriend raised his gun to the cab driver, hit him on the head, then dragged him into an abandoned building. None of this—the assault and battery, the kidnapping, the carjacking—was supposed to happen. Kiana could rationalize stealing from other criminals, but this cab driver was making an honest living. She was violating the unspoken moral code she had set for herself when she began robbing drug spots: never hurt innocent people. After returning to the cab, her ex-boyfriend drove toward their intended destination. Not long after, they heard the sound of helicopters above, followed by sirens. Later at her trial Kiana would learn that the cab driver regained consciousness and managed to call 911 on his cellphone to report the carjacking. When her ex-boyfriend realized that they were being pursued by law enforcement, he led police on a high-speed chase through New York City. The chase ended when their car crashed into another vehicle. Getting out of the car to face the raised guns and commands of law enforcement, Kiana describes a scene that has haunted her for years. Pools of white liquid covered the pavement near the wreckage. The driver of the car they hit, who would later succumb to his injuries, had recently left the grocery store. The white liquid was the milk he purchased for his family.

Most of the crime narratives women described did not have endings as dramatic as Kiana's. However, the escalating nature of criminal activity that began for one reason and evolved in unanticipated ways, was a theme not uncommon among respondents. Like Kiana, some women's entrée into criminal involvement was related to economic or social marginality. The unrelenting toll of poverty, for example, was weathering and the chance to take control, even at the risk of imprisonment, was a grasp at agency. In Kiana's case, it meant weighing unknown risks against the known reality of single motherhood, bills, and stress. In negotiating her choices, Kiana didn't embrace criminal activity without reservation, and nor did she view struggling to put food on the table as inherently noble. No matter the choice, Kiana felt that one thing was sure: She would lose. Kiana's story captures the interplay between marginal identity and how women frame their arrests and convictions. The subject of this chapter is this dimension of duality at the margins.

AGENCY, MORALITY, AND POSTCARCERAL NARRATIVES

One of the challenges of writing about formerly incarcerated persons' experiences before, during, and after imprisonment is acknowledging the structural and systemic forces that disproportionately impact marginalized groups, while still validating an individual's agency in making personal choices. The application of theoretical and conceptual frameworks is required to distinguish narrative from generalizable findings, yet it is also important to avoid prioritizing the systemic to the exclusion of the self. This chapter wrestles with this tension by examining how women who engaged in criminal activity interpreted the repercussions of their actions. Women are not passive bystanders in the own lives, nor do they view the institutions charged with responding to criminal activity as neutral entities. When participating in crime, women assert their agency ever aware of what's at stake: the risk of further marginalization. In this way, the women I spoke to grapple with a very specific type of agency, moral agency, in explaining the decisions they made and the role of the courts and state actors in impacting their lives.

Moral agency, or the choice to engage in acts perceived as moral or immoral, is pervasive throughout women's carceral narratives.[2] The framing of moral agency is, in part, shaped my women's intimate knowledge of what it means to be denied agency. Imprisonment, for example, is a state-sanctioned form of agency deprivation.[3] And before prison, women also experience limited agency in the relationships and institutions that minimize their humanity. The denial of agency, however, does not mean that women did not try to reclaim agency and create space for themselves in a world that either didn't see them or saw them only through the lens of criticism and moralistic judgment. When women speak about agency they do so in nuanced ways. One is not limited to only "having agency" or "not having agency" in a fixed or static sense of the concept. Rather, agency ebbs and flows depending on the circumstances impacting a woman's life. Women's explanation of their criminal past reveals that agency is informed by a complex moral worldview that adopts mainstream norms while criticizing the structures and institutions that shape their postimprisonment experiences. As it relates to criminal activity, duality at the margins is not only a result of one's criminal record, but is also shaped by how women come to make sense of criminal activity and the criminal justice system. In the stories that women tell, the common thread uniting their experiences is how their marginal identities as justice-involved mothers figure prominently in the choices available to them and decisions they ultimately make.

"I Did It for Me"

When Kiana initially discussed her decision to rob drug spots, she pointed to her economic needs, specifically citing overdue electricity bills. As our conversation progressed, the rationale became more nuanced. Describing how she explained her conviction to her young sons, she states:

> But I don't know. I think they kind of understand for some odd, crazy reason that I went away, and for whatever reason that I did it, I definitely didn't do it for them because that's not a reason to be robbing, sticking up people for them. I did it for me. It was an easy way out for me. But I think they understood and I think they forgave me for that. . . . It was hard though. It was definitely hard.

For some readers, Kiana's explanation that crime was "an easy way out" may not make sense. But for Kiana it was an easy way out, even if "easy" departed from the conventional understanding of the word. She was a single mother with a seemingly unending stack of bills, trying to make ends meet month after month. The choice between facing a future of more of the same or joining her ex-boyfriend to make more money in an hour than she made in several months combined, made the latter option feel like a risk worth taking. In retrospect, Kiana regretted her decision and also learned that the criminal justice system operated by a set of rules that she was ill-equipped to understand. For example, she was frustrated that she was convicted of both robbery and kidnapping. While she helped to plan a robbery, it was her boyfriend who assaulted and kidnapped the cab driver.[4] Ultimately, she came to terms with her conviction by rationalizing that her previous crimes had caught up with her. In her words: "That's what I get for robbing all them weed spots."

Like Kiana, forty-eight-year-old Diana, a white mother from New York, engaged in a financially motivated crime. Her marriage was crumbling after she discovered that her husband was unfaithful. She wanted to leave the relationship but also felt that she should try to keep her family intact. In what appeared to be reckless behavior, Diana felt that getting arrested for embezzlement would signal to her family just how miserable she was in her marriage.

> *Geniece:* The situation that happens with you going to prison how did that come about?
>
> *Diana:* It's a long story. I had a job at a law firm. I started off as a secretary. And my boss was a malpractice lawyer. I worked in billing. It was a small firm, like four attorneys. And I would use it against her like you want to steal from people, then I'll steal from you. And the thing was I knew was going to get caught.
>
> *Geniece:* You knew you were going to get caught?
>
> *Diana:* Of course. I knew I was going to go to prison. Maybe that was the only way I get away from this man [her husband]. . . . I don't know what I was thinking, but I wasn't thinking right.

Upon reading Diana's account, one might ask: Why didn't she just leave? Why did she continue to do something she knew could lead to her arrest? The easy answer is that she didn't care. The least probable answer is that she wanted to go to prison. The truth, however, is far more complex. First, and this holds true for other women as well, limiting explanations to solely sociological and criminological reasons without acknowledging underlying psychological conditions, like depression, does not provide a complete picture. While few women discussed diagnosed mental health illnesses, the possibility that this played a role in their actions is supported by data.[5] Second, like Kiana, Diana expressed a desire to be understood by those around her. In her case, she wanted the problems in her relationship acknowledged and felt powerless to do so within the confines of a dysfunctional marriage. When she began to embezzle, Diana's sense of right and wrong aligned with normative views of crime. She knew that her actions violated the law and would result in consequences. Yet, because she "wasn't thinking right," she felt that the intended outcome (attention and acknowledgement from family) was worth the risk.

At forty-nine years of age, Olive, a Black mother of four, was arrested more than any other women with whom I spoke. In total, she estimated that she was arrested forty-eight times for reasons related to drug use or sex work. As a child, she describes struggling with self-esteem and feeling like an outcast among her siblings. She ran away from home several times before becoming pregnant at the age of seventeen. By the time that she was twenty-five years old she had three more children and was overwhelmed. It was at that time in her life that she was first introduced to crack cocaine. Initially she didn't like the drug's effect on her body, and after one use didn't try it again for years. The next time she did use it, however, addiction consumed her life. Once she was addicted, other aspects of her life also became unstable. For example, she was in a relationship so abusive that it almost resulted in her death. After her ex-boyfriend beat her beyond recognition, she was in a medically induced coma for over a month. Following the incident her addiction to drugs only increased, as she struggled to cope with the emotional and physical pain of the violent attack.

> *Olive:* I had no idea it [drug use] was going to take my life to destruction. I had no idea that that moment right then was destruction. . . . Twenty-five years later I regret running the streets. Doing anything by any means necessary to get money to buy more. My morals, my values went down the drain. Beat up, beat down, beat around because of a material substance that I allowed to take over my life. But I won't do it again. . . . You know what I mean?
>
> *Geniece:* Right.
>
> *Olive:* Because life is still life. It's not going to change. And the situation that you think you're running from, it's not going to go away. It's still there.
>
> *Geniece:* Right.
>
> *Olive:* It's not going anywhere. If anything, it's enhanced. And it took me twenty something years to admit this. I have a problem with chemicals.

Olive, like Kiana and Diana, illustrate how criminal involvement was connected to other destabilizing factors in their lives. Contextualizing their actions within their preincarceration narratives did not negate their role in the crime they committed. Rather, understanding the broader context for criminal activity demonstrates how moral agency is subject to conflicting values and beliefs that a person holds. Agency, therefore, is not only demonstrated when one makes the right choice at the right time. Agency is also expressed when one freely makes a choice that they recognize as potentially detrimental. One can weigh the consequences of an action, recognize the negative impact of that action, and still chose to commit a crime.

SHARED BLAME AND THE DEPRIVATION OF AGENCY

While most of the women I spoke with accepted sole responsibility for criminal activity, some women held others partially responsibility for their involvement in crime. This was true for Tanya, a forty-one-year-old Black mother of three. She viewed her choice in a partner, rather than the criminal act itself, as the most significant factor that led to her arrest. When we met, Tanya had recently served two years in prison for home invasion and was in the process of completing five years of probation. Eager to begin her life without the mandatory check-ins with her probation officer, she looked forward to finding a job and reestablishing her relationship with her children. When I asked Tanya to tell me the events that resulted in her arrest and imprisonment, she explained that she was a naïve accomplice in a home invasion and didn't realize what was happening until the crime was already in progress.

> *Geniece:* How did he [boyfriend] contribute to that [the role in her arrest]?
>
> *Tanya:* Well, he put me in a situation. We were just supposed to get marijuana, I'm gonna tell the truth, I'm not gonna lie. And he ended up doing a home invasion that's armed robbery. So because I didn't get the marijuana I'm the one that the cops caught on.

Toward the end of our conversation I asked if Tanya wanted to share anything that she had not yet discussed in the interview.

> *Geniece:* Is there anything about your experience about being a mother that you think is really important that I haven't addressed?
>
> *Tanya:* My situation is kind of different because I didn't put myself in trouble . . . when I think about it I did because I was going to get drugs. It was what it was, you know what I'm saying? To know that we, when we're doing things we don't think about the consequences, we don't think about what's around us.

Tanya's intention on the night of her arrest was to purchase drugs. Her primary mistake, she believes, was placing herself in a relationship and in a situation that led to her unintentional involvement in the more serious crime of home invasion. Tanya's experience resembles Kiana's, by showing how quickly one act of crime can evolve into another. When women weigh the risks associated with criminal activity, they do so based upon their *own* moral guidelines, whether it's justifying robbing drug spots or engaging in a nonviolent offense. What they realize only after the fact, is that their association with other criminally involved people elevates their risks in ways they did not anticipate. Engaging in crime, then, is not solely about accounting for the possibility that an act will lead to arrest. Rather, women also face the possibility that the actions of others will impact their own marginal status and jeopardize their freedom.

Similar to Tanya, Ariana described the extent to which she saw her arrest and incarceration as both a result of her choices and her boyfriend's influence.

> *Geniece:* Okay, and when you were incarcerated, did you feel like there was someone that you blamed for the whole situation? When you looked back on . . . ?"
>
> *Ariana:* I blamed John, and I blamed myself for this. There's nobody else to blame. It's me and I blame him.

Thirty-six-year-old Rashida, who was convicted of assault after stabbing her boyfriend in what she describes as an act of self-defense, also explains her reaction to her conviction:

> I wasn't angry towards the court system, I wasn't angry towards the system, period. The system has nothing to do with me being upset, it was more the guy, the man, that's what had me angry, like—like that type angry, like why did you do this to me? you know, to the point I have to protect myself.

In considering women's participation in crime over the life course, some criminologists have compared the extent to which single women and women in relationships engage in crime.[6] Extending findings to policy, however, must be done cautiously. When the social networks in which women are embedded increases the likelihood that partners may themselves be criminally involved, long-term relationships or marriage may have a deleterious effect on women's criminal trajectory.[7] Knowing the social and relational factors that affect a woman's criminal status is useful, but not because institutions should dictate to women what they should or should not do. Rather, understanding the vulnerabilities that keep women in relationships they would otherwise leave can inform women-centered approaches to mitigating risk.[8]

Women who stated that coercion or pressure from a partner was a part of the reason they committed a crime, noted that economic need was often a factor. There was however a notable exception. At sixty-three, Ana was the oldest women I interviewed, and that was not the only attribute that distinguished her from other women. She left Puerto Rico as a teenager, hoping to pursue an education. Shortly after moving to New York City to live with her older sister, she enrolled in a secretarial training program, got married, and started a family. Thirteen years into her marriage, she and her husband divorced after she learned of his infidelity. It was difficult balancing single motherhood and work, but after years of careful saving she earned enough money to buy out the owner of the small convenience store where she worked. Owning that convenience store was Ana's piece of the American dream. By then, her children were out of the house and she was ready to pursue a relationship. She began dating a man who frequented her store, a decision she describes as the worst mistake of her life.

> Ana: I met this guy he went to the store. I met him and I knew he was into everything. I knew he was a drug dealer, I knew he was into everything. But, you know at that time [I] didn't have the mind that I have today and . . . got into the relationship with him. He used to send me to Puerto Rico, take money here, take money there. He used to deal [illegally] with people . . . so when my crime [happened] I used to make phone calls. I heard everything, all his plans. . . . So, I was involved. I was blind. Sometimes I feel that I was manipulated.[9]

After years of living in New York she relocated to Florida where she was soon arrested for being an accessory to a murder orchestrated by her boyfriend. Just before Ana was arrested and charged, she received a phone call from a Florida detective who asked that she go to a local precinct for questioning. With no lawyer present to provide her with counsel, she didn't realize that the questions she answered could lead to her arrest. She described how she felt after being charged:

> Geniece: How did you feel when you realized what was going on?
>
> Ana: That I was the stupidest person in this world. That you can't trust nobody in this world. That I was the ugliest person in this world when I put my family aside for this relationship. It's the way I feel.

Ana's description of her arrest echoes a familiar theme expressed by women in chapter 2 who attributed their arrests to negative relationships. In Ana's case, however, pregnancy was not a contributing factor nor was her relationship influenced by her need for economic stability.

In fact, she was successful in her own right and enjoyed more financial security than she had at any other point in her life. Like Tanya, she recognized her choice to engage in law-violating behavior, but also felt that she would have never been placed in the situation to violate the law had it not been for her partner.

Part of Ana's self-critique was also a result of the stage in life at which she was arrested and the fact that she had no prior criminal charges. When she was sentenced, Ana was in her fifties, which made her an outlier for a first-time offender. During our conversation, the heaviness of "what-ifs" and "could-have-beens" weighed on Ana. She wept while discussing the grandchildren she was unable to help care for, particularly a granddaughter with a physical disability. For all her years of struggling as a single mother and the long hours she invested in her business, it was her relationship with a man that upended her life. Despite her age and untarnished past, Ana lost ten years to prison at a time in her life when she thought she might otherwise be preparing for retirement.

WRONGFULNESS, SERIOUSNESS, AND FRAMING REPEAT OFFENSES

The disconnect between how women view their criminal activity and how the criminal justice system formally labels them is due in part to one element of moral framing: the difference between wrongfulness and seriousness.[10] Criminal seriousness is shaped mostly by a crime's potential harmfulness to others, while wrongfulness is shaped by mediating factors such as underlying reasons or motives for the crime.[11] An enduring tension among scholars opposed to the expansion of carceral institutions is the possibility that distinctions like wrongfulness and seriousness or violent and nonviolent offenders will help some members of the incarcerated population at the expense of others. For the individuals most directly impacted by these distinctions, incarcerated and formerly incarcerated people, this tension also exists, albeit in a different form. The majority of women I interviewed were never arrested or imprisoned for inflicting injury or physical harm on another person. However, few of the women believed that there were no victims as a result of law-violating activity. Whether obvious or not, they often felt that there was always a victim: the family members who watched in despair as they struggled with drug addiction, the children who suffered the pain of separation when they were incarcerated, and the offenders themselves, many of whom began life witnessing the struggles of their own crime-involved family members. Respondents, however, acknowledged the difference between so-called victimless crimes and those that directly harmed another person. It was this distinction that most significantly shaped how they understood their role in a criminal act.

Often, *what* is viewed as a legal wrong and how it is punished is influenced by *who* commits the act in question. One need look no further than the example of marijuana's legalization and its emergence into a billion-dollar business to see how wealth and political power determine who profits and who is penalized.[12] When Ana was sentenced as an accessory to murder, an ostensibly serious crime, there was little consideration by the court that a woman near sixty with no criminal history might fear for her own safety and the well-being of her family when she relayed information or money to parties who committed violent crimes. Thus, when examining how women interpret their moral agency, it isn't enough to understand how they make sense of their actions and convictions. It is also important to interrogate the context of their criminal charges and the response by the criminal justice system itself.

The distinction between seriousness and wrongfulness also highlights differences between the framing and adjudication of crimes by the legal system and that of individuals.[13] Women's stories reveal that the stigma women associated with particular crimes was not necessarily a result of public perception, friends, family, or even how the criminal justice system labeled the crime.[14] Rather, women provided nuanced accounts of how the underlying factors that resulted in their conviction shaped how they viewed themselves and how they expected others to view them. Most surprisingly, within the context of their broader carceral narratives, women who committed multiple crimes perceived to be less serious were sometimes *more* likely to struggle with reframing their negative criminal identity than women who committed one or two serious crimes. Why? The seriousness and sometimes the wrongfulness of a single act committed by a first-time offender meant that crime was an anomaly, motivated by what a woman believed was a morally just reason. Repeated crimes, especially a "victimless" crime like drug possession, was one some women viewed as a personal weakness.[15] Repeated interactions with the criminal justice system made it difficult for women to frame a crime as an anomalous act. As a result, women who cycled in and out of police stations, courtrooms, and jails saw those experiences as tangible reminders of their perceived shortcomings.

TABLE 3   FREQUENCY OF CRIMINAL ACTS AND MOTIVES REPORTED

Number of Instances Reported*	
Crime	
Assault	17
Drug Related	48
Embezzlement/ Identity Theft/Fraud	4
Murder Related	2
Prostitution	7
Robbery, Burglary/ Petty Theft	12
Motives	
Addiction	28
Assisting other party	3
Economic Gain	26
Emotional Duress	3
Force	2
Naïve Accomplice	2
Self-Defense	6
Willing Participant	6

*These are the total instances of offenses and motives described across all seventy respondents

Table 3 summarizes criminal activity and motives reported by women. It is important to note that a number of respondents participated in more than one criminal act. For example, those who engaged in drug use sometimes sold drugs. Notice also that addiction and economic gain are the most highly reported motives reported by women. This is not surprising since drug-related crimes comprise the highest number of criminal acts committed by women in the United States.

One of the reasons why some women with repeat offenses were self-critical was that their repeated contact with law enforcement seem to substantiate claims that they were unwilling to change. Because the majority of these women were arrested for drug offenses, the role of addiction further called their morality into question. While drug addiction is widely understood as a medical disease, the language of the law often elevates the (im)morality of the offender above the gravity of their illness.[16] As a result, it can be difficult for a woman to challenge the moral legitimacy of the institutions responsible for labeling her if she has a lengthy criminal history. By comparison, women with one or two interactions with the legal system, even for serious crimes, may find it easier to informally dispute the carceral narratives scripted and formalized about them by the criminal justice system.

While crimes were sometimes described as directly or indirectly benefiting another party, most women indicated that their crimes did not have entirely altruistic motives. This was most clearly evident among women who were charged with drug-related offenses. Some women saw their drug use as driven by selfishness. Others saw their drug dependency as a result of underlying emotional problems. Viewing criminal activity within the broader context of psycho-emotional problems allowed women to see their behavior as a result of factors that stemmed from childhood, destructive relationships, or the overwhelming toll of financial and personal distress. The same line of reasoning was evident for women who committed property and assault crimes. Benefiting personally from a crime might appear selfish, but if respondents were not in a healthy emotional or mental state they framed a seemingly self-centered act as a way to cope with external factors beyond their control.

When Marcia began using drugs in her mid-twenties it derailed many of the aspirations she had for herself and her family. Reflecting on that time in her life, she believes that her entrée into using crack cocaine was a result of immaturity.

> Geniece: So, were you—at what point in your life would you say that drugs entered the picture?
>
> Marcia: When drugs entered the picture?
>
> Geniece: Um-hmm.
>
> Marcia: When I was in my twenties. Because I didn't know nothing about it and I got turned on them then. Everybody have their own path to go down and you know, you don't know—you don't know where it's going to lead you. You know what I'm saying. So, I took that path and that path gave me a real bad fall—which it was with some of my kids. And now I don't do that. But I thank God my kids are still in my life. They're grown, but there's only one I don't see. But all the rest of them I see. They call me, they come by. You know, so, I'm happy with that. And when it's time for my other little baby, he will find me. He will find me.

Marcia does not excuse her criminal past but neither does she allow her past mistakes to define her. The distinction she makes between her criminal identity and how she viewed herself after imprisonment is what Shadd Maruna describes as reclaiming the "old self."[17] Marcia's decades-long battle with drug addiction lasted until her early forties and once she was in recovery she hoped to return to the person she was prior to her "bad fall." In other words, Marcia "the drug addict" was not her "real self" and thus should not define who she was at forty-nine. Respondents who adopted this framing tended to view themselves as both redeemed and transformed. They did not see themselves as victims of uncontrollable circumstances who felt destined for failure, but rather as good people who made unwise decisions.[18] Given their marginal status, this was a way for women to acknowledge the relationship between their outsider status and who they were beyond a label. As Potter notes, being a criminal offender is not a characteristic endemic to one's identity, but rather a situation that is a part of a person's history and shapes their future.[19] Like Marcia, Becky, a white thirty-two-year-old mother of one, describes her former drug use in redemptive terms:

> I'll say this. Illegal things got me to lose my daughter. When I was living by the rules, the correct rules, what I'm supposed to do, everything was great. When drugs and crime came into play, it went downhill and it went downhill quickly. And I always thought—I thought for eleven years that I could bullshit the system. And you can't. And I've got to say I'm grateful that I didn't because I learned a lot going to jail, believe it or not. It got me clean, I think it saved my life and I think it's changed me. I'm not saying that I wish—if years ago that I wish this would happen to me, no I wouldn't have wished it on me, but I can say I'm grateful things did happen and I did go to jail luckily enough for a long, long period of time and I have an opportunity again to be a mother again.

Not only does Becky view her drug addiction as a mistake that led her down a difficult path, but she also points to how prison altered her trajectory. For Becky, acknowledging the role of prison in shaping her future meant accepting accountability for her actions. By recognizing both the unpleasant and positive parts of her past she was able to describe the totality of her experiences as having a great purpose.

Thirty-nine-year-old LaToya was one of the only respondents to admit to ongoing substance abuse. A Black mother of five children, she was candid about her present addiction and the fact that she felt unable to maintain sobriety. Her drug use was personally costly, particularly in her role as a mother. After the birth of her sons, drugs were found in their blood sample. She soon lost custody and when we spoke she had no information regarding their whereabouts. When I asked her to describe how she felt about losing custody of her children, she stated:

> It's me. It's no other way to put it. It's me and my addiction. That's it. It's me and my addiction and being selfish and greed. That's not cool. That's how I

think and how I do. Maybe I shouldn't think that way but hopefully as time goes on I can look at it another way and think about it. I might hear something from somebody that make me think about it different or see things in a different way. I don't know.

LaToya's framing of her stigmatized identity does not involve disputing the particular offense, but rather demonstrates her willingness to change if given the necessary resources. The onus is placed on others, something that most of the mothers I interviewed were reluctant to do. While other respondents like Becky and Marcia, who were convicted of drug-related crimes, framed their decision to improve their lives as self-directed, LaToya hoped that she "might hear something from somebody" that would change her way of thinking. In this way, LaToya's comments are unique and shed light on how ongoing addiction may influence how one frames recovery.

It can be tempting to elevate examples of some women's journeys and generalize them to demonstrate that marginality does not preclude an applause-worthy redemption story or, conversely, that marginality justifies exclusion. Becky, for example, saw jail as one part of her recovery. Her experience is her truth but it also does not negate the very real harm carceral institutions inflict on women and men each day. Similarly, LaToya's personal struggle with drugs does not mean that she is unworthy of motherhood, unable one day to recover, or that all mothers with a past of addiction will struggle in the same way. These tensions often coexist because marginality looks different for each woman and existing on the margins means wrestling with competing narratives about how a woman sees herself, how the world sees her, and how she is *expected* to feel about her place in the world. At a broader level, how women describe their experiences with crime illustrates the varied ways in which criminal history shapes their view of their marginal status. To further unpack the moral agency that women exercise vis-à-vis their relationship to the criminal justice system, I return to Trisha, whose case reflects how power structures reinforce the dynamic between marginal status and criminalization.

A MISCARRIAGE OF JUSTICE

On the night of the incident that led to her arrest, Trisha was doing what she had done in weeks prior: she was out socializing with friends. Life for Trisha had recently turned a corner and she was excited about the future. Although she was still wrestling with feelings of anger toward her mother, whom she blamed for marrying the man who abused her, she had also made significant changes in her personal life. She ended a long-term relationship with her son's father after she disclosed her sexual orientation and that she wanted to be in an exclusive relationship with a woman. When she came out to her boyfriend he was supportive and encouraging, a reaction that put her worst fears about his response to rest.

While out that evening, a man with whom none of the women were acquainted approached them and began to make vulgar sexual comments. Trisha and her friends thought that they could diffuse the situation by disclosing that they were lesbians and had no romantic interest in him. His comments, however, turned from vulgar to threatening. The interaction soon turned violent, with Trisha punching the stranger and then fleeing with her friends. What happened after that brief encounter remains a mystery, according to Trisha. She argues that another person, an unidentified male, intervened and attacked the man. However, the closed-circuit video from a nearby business, which the prosecution used to buttress their case against her, only captured her and her friends' interaction, not the deadly attack that took place moments later. Because only she and her friends were on film, that evidence proved to be enough for the jury to convict her and her co-defendants.

Throughout court proceedings Trisha vehemently denied her role in the victim's death, even turning down a plea deal. She knew that refusing a plea deal against the advice of her attorney was risky. But to Trisha, accepting a plea deal meant lying and lying meant that she would have to compromise her moral values. Ultimately, Trisha believed that no matter what she said, the jury would make their decision not based on the truth but rather their own biases. Explaining her cynicism in the judicial process Trisha told me:

> We got shitted on. The jury was all white. . . . You're getting people from the area that just commited this crime. They don't want us gay people out there anyway so of course they going to go against us. So I got [nearly a decade] . . . well they offered me [a reduced sentence] but I said . . . what's the catch?" they said "well, you got to plead guilty." I said "I'm not pleading guilty. I have morals and beliefs and just because I'm a lesbian doesn't give the next person the right to disrespect me. What happened to self-defense?"[20]

At the beginning of her prison sentence Trisha tried to challenge the verdict, believing that it was a miscarriage of justice, rooted in racism and homophobia. With little faith in her overworked and underpaid public defense attorney, Trisha spent the beginning of her sentence in the prison's law library, searching for a way to contest the verdict on constitutional grounds. Believing that the judge's instructions to the jury were misleading, she contacted her attorney and inquired if the legitimacy of the verdict could be challenged on the basis of inaccurate jury instructions. Impressed by her research, her attorney appealed the decision and was successful in allowing Trisha's case to be heard once again. Despite this victory Trisha found her options limited. Ultimately, she was presented with the same option she faced when initially charged: Plead guilty or face a lengthy prison sentence. By the time she was offered the second plea deal her mother had died and she knew the pain of separation from her young son. Although pleading guilty went against her morals, being present for her son was more important.

> *Trisha:* And I got from [a reduced sentence] and the other [defendant] one got [a reduced sentence]. I ain't going to say it worked out but it was a lot better. I had at that point in order for me to get that deal, I had to plead guilty. At first when they came over to me my morals and beliefs was more important to me than anything. The second time I had already lost my mother, I already knew what it felt like to be away from my son and I already knew that the system was just trash. So, I was like right now I need to swallow my pride, my morals, and beliefs and think about my son.

Although she was successful in getting an appeal, even that proved to be a Pyrrhic victory because she ultimately had to confess guilt to a crime she didn't commit. In Trisha's mind, her criminal record was not a constant reminder of a criminal action, but rather a reflection of a broken legal system. Her rap sheet wasn't evidence that she broke the law, but rather proof of a system that, in her words, was "just trash."

Within the context of criminal behavior, moral agency primarily focuses on the decision to engage in or refrain from a law-violating act. Conventional views of crime and law also portrays the criminal justice system as the default arbiter of morality and those who violate the law are subject to the stigma of a criminal label. For Trisha, like other women who challenged the legitimacy of their arrests and conviction, the criminal justice system was not a neutral adjudicator of guilt or innocence. Furthermore, Trisha's view that the criminal justice system discriminated against her and her co-defendants because of their sexual orientation gave her the confidence that it was her, not the criminal justice system, that held the moral high ground.[21]

Trisha's account also illustrates the tension between critiquing flawed institutions, while relying upon the very same system to prove one's innocence. For example, her claims that the legal system was biased against her and her co-defendants because of their sexual orientation is substantiated by research. In their study on LGBTQ youth Nadal and colleagues found that young people who identified as LGBTQ reported feeling discriminated against by the criminal justice system specifically because of their sexual orientation.[22] Moreover, the compounding impact of race and social class further exacerbated discrimination. So, even while articulating the illegitimacy of the courts to adjudicate her case, Trisha also saw the courts as her only way to demonstrate her innocence. This duality, criticism and acknowledgment of necessity, speaks to what Monica Bell describes as legal cynicism.[23] Although Trisha was deeply cynical about fairness within the criminal justice system, she also hoped that within the narrow context of her appeals process the judicial system could potentially work on her behalf. Thus, while viewing the legal system as inherently biased, Trisha was willing to invest her time and limited resources in using the same system to rectify the legal status of her and her co-defendants. For marginalized people the luxury of complete dissociation from flawed institutions is one that they can ill afford. They recognize that because of their status the very institutions that structure their marginality are sometimes their only avenue of recourse.

Other women, like Dani, criticized the manner in which the criminal justice system labeled them without addressing the underlying issues related to arrest. Specifically, Dani criticized the judge, whose statement during her sentencing focused on her tarnished morality while inaccurately describing her upbringing.

> *Dani:* And it's not just the fight, but I think they didn't, they're so quick to put people in prison. And sometimes I think some people need to go, and I'm not saying I shouldn't get no prison time, but I think that they never offered me a way, like in patient . . . 'cause of my drinking. It never was offered to me, and I felt like that I was wrong, and because I'd never committed crime. I had no record, only judge I stood before was traffic judge. And I felt like they were being very inconsiderate. . . . It wasn't like I was a person that committed crimes over and over again. The judge was very mad, it wasn't because he felt like I came from a good family. And he said I should be ashamed, and I was like oh really like please, like whatever you know? That don't mean anything, I mean you can come from, you can live in a house where you have two working parents. That doesn't mean that it's not dysfunctional, that's the way I feel.

Likewise, Jane, a white mother from Massachusetts, was also critical of the criminal justice system. Her criticism was based on what she saw as broad, systemic inequity that had a disproportionately negative impact on marginalized populations.

> *Jane:* Everybody makes mistakes. And I would say 80 percent of the world does something wrong, it's just a certain percentage gets caught, okay? And if you do a crime, okay let's say a Lindsay Lohan, a Paris Hilton, a Matt Damon, they do something wrong, they go to the prison, it's not a big deal. It's not a big deal to the world. Their kids are not taken away, they don't lose rights to jobs. It's not a big deal.
>
> But when the poor people or the minority groups end up in prison, they want to pull away the children, they want to give them a stupid amount of time for a drug-related crime, which is ridiculous. People will murder—this guy who killed somebody in California, this bus driver, MTA worker, whoever he was, he got manslaughter, which is only like two to four years, we have women in prison serving twenty-five to life for drug offenses, which is ridiculous. And most of these women are mothers. And most of these women are single moms and most of them come from very poor neighborhoods.

While their status as formerly incarcerated women meant that their supervision by correctional institutions dominated our conversations, at times women provided subtle or explicit critiques of how other institutions displayed weak moral standing. For twenty-five-year-old April, a white mother from Massachusetts, both the criminal justice system and the health care system held little moral legitimacy and affirmed her view that poverty and homelessness shaped how institutions viewed her. Her experience navigating pregnancy during and after jail offers an illustration of how both her economic and socially labeled moral status impacted her care.

> *April:* And then I had to find prenatal care, I got out of jail, I didn't get any prenatal care really in the jail, I just got prenatal vitamins, that was it. . . . I don't know what else I could get but finding a prenatal hospital out here was really hard too.
>
> And then when I finally did call a place, they didn't have an appointment available for a couple months. . . . So I had to get a prenatal look at a homeless shelter that had a doctor that works there. And he wrote me—luckily he could write me a prescription for prenatal vitamins, otherwise I had been buying them from a grocery store, and they're like fifty dollars at the grocery store. . . . I was panhandling, sitting on the sidewalk begging money to buy prenatal vitamins and bus passes— it was so humiliating. And going to churches to get food where they serve the homeless people, and it's all a bunch of old, cracked out— and then me, I'm all pregnant. It's just so inappropriate, I'm so afraid of someone bumping into my stomach or whatever.

And then I went all over Massachusetts trying to find parenting classes, different things—then the prenatal doctor appointment I went to, I ended up hating the midwife so much so I had to leave and find a different hospital to give birth in because she was very rude to me. You know they ask you, they interview you to get all your background information? So I'm planning on living in a shelter, because they ask about your living situation, asking what support you have. I'm like, well basically none, just my friends and stuff like that. She asks, "Have you ever been incarcerated?" I'm like, "Yea, I just got out of jail." . . . I like the more natural medicine and stuff like that. So they have a birthing center at Cambridge Hospital and I said that's where I want to give birth. And you can do it in the water. . . . And she was like, "Oh, only normal people can do that." And I was like, "What? Well I gave birth to my daughter at home in the bathtub all by myself with no midwife, I know how to—" She's like, "No, you're homeless, you're a criminal, you can't—we only let normal people give birth in that place. You have to give birth in the hospital, because we don't know what you're going to do." I was like, "What?" I was so offended." . . . So Mt. Auburn Hospital, I just went there and they were totally fine, they didn't even ask me any questions—I told them the whole situation, I was like, "Cambridge Hospital said I'm not normal." They were like, "Oh yeah, you can give birth here."

I gave birth at Mt. Auburn, the nurse never even came in the room. I told them I wanted to do it by myself and they let me do it by myself. They put me in a room, they had a bathtub in there, they closed the door and they were like, "Buzz if you need us, buzz if the baby comes out and we'll come in and help if you want." So that's what I did, I gave birth alone in the hospital, the midwife came in and I was holding the baby, and she was like, "Oh, you want me to cut the umbilical cord?" And I was like, "No, not yet." Because I read that if you stay attached to the placenta longer, it's better for the baby. . . . It was alright, but it's hard, because you don't know. I didn't know where to look for prenatal care. I didn't know what places. Everything is hard.

April's desire for a birth plan with little medical intervention put her at odds with health care workers, not because her wishes were unsafe or against protocol, but because of her status as a formerly incarcerated woman. She wasn't "normal" according to the nurse she spoke to, implying that her ex-offender status justified limiting her options for childbirth. Women like April did not view their morally compromised status as ex-offenders as an automatic disqualifier in their ability to offer pointed critique of institutions. In challenging the legitimacy of their convictions, sentences, and treatment by institutions, women illustrate yet another way in which they create space for themselves by critiquing from the margins.

THE CARCERAL NARRATIVE IN THE REMAKING

The word *ex-offender* connotes the past, former, a status that once was but is no longer. Yet, in daily life, standing before a judge, speaking with a health care provider or a social worker, it is treated as a present indicator of who a woman is. The ex-offender label acts as a scarlet letter, in both seen and unseen ways, shaping how women navigate a world that is quick to judge them yet slow to recognize the fullness of their stories. Women's appraisals of their arrests, judicial proceedings and incarceration, offers insight into how they perceive themselves as a part of a broader ecosystem of (in)justice in America. By examining their experiences with criminal justice processes we gain necessary context for understanding their postincarceration journey.

A large part of the reason why ex-offenders' moral agency is lost amid discussions of incarceration, is that if not analyzed through a nuanced lens, those discussions run the risk of spotlighting cultural arguments focused on individual criminality at the expense of systemic inequities.[24] The individual, however, does not exist apart from the collective, just as the decisions of criminally involved women do not exist apart from abusive histories, discrimination, poverty, and weak social support systems. For example, understanding why Kiana made the decision to get into that yellow cab and the other crime narratives women share bridges the gap between the macrocauses of crime and the intimate details of their lived experience. We might also look at April's experience in seeking prenatal health care. As a white woman her race may not have been a barrier to maternal healthcare, but she was also homeless, a single mother, and an ex-offender when she sought help for her second pregnancy. To date there has been little in the way of research that examines how formerly incarcerated pregnant women navigate the healthcare system. What we do know, however, is that individuals with a criminal record report negative experiences with healthcare providers.[25] Thus, when formerly incarcerated women describe their experiences with social institutions, they illustrate that carcerality is not limited jail or prison, but extends to institutions that evaluate their humanity based on their relationship to the criminal justice system.

The carceral narratives of most formerly incarcerated women are being written long before imprisonment.[26] This does not mean that a woman is destined for a life of marginality, but rather that how the world sees her from early on in life increases the likelihood that she will one day be criminalized. In recounting the details of arrests and crimes, women illustrate that the marginality that their status creates does not mean that they are spectators on the sidelines of their own lives. They can challenge the legitimacy of the legal system like Trisha, just as they can place their conviction within the context of their relationships, like Ana.

A part of the process of challenging institutional "official" accounts surrounding their criminality is inserting themselves into their own narratives. They may not wield power in the ways that judges or correctional officers do, but they do own their stories and those are the stories that they share with their children and their loved ones. What women reveal in discussing their criminal involvement is that their framing of law-violating behavior provided a means by which they assess and reassess their moral interpretation of criminal acts, while pointing out the tensions and conflicts within themselves and in the people and institutions around them.

CHAPTER 4

The Duality of Marginalized Motherhood

A 2007 survey by the Pew Research Center reported that the general public believed mothers faced more complex challenges in the twenty-first century than at any other point in the previous thirty years. What struck me the most about the report was not its findings or even the broader policy implications of the study. Rather, it was the less than subtle message conveyed right in the article's title: "Motherhood Today: Tougher Challenges, Less Success."[1] The mothers represented in those findings were trying to balance childcare, career demands, and negotiate their personal goals with those of their partners. Indeed, the centuries-old tightrope of societal pressures and expectations women have had to traverse was on full display.[2] What remains telling, however, is that the manner in which motherhood is framed and *who* is centered in discussions around motherhood evolves to reflect what is valued and esteemed in our society.

According to legal scholar Dorothy Roberts, the meaning of motherhood is largely a social one. Roberts notes that motherhood is a complex social role and holds varied meaning depending on the social context.[3] In one sense, motherhood refers to the experience of mothering. That is, the way a woman feels about her role and how her unique experiences frame her understanding of that role. Second, motherhood can refer to the relationship between mother and child. From this perspective motherhood is evaluated as a tangible and observable relationship. Lastly, motherhood can more broadly be construed as a socially

90

constructed identity influenced by societal norms. Thus, when we consider motherhood today, or really at any point in this country's history, it is clear that it has rarely included the experiences of mothers like those at Mother's Love, Helping Hands, Inc., or Restoration House.

For so long, the manner in which we collectively speak about, write about, and even research motherhood has been through an exclusionary sensibility that privileges middle-class experiences, whiteness, and hegemonic patriarchy.[4] Therefore, in order to fully appreciate the complex forces impinging on formerly incarcerated women, it is necessary to decontextualize what motherhood means as a project of mainstream/white cis-womanhood.[5] A narrow conceptualization of motherhood is both limiting and problematic in a world that excludes formerly incarcerated mothers from staking claims to the very version of motherhood used to evaluate their ability to reintegrate into society. So, when we marginalize or ignore the various ways in which motherhood exists, where does this leave the most vulnerable of society's mothers? They are usually sidelined by policies that disproportionately harm them, by rhetoric that belittles their existence, and by a world that more often than not pretends that they simply do not exist.

Any analysis that examines the intersection of motherhood and criminality without interrogating the concept of motherhood itself assumes a singular and flat notion of motherhood within its framework. To assume that motherhood exists as a static or fixed category is to overlook how marginalized women have conceptualized their roles in the face of societal exclusion. For formerly incarcerated mothers, the challenge of navigating their ex-offender label and their identity as caregivers is a constant reminder of their outsider status. Their challenge is a particularly difficult one because for them motherhood does not necessarily confer esteem, nor is it a neutral site of gendered parenting. It is an identity that is questioned and contested time and time again.[6]

In this chapter I examine how women grapple with their own expectations for motherhood within the broader context of mainstream representations that often elude them. A common theme in the varying methods women implement to manage the stigmatization that defines much of their interactions is the careful balance they strike between their outsider status and their desire to be accepted and judged as "good mothers."[7] In this way, the duality of marginalized motherhood means that women negotiate their ex-offender status while asserting the values and aspirations that epitomize normative standards of middle-class motherhood.[8] Existing on the margins of society while occupying the socially important role of mother means that women are constantly recalibrating the image of themselves as valued caretakers against the societal caricatures of crime-involved women.[9]

Postincarceration success is often measured by employment status, reintegration, and, most significantly, nonrecidivism. While women identified these as important goals, there was also an acknowledgment that to some extent their employment, housing status, and social inclusion was out of their control.[10] Therefore, using those criteria as markers for successful reintegration meant that if employers remained skeptical or landlords refused to rent to them, they would forever remain bound to their marginal status. As such, part of redefining their roles and challenging normative definitions of a "good mother" meant expanding the definition of successful reintegration to include the long-term success of their children.[11] This measurement of success can't be measured in three years, the typical time frame used to measure recidivism, nor can a decade fully measure their postincarceration trajectory. Framing success in this way means that women desire the kind of open-ended standard of evaluating success allowed for women without a criminal record.

Women want the opportunity to reflect on their personal triumphs, and children's accomplishments, and articulate a "victory in the face of obstacles" narrative, rather than the more rigid short-term goals imposed upon them. In discussing their understanding of motherhood and the strategies they implement to avoid marginalization, I don't frame motherhood as a moment-specific life event that leads to a particular set of outcomes. Rather, I lead with the perspective that motherhood is a dynamic and ever-changing experience that formerly incarcerated women evaluate, adjust to, and critique as they navigate their own postimprisonment journeys.

"I'LL GET THERE SOMEDAY"

Growing up, twenty-eight-year-old Cadence's world felt small. She was raised in Brooklyn during the 1990s before the trendy cafés and remodeled brownstones, emblematic of borough-wide gentrification, pushed out poor, mostly Black and Brown, residents. After her father was sentenced to prison for drug possession, her parents divorced and her mother enrolled in school, eventually earning a degree in teaching. While she admired her mother's hard-working stick-to-itiveness, the two were never really close. It was her father, for all his shortcomings, that she looked up to, and his absence left a palpable void in her life. Once he was gone her interest in school waned and by eleventh grade she had dropped out. She earned her GED not long after leaving school but found herself unsure of what she wanted to do and who she wanted to become. This unsteadiness, coupled with what she describes as her naiveté, made her susceptible to the empty promises of neighborhood boys, like the father of her first two children. After giving birth to her first child she decided that the retail jobs that barely allowed her to make ends meet were no longer a viable way to secure a future for her and her child. She enrolled in community college but dropped out a few months later after reuniting with her boyfriend and becoming pregnant with her second child.

Cadence was able to stay with her mother and stepfather until she gave birth to her second child, but soon her mother's rules and expectations became unbearable. So, with no other options for housing she relocated to a shelter while continuing community college classes and working as much as possible. Within six months she was able to save enough money for a deposit on an apartment and, with her young children in tow, she settled down in a place of her own. Not long after she moved she began a retail position at a high-end department store in Manhattan. For Cadence, life was finally looking up. No sooner had she acclimated to her new job, however, than problems began to emerge. After applying to several other positions within the store and realizing that she might never be promoted because her supervisor favored other employees, she was both discouraged and angry. It was around this time that she began dating a customer to whom she expressed her workplace frustrations.

As was the case following her father's incarceration, the company of a boyfriend was a welcome distraction from the challenges of reality. It was for this reason that she believes she took his suggestion at retaliating against her supervisor seriously. The plan was simple enough: She would activate hundred-dollar gift cards while selling them to her boyfriend for a fraction of the price and the two would split the proceeds. Initially her plan seemed to work, but Cadence had not considered that like any other piece of merchandise, the store checked the inventory of gift cards against daily earnings. One day, as she was working the register, law enforcement approached her and placed her under arrest. Even before they read the charges, she knew why they were there.

When Cadence was arrested and charged with grand larceny she was pregnant with her third child and had already decided that she was going to keep the baby. Like some of the other women I interviewed from New York, she spent part of her sentence at Riker's Island before being transferred to Bedford Hills, one of the few women's prisons that provided mother-infant care services. Unlike her two older children, for whom she struggled to explain her absence, Cadence viewed her relationship with her third child as a blank slate. Her youngest child never experienced the pain of prolonged separation and was too young to understand the unusual circumstances of her first few months of life. In her young daughter's eyes Cadence saw an opportunity to fulfill her goals as a mother, unencumbered by the weight of a label that stigmatized her.

When Cadence and I discussed how she wanted to parent her daughter, who currently resided with her at Mother's Love, she was candid about the fact that despite being a mother of three, she felt like a novice. She didn't view her own mother's parenting style as a helpful model, nor did she want to repeat the mistakes she made when raising her two older children. When describing the practices, skills, and methods she wanted to define her postincarceration parenting style, she spoke mostly from a place of aspiration, focusing on the future. Drawing upon a fictional character, she described her ideal version of motherhood:

> I'm a mother that's trying to be a better mother, you know what I mean? . . . And . . . in my mind that's like Betty Crocker, you know . . . I'm baking, my kids have cookies, you know . . . and I'm also working and I'm getting them everything that they want, plus I'm giving them kisses and I'm reading bedtime stories and for some reason that just can't happen. Like it's just not, I don't know from where, you know, but then women really didn't work. Betty Crocker stayed home and cooked like, you know, all day and cleaned house and I want to be all that in one, but you know, so . . . I don't know. Just finding my balance in it and just . . . doing the best that I can and also just learning more patience because it takes a lot of patience. . . . But, you know, trying to know also that I can put that to the side and make time for the kids too and it's hard, but, you know . . . I'll get there someday.

When Cadence spoke of her aspiration to embody the characteristics of Betty Crocker she didn't use qualifying statements or add caveats indicating that she knew Betty Crocker was a fictional character. It seemed that Cadence truly believed that Betty Crocker was a real woman, or at the very least, a symbol of what a real woman ought to be. To her, this meant that her present inability to attain the very qualities to which she aspired not only substantiated her perceived shortcomings, but outlined a model for idealized motherhood.[12]

Cynthia, a white mother from New England, didn't reference Betty Crocker, but like Cadence she described similar practices that she viewed as illustrative of aspirational motherhood. When asked what she believed a mother should be, she responded:

> Just loving her and kissing her and taking her to school and practice or whatever she has, being responsive . . . making brownies and watching movies, and just doing mom stuff.

For both women motherhood meant deftly managing the domestic sphere while being fully present and available to children. This version of motherhood, set against the backdrop of weekly court-mandated meetings, employment requirements, probation, and the various formal and informal constraints that circumscribe an ex-offender's daily activity, can prove to be both exhausting and elusive.

For women like Cadence, the myth of Betty Crocker casts an almost suffocating shadow, not solely because it is unreal, but because it is rooted in something *very* real. Historically, idealized representations of North American womanhood are white and middle class and any deviation from that norm has been viewed as lacking, insufficient, and often deviant.[13] When viewed within the context of postincarceration, women understand that demonstrated rehabilitation is their most valuable currency in proving their success. Women therefore framed and defined goals accordingly.[14] Some women I spoke to described aspirational models of motherhood that were more accessible to them than those described by Cadence and Cynthia, making the goals seemingly more attainable.

Soon after her arrest for petty theft at nineteen, Aaliyah learned that she was pregnant. While in jail she spent much of the time reflecting about what motherhood would mean for her future and the kind of future she wanted to create for her child. Recalling how the ridicule she received within her own family led to insecurities about the color of her skin and intellect, she was determined to instill self-worth and body-positivity in her young daughter. Using other Black women as examples, Aaliyah outlined her vision of aspirational womanhood and motherhood.

> But all the times I wrote I would look at my poetry and I would say, how come nobody is looking at my poetry? I can always do the good stuff. I know this is good stuff. . . . She [her sister] would write about flowers and young love, and I was writing about Harriet Tubman, about black women being strong. This was what I was writing when I was younger. Like strong women

have always influenced me. There is something about strength, it's beautiful. Like to see a strong woman, that's what I'm saying, men would not be who they are if it wasn't for women, because we're so strong. Obama yeah he the president, but you always hear about how Michelle Obama she was a better lawyer. She was a better student. Come on. She felt strong.

Even I watched my grandmother. My grandfather was the provider. He went out and made all the bread. But I'm telling you, she controlled how he spent that bread. She controlled how he washes, how he cut his hair. She controlled how he ate, slept, everything. My grandfather and my grandmother have been together sixty years. They celebrated their anniversary last week. And never has my grandfather went shopping for himself. She always washed clothes. She took care of all the kids. How can a woman do all of that? She took care of her twelve kids and of my daddy's seventeen. My grandfather was always at work. She did it all by herself. . . . My grandmother is such a strong, strong woman. . . . She spoke her mind all the time. If you don't like it, what are you going to do about it? You can be big as a mountain, you try to put something on my grandmother and she would take up a broom, a stick, anything. . . . She was firm in her word. She was a strong woman.

In comparing the aspirational exemplars Cadence and Aaliyah describe, one difference is striking: Cadence's model of womanhood and motherhood makes her feel that she has fallen short. She hopes to meet the goal "someday" but all the expectations she has set for herself leave her feeling exhausted and overwhelmed. By contrast, Aaliyah identified specific characteristics in each of the women she references that she saw as attainable. Even her reference to Harriet Tubman underscores the aspect of motherhood she views as essential: strength. To be sure, the emphasis on strength and more specifically the prototype of the "strong black woman" can be problematic if it privileges unflinching stick-to-itiveness at the expense of emotional expression and mental health.[15] Nevertheless, the concept of strength is far more malleable than a more-perfect-than-life fictional character, in that it allows women to define and embody their own version of strength and adjust it to meet their circumstances, experiences, and sociocultural context.

Bridgette, a fifty-eight-year-old Hispanic mother from Massachusetts, also drew upon a model of motherhood rooted in her assumptions about cultural approaches to parenting. Like other women I interviewed, Bridgette had a difficult upbringing. She was raised in low-income housing and grew up in a physically and emotionally abusive household. As an adult, her abusive experiences continued, first with her ex-husband, who was physically violent toward her during her first pregnancy, and more recently by means of her own adult children. As one of the older women at Helping Hands, Bridgette's responses took on a reflective and wistful tone when she described the impact of her past decisions on her adult children. In describing her relationship with her son, she expresses both regret and sadness at how she raised him and how that may have impacted their current relationship.

> *Bridgette:* I'm done with my son! I was in a battered women's shelter, my son threw a cup of hot coffee at me. He went to court today. I went to the hospital and I told them that I was psychotic and had a nervous breakdown, and I made the whole thing up, which an outright lie. But he's on five days probation, what am I going to do? Put him away for five years? So he's a little violent. He's got three kids from three different mothers. The first mother he burnt her face with a cigarette, the second one kicked the door down, she left him, the third one left him. He's a woman beater. I blame it all on myself. I do.
>
> *Geniece:* Why do you blame it on yourself?
>
> *Bridgette:* I don't know. I didn't—I wasn't consistent. I wasn't an African-American mother.
>
> *Geniece:* What do you mean by that?
>
> *Bridgette:* I wasn't a strong woman. You look in the news, what do you see, who rapes everyone? White people. I mean, African Americans when they say "no" to their children, they mean it. As much as you love your child, I always said it, as much as you love your child, you stick to your words, African-American mothers.

When describing what she saw as parenting practices universal to African-American mothers, Bridgette nodded toward me as if to indicate that I, as a Black woman, was familiar with those practices. The presumption of our shared knowledge also conveyed that I too must have understood why she struggled to raise her children. By comparing herself to something she was not and could not be, Bridgette's description of African-American motherhood is not only aspirational but also unattainable. According to Bridgette, the assumed strength and disciplinary practices that African-American mothers possess exists because of the particular cultural and social context these mothers inhabit. In this way, African-American motherhood wasn't something to strive for, but rather an ideal type rooted in stereotypical notions about Black women that helped to justify her perceived shortcomings as a parent.

The juxtaposition between women and the models they describe might at first seem counterintuitive. By identifying representations of motherhood that a woman describes as superior to herself, she seems only to invite scrutiny and criticism of her own parenting abilities.

Drawing these distinctions, however, illustrates how models of aspirational motherhood is a way for marginalized mothers to align with, not merely distinguish themselves from, the versions of motherhood that they esteem.[16] Because it can be challenging for individuals viewed as morally compromised to present a convincing case about their moral strengths, disconfirming a stereotype can be executed by aligning oneself with normative or idealized representations of social figures.[17] Demonstrating that they value and embrace the norms and standards delineated by institutions, such as transitional organizations and social services, can be a way for women to signal their allegiance to and acceptance of the kind of motherhood valued by wider society.

It is indeed the case that being rewarded for embracing a particular brand of motherhood in order to demonstrate progress or success is both classist and racist, as it limits the range of possibilities afforded to marginalized women.[18] Nevertheless, attempting to conform to these models of motherhood is a way for women lacking social and cultural capital to demonstrate their commitment to postprison expectations of reformation and rehabilitation. The duality of marginalized motherhood is such that women don't choose their outsider status; These identities are socially imposed upon them.[19] What they do choose, however, is the manner in which they navigate their identity, the extent to which they challenge labels, and, most important for women, what they tell their children about who they are as mothers. So, when Cadence finds herself struggling to meet the standards of Betty Crocker or Aaliyah idealizes Michelle Obama and the strength of her grandmother, it is not solely the distance between these women and their role models that matters. The fact that the template upon which they base parental success aligns with broader views about acceptable versions of motherhood reveals that they want what society and the institutions that organize their lives say they should want. In the period following incarceration women are not only tasked with acquiring new skills and earning a living, they are engaged in the informal discursive project of articulating a moral ideology centered around the most salient role in their daily interactions: formerly incarcerated motherhood.

The examples of motherhood that Cadence, Aaliyah, and Bridgette invoke show that their view of motherhood does not deviate radically from normative expectations of what mothers are supposed to embody.[20] This is significant for two reasons: First, at the level of public opinion, poor single mothers, particularly those with criminal records, are often viewed as undeserving of their roles as mothers, the identity that centers much of their postrelease experiences. This line of reasoning assumes that to commit a crime and therefore defy the unspoken oath of sacred motherhood is to abdicate any claims a woman might have on mainstream representations of mothering. However, the women I spoke to are not only aware of what society values in mothers but they embrace many of those characteristics.

The second reason women's articulation of their aspirations for motherhood is important is because as they begin to rebuild their lives after incarceration, they are measuring their success and failure by a standard of motherhood that can prove to be elusive. Not elusive because of a lack of desire to attain their stated goals, but because the goals they set for themselves can require economic resources and social support that can be difficult for formerly incarcerated women to attain. For example, Cadence's Betty Crocker image most clearly portrays a version of motherhood that has long eluded women who were not middle-class or white. This is not because minoritized populations don't hold conventional views about childrearing or prioritize their families. Rather, inequitable economic structures and a dearth of social programs to address poverty means that in order to comfortably provide financial support for a family, two working adults in a household are often a practical necessity.

Beyond economic factors, women also illustrate the differences between middle-class white representations of motherhood and marginalized motherhood. Aaliyah, and to a lesser extent Bridgette, focuses on the characteristic of strength that she believes to be a key hallmark of Black matriarchy and motherhood. Still, in each case there is a perceived gap between who they are and who they aspire to be. For Aaliyah it is the lack of social and familial support that stands in the way of her goals, and for Bridgette it is her perception of her own cultural deficiencies.

"SOME MOTHERS JUST DON'T CARE"

When Nadiege, a thirty-one-year-old Haitian-born immigrant from Brooklyn discusses motherhood, she is careful to distinguish her criminal past from her parenting skills. Because her son was a baby when she was incarcerated, Nadiege was able to avoid separation while in a mother-and-infant prison program. As a result, she did not feel that her criminal involvement tarnished her status as a mother. This was one of the reasons that she was critical of other women she met at Mother's

Love, who seemed to prioritize themselves above the needs of their children. She describes a recent incident at Mother's Love that illustrates her critique of inattentive mothers:

> *Nadiege:* Girls come to me and ask me what my story is, and it doesn't matter. I'm not getting high, I haven't used drugs, I do drink alcohol, and no I don't feel the urge to use drugs again because it's not something that I need to do. I have three kids, and I'm not getting any younger. I want to be a positive person in my children's' lives. . . . I'm not going to that selfish person that you guys are making excuses to be, because that's what it always is. Women come here and make excuses because they want to get high. So, they pick up that "addiction" word and use that, you know what I'm saying?
>
> *Geniece:* You mean as an excuse or something?
>
> *Nadiege:* Like as an excuse! "Oh, it's an addiction," "Oh, it's the devil." Get the fuck out of here! What are you talking about? No, you want to get high! If you wake up every day and think about getting high, you're going to get high. . . . Don't give me that bullshit excuse about the devil or that it's your addiction . . . my kids are good enough reasons for me not to get high again, you understand what I'm saying? That's that negative aura that people bring in here. One girl split the program for like two days, dropped her kid off, and abandoned her child. She didn't leave any clothes, no diapers, no money, and no formula. . . . She comes back on the 4th of July, she drops off the car, she goes and gets her phone, she goes to sleep. Then she jumps in the pool. Why are you smoking crack? Do you seriously understand that this program is here to help you? Ok, well let me go out and smoke crack too. Let them give me fifteen hundred dollars so I can go and smoke crack. I'm not saying it's not fair, I'm just saying what kind of an example is that for everybody else? I got into an argument with somebody yesterday about that. That's just making up excuses. She called me selfish yesterday, but I'm not selfish. She's selfish for abandoning her child for two days.

In recounting another resident's experience, Nadiege not only draws attention to that mother's weaknesses but also to her own perceived strengths. While Nadiege speaks at length about the neglectful behavior of the other woman, she also reveals quite a bit about herself. For example, she believes that one's role as a mother should trump any and every aspect of life, even when one is struggling with drug addiction. Addiction doesn't provide a context for understanding what appears to be careless behavior because, to Nadiege, motherhood should always be the context through which all other behavior is regulated. One of the reasons that Nadiege was so critical had to do with the fact that she too struggled with addiction in the past and still managed to care for her children. To her, other women in the program failed to maintain their sobriety because they lacked the desire to create a stable environment for their children.

The emphasis that women like Nadiege placed on her strengths vis-à-vis the weaknesses of other mothers reflects what Crocker and Major call strategic comparison.[21] According to Crocker and Major, individuals from stigmatized communities may sometimes compare themselves to other members within their in-group in order to create a buffer between themselves and criticism from wider society. Specifically, marginalized individuals identify people whose actions or behaviors they view as more reprehensible than their own.

Comparison to peers is a natural and expected part of social interaction. In some ways women's comparisons to other mothers are no different than a scholar comparing herself to a counterpart in the same field of study or an athlete comparing their success to their nearest rival. The key difference, of course, is that when the person executing the comparison occupies a socially sanctioned and marginalized identity, the comparison exists within the context of shared disadvantage. Moreover, strategic comparisons of this kind aim to substantiate the claims that women make about a contested identity like postincarceration motherhood because institutions have compared *them* to normative standards and have found them lacking. For example, Nadiege's framing of other mothers' inability to appropriately address their addiction resembles the personal-responsibility narrative used in policy and media representations that would likely be used to negatively judge women like herself. Strategic comparisons also illustrate how the duality of marginalized motherhood is deployed through the bifurcation of an internal logic in which one inhabits both a marginal space while juxtaposing one's perceived moral superiority against the moral failures of peers.

The sentiments shared by Nadiege are echoed by other women I interviewed. Like Nadiege, Grace, a mixed-race twenty-year-old mother from Massachusetts, viewed other mothers' decisions as a result of their unwillingness to change. Explaining her own postincarceration trajectory, she stated:

> And it's sad to say, but some mothers just don't care, you know? And then, there's the ones who do, and really wanna be there for their kids, and just everything's getting in the way of, you know—and I just feel like, I don't know, shouldn't nothin' stop you. And that's the way I thought about . . . When I got out [of jail], my son was still in DCF custody, so my frame of

mind was nothing can stop me.[22] You know what I mean? I did what they wanted me to do before they even asked me to do it.

While acknowledging that "everything's getting in the way" of providing for their children, Grace also felt that if there was enough will power, desire, or determination, nothing should or could effectively hinder the efforts of her peers' reentry process. The individualistic nature of Grace's and Nadiege's responses mirrors the tone and tenor of programming at many correctional institutions and reentry organizations.[23] Success is framed primarily as a marker of individual effort, which of course means that failure also rests squarely on the shoulders of individuals. The fact that some formerly incarcerated women reiterate that perspective is not surprising. If the reintegration process is based on principles of individualized goals and accomplishments, then it stands to reason that those same standards might be applied when discussing the actions of their peers in reentry programs.

When thirty-six-year-old Vickie arrived at Mother's Love she had recently given birth to her second child and was determined to maintain her sobriety. Although she found it difficult to manage the competing demands of motherhood and addiction, she was also critical of mothers who weren't able to overcome their addiction for the sake of their children.

> Because when I see people and they struggle with drugs and you know they use drugs and they have for years and they still struggle with it. I right away, I might label . . . when are they going to get high? It's just a matter of time for them.

In focusing on what she viewed as other women's lack of resolve or willingness to change, Vickie frames their drug use as a moral failure, rather than an illness. Similarly, thirty-six-year-old Carissa, another resident at Mother's Love, was critical of mothers who she felt failed to take advantage of available resources offered by the transitional organization.

> I think it's a good organization you know? . . . But even though it's willing to help people, you got to want the help, you know? If you're not willing to do what you've got to do for yourself and your children, this is not the place for you, you know what I'm saying? . . . Some people just don't want to be helped, but they come here and they waste a bed for somebody else that wants the help you know? . . . And I, you know like how some, as the saying goes, one bad apple spoils it for a lot, for the rest. . . . And if you don't want to change, then I don't think this is the place for anybody. . . . 'Cause they

want to help you, but you've got to be willing to help yourself, you know? Because nobody here's going to hold you by the hand, and take you step by step. . . . They're going to explain what you need to do, and we all grown, you need to go and do that.

Again, embedded within each of these critiques is the notion that both the highs and lows of postincarceration are individualistic in nature. Not individualistic in the sense that each person's journey is unique and shaped by their lived experiences, but rather a product of their ability to work hard enough to overcome even the most complex of obstacles.

In group meetings within jails and prisons and parenting classes at transitional organizations, women have been told what it means to be a "good mother."[24] Being a "good mother" within the context of spaces that evaluate their character and morality is not merely a subjective exercise without tangible consequences. Correctional institutions and transitional programs are powerful and this reality does not escape women. The strategic comparisons that women engage in reproduce the kind of value-based metrics used to assess their morality, worthiness, and rehabilitation. More than anyone, women recognize that failure to meet expectations can result in serious repercussions. So, when formerly incarcerated women seem to cast aspersions on other women with criminal records it must be understood within the broader context of the carceral communities that they inhabit. Women can simultaneously exercise agency in how they execute and articulate personal morality in judging others, while reproducing the evaluative framing used by the judges, attorneys, correctional officers, and social workers who play a significant role in determining their freedom status. For each woman, their view of morality is malleable, shaped by a combination of preincarceration and postincarceration experiences that creates a perceived benefit or penalty for the version of motherhood that they embrace.

"I TRIED MY HARDEST"

The day that a woman enters a hospital to have a baby can be both an exciting and an uncertain time. By her fifth time in the labor and delivery ward, however, there was a sad inevitability that weighed on LaToya. The routine was predictable: The baby would be delivered, routine screening would be conducted, the presence of crack cocaine would be detected, followed by the flurry of paper work and social workers.[25] Once again, LaToya would leave the hospital empty-handed, seeking consolation in the very substance at the source of much of her life's regrets. When I met LaToya at a Boston coffee shop she had already lost custody of her five children and many of her other relationships were fractured, unable to weather the challenges that come with addiction. Motherhood for LaToya was a reminder of her greatest losses, but it was also a source of hope. As she described her experiences as a mother, she reflected on her own childhood, stating that her mother spent more time with male companions than with her and her siblings. When I ask her how she felt about her mother's actions she responded that she harbored no resentment. After all, she reasoned, her mother was young and wanted to have fun. She did not feel that it was her mother's responsibility to ensure that she and her siblings didn't engage in negative behaviors, so it was unfair to hold her responsible for her own drug addiction that plagued her since adolescence.

When I asked LaToya to describe how she viewed herself as a mother, she spoke mostly of her intentions, wistfully imagining what might have been. The devastating consequences of addiction made it such that her discussion of motherhood centered on her potential, rather than on the fraught relationships that defined her reality.

> *Geniece:* How would you describe your experience of being a mother?
>
> *LaToya:* It's hard. You gonna have me crying. I don't think it would be hard though if I wasn't on drugs. I think I'd be a good mom, a good provider because I'm a good person, I have a heart of gold. Don't get me wrong I'm not perfect or anything but I think I'd be a good mom if I wasn't into the streets or the drugs, I think I'd be good . . .
>
> *Geniece:* What do you think is most rewarding about being a mother?
>
> *LaToya:* It's being a mom. But I'm still not ready to take care of my kids or have them back in my life right now.
>
> *Geniece:* What thing is the most difficult, the one thing that is the hardest thing about balancing . . .
>
> *LaToya:* I can't answer that because I don't know. I'm not with them I haven't been with my kids in twenty-one years so I can't tell you. . . . It's not even funny, I fucked up my life. Excuse my language but it is what it is. I fucked up and I gotta deal with it. I wanna cry but I'm trying to hold back.

One might read LaToya's account and find her use of terms like "good provider," "good mom," and "good person" at odds with the actions that resulted in the custodial loss of her children. Goodness, however, is a loaded term, one with moral connotations that shift depending on who uses the word and whom it refers to. As a complex and malleable social role, motherhood is not only defined in relation to other people but also in relation to a concept and ideal. LaToya was aware of the toll that drug addiction had on the material and practical aspects of her role as a mother. However, she also saw her feelings toward her children and her desire to change her life as indicative of who she was as well. This distinction might seem moot since her actions, drug use during pregnancy, led to potentially life-long consequences for her children. Indeed, by her own admission, LaToya viewed herself as primarily responsible for what happened to her children. But she also felt that her willingness to admit her present inability to care for them was evidence that she was a good mother.[26] In other words, being a good mother for LaToya meant acknowledging that the best thing that she could do for her children was to love them from a distance.

The notion of "good motherhood" is not uncommon among all mothers striving toward a version of idealized parental success, but it is particularly salient among morally compromised mothers.[27] When released from jail, prison, or correctional supervision, women still experience being morally judged in their daily interactions. Difficult access to housing, employment, and children is a regular reminder that a criminal record exacerbates the existing challenges faced by those who occupy marginal identities along the lines of race and socioeconomic status.[28] Aiello and McQueeny note that incarcerated women try to prepare for these challenges by renegotiating their identities as mothers and distancing themselves from their incarcerated identity.[29] This strategy, however, is complicated by the fact that the stigma of ex-offender motherhood is also shaped by their identity before motherhood and hinges on the outcome of their future relationship with their children. In this way, being a "good mother" by conventional standards is not solely an evaluation based on the present, but also on the past and the future.[30] Therefore, one's experience as a formerly incarcerated mother, even when seemingly positive, is subject to caveats and qualifiers by people and institutions who use the ex-offender status as a lens through which women are judged again and again.

In chapter 1 we saw that for formerly incarcerated women marginalization begins not at the point of arrest or sentencing but during their formative childhood years. Indeed, many incarcerated mothers have faced a lifetime of being labeled as "bad" girls, "bad" daughters, and "bad" partners.[31] Similarly, a woman's status as a morally compromised mother does not begin and end when she is convicted and released from prison. By the time many women enter prison they have already experienced layers of stigma, such as family dysfunction, intimate-partner victimization, and poverty that can make their roles as mothers vulnerable to formal and informal critiques. Moreover, because motherhood is an evolving social role largely influenced by child-parent relationships, the sometimes rigid standards to which women are held by evaluative entities like reentry programs can be incongruent with their own experience.[32]

For life-course theoretical framing this is significant because the working assumption is that becoming a mother shapes future actions. However, without attending to the ways in which motherhood changes for a woman throughout her life and how her own understanding of what it means to be a mother shifts, it can be easy to measure the salience of ex-offender motherhood solely based on her relationship to the criminal justice system. In their framing of motherhood, women understood the challenges their peers faced, even when some drew comparisons between themselves and those whose actions they viewed unfavorably. As a result, most women resisted describing other women as "bad mothers," which they felt implied a fixed and lasting moral status. While women might identify problematic behavior, they viewed them as lapses in judgment, rather than a final pronouncement of a woman's character.

Like LaToya, Rashida, who was arrested for assault, defined her role as a mother based on her intentions toward her children, rather than her criminal history. Reflecting on motherhood she stated,

> I tried my hardest to make sure my kids grew up the right way. So yeah, I think I'm a good mom, because I got them to the point they are now.

Forty-forty-year-old Juanita also underscores this sentiment as she explains her feelings about motherhood:

> I think that I'm a good mother, and I think that I'm doing the best that I can, to be there for all of my kids. Whether they want me there or not, I'm trying the best that I can. Like I know that I messed up in my life, and I know that I need to move on. So if my children want to keep me in their paths, then I have to keep moving.

To Juanita, being a good mother is defined not by the past but by her orientation toward the future. Her desire to "keep moving" is what makes her a good mother, because it demonstrates that she is able to alter the course of her life in spite of past decisions.

In addition to framing motherhood based on their future intentions, rather than past behavior, some mothers pointed to their parenting philosophy as illustrative of their strengths. Tammy, a thirty-seven-year-old mother of nine children, explains her perspective on parenting:

> I think of myself as a mother as a good parent, trying to be some good parent, a respectful parent, a God-given parent. I look forward to the future with my children. Instead of keeping them all in bubbles, I want to just be free with them, be free with my kids instead of holding them, holding them hostage, you know what I mean.

Sage, who was in the process of regaining custody of her children, also explains why she rejected an overprotective approach to parenting:

> I would have to say I think I'm a good mother. I think I'm a good mother, but I'm a real mother. I know that and I'm always . . . I know what my defects are and I'm always trying to work on that. I'm an attentive mother. I'm definitely a nurturer. I'm a good communicator with my oldest son. I mean he just says it all. But I think what I provide as a mother, I'll say, I try to give them the whole package. I don't try to shelter them from the world, but I do try to guide them.

What women demonstrate in how they frame motherhood is an ability to straddle the expectations of a normative, institutionally sanctioned version of motherhood with their own values rooted in their lived experiences. The act of balancing and negotiating their roles as mothers is an unwieldy process, filled with the expectations and burdens of postimprisonment. At times a woman may invoke a narrative critical of other mothers even when acknowledging the tenuous nature of her own status within society. Inhabiting spaces of contradiction and critique, however, is not a justification for delegitimizing women's roles as parents. Motherhood for most women is a socially complex role, fraught with competing demands. But for these mothers there is the added burden of fulfilling expectations that often seem in flux.

"MEANT FOR SOMETHING GREATER"

Toward the end of each of my conversations with women, I asked them to share the dreams that they had for their children. The question was centered on their children, but it wasn't long before I realized that it was just as much about the woman's dreams for herself as it was about the dreams that she had for her child. Who their children were and would one day become was, for many women, a direct reflection of how they saw themselves as mothers. Aggregate data on children of incarcerated parents substantiates the tone of women's responses: Children of incarcerated parents are more likely to be victims of abuse, engage in risky behaviors, and be incarcerated as adults.[33]

In one study analyzing the incarceration of adult children who had an incarcerated parent, 8.5 percent of adult children who had an incarcerated father had themselves been incarcerated, while 21 percent of adult children with an incarcerated mother had been incarcerated.[34] Because children of incarcerated parents are already at risk due to contextual factors, such as experiencing community-level crime, the possibility of incarceration reflects both intergenerational and structural risks.[35] It is no wonder then that for the women I spoke to, protecting their children from the most negative consequences of parental incarceration was a key priority. To them, the successes of their children provided tangible evidence that despite their imprisonment, they had managed to help their children navigate and avoid the pitfalls that led to their own incarceration.

By the time I interviewed Aaliyah I thought I knew what to expect. I didn't know the specific details of her story, but having conducted a few dozen interviews by then, I thought I might be adept at compassionately yet objectively exploring topics ranging from childhood victimization to intimate-partner abuse. Yet, there I was in the small private parlor of Mother's Love's residential housing on the verge of tears. What moved me in a way that I had not anticipated was Aaliyah's almost unflappable optimism about her daughter's future in spite of circumstances that robbed her of her own childhood. When I asked Aaliyah to describe her hopes for her daughter, she was enthusiastic about the future and confident in her ability to help her daughter realize her potential:

I can't wait to tell my daughter, "You're beautiful," no matter what people say. I can't wait to tell her, "You can be anything you want to be." I can't wait to just fill her with so much self-esteem, just to love her. I can't wait to make her believe in herself. I can't wait until she can be able to say, "I can do anything I want to." I can't wait for that day when somebody tells her she can't and she proves them wrong. I just can't wait to see that. I can't wait until she becomes something that is so big in life. I can't imagine it. I don't know if she is going to be a star. I just know that she is meant for something greater. I just can't wait for that day. She is going to be somebody better in life. I just want her not to make the same mistakes I made. . . . I have to teach her how to be extra smart and extra cool and ambitious. . . . With her I know I'm going to rise. So, it's just like I want her to be different. I want her to be determined. No matter what obstacles she faced, she can do it. I don't ever want her to be like, I can't. Because even now sometimes I feel like I can't do it, because I'm so used to that frame of mind. But I want her to always be like, oh, I can do it. I'm pretty enough, I'm strong enough, I'm smart enough, I'm tough enough. I can do it. I want her to be like that.

Aaliyah saw the fates of her and her daughter as intertwined. Her daughter's ability to succeed was dependent on her own ability to instill confidence and self-esteem within her child. The extent to which she felt her daughter's success was fostered or impeded by her own experiences influenced how she viewed her reintegration process.

Summer, a twenty-six-year-old white mother from New York, further underscored how women view their own success in relation to their children's outcomes:

> So, I just want my son to have a really good life and make good choices and I want to be able to be in Adrian's life as much as I can because I failed the first time at being a mother, I'm not going to fail the second time. . . . I can't change the past but I can only make the future better.

Summer's dreams for her son reflect her own desire to change the existing narrative that she had about who she was as a parent. Formerly incarcerated women are constantly evaluated based on their pasts, long after they leave transitional homes and complete court-mandated programs. A future-oriented focus that centers on the outcomes of their children makes women's postincarceration experience less about them (and their pasts) and more about their ability to model success vis-à-vis their children. Thirty-one-year-old Isabelle also underscores this sentiment, by drawing a connection, not only between her past and her goals for her children's future, but also to the broader context within which her children were raised:

> Dreams I have for them? God . . . I just want them to have the best lives that they can have and do everything they can do and go to school and have their own lives, you know what I mean and hopefully they're not—not happen what's happened. My grandmother is an alcoholic, my mother is an addict, and now me, my sister, my cousins, my whole family, aunts uncle. I'm hoping it doesn't happen with them. I'm going to do everything in my power to try to prevent that. You know what I mean? Everything. And I'm not going to keep anything from them. This whole story here when they get old enough I'm going to tell them what happened.

Twenty-eight-year-old Elise, a Black mother from New York, hoped that one day her six children would be able to look beyond her past and criminal record. Describing her goals for the future she stated:

> My dream is for my other kids to just accept me one day and to know that I never did stop loving them. To one day be there. Be in their lives every day and for them to know that I'm here. And to just have some time of relationship with them [*crying*] . . . sorry. My dreams for my son now is for him to know his sisters and brothers and for them to not feel some type of way because I take care of him and not them. My dreams are to send my son to college and go back to college myself. And that's it.

Like Aaliyah, Elise connected her hopes for her children with how she wanted them to view her as a mother. She feared that if her children could not look past her criminal record that it might impede their own future. Given research findings that show that parental incarceration can result in a rift between parents and children leading to deleterious childhood outcomes, Elise's fears were not unfounded.[36] Another goal she mentions, her children's enrollment in college, was also a recurring theme in women's responses.

Wanting one's child to excel in school and one day attend college isn't particularly unusual for parents. However, when that parent is a formerly incarcerated woman, the centrality placed on higher education challenges existing views about the outcomes for those children.[37] Most of the women I interviewed received little if any education while incarcerated. Those who did receive educational classes in prison typically participated in training groups that focused on parenting and life skills. This was also true of the educational classes they received in postprison transitional organizations. A number of women I spoke to wanted traditional academic education for themselves, feeling that it would prepare them for the labor market, and wanted the same for their children. However, if they were unable to access higher education for themselves, then their hope was that their children would be able to reap the benefits of higher education. Women didn't only want to keep their children from repeating their mistakes, they wanted them to move forward and upward in achieving the goals that had eluded them.

Cadence, who aspired to be a modern-day Betty Crocker, also saw her success as a parent tied to her children's education. Discussing her goals for them she stated,

> I definitely want them to finish school and then, you know, I don't want [her] to like boys and all that stuff . . . later like after college and all that.

Likewise, twenty-eight-year-old Khloe from New York saw her daughter's education as a way for her to avoid Khloe's mistakes while also achieving success:

I don't know like I don't want her to go through the pain of addiction of prison life and I just want to finish school and go on to college and get a career and meet a nice guy and have kids after she is married, and I want her to have "the American dream," and I was nowhere close to that. I just want her to follow her heart and do what she loves and I will support her even more.

The directional pathway of parent-to-child intergenerational outcomes is one that women acknowledge in explaining how their pasts impact their children's future. But women also understand the constraints of their own futures in light of their criminal records. As a result, they view their children's outcomes as a means of substantiating their postincarceration success. In this way, the parent-to-child pathway runs concurrent to that of the child-to-parent pathway. Women understand the significance of protecting their children from problems that increase the likelihood of incarceration, but they also believe that their children's accomplishments can influence how they are viewed as mothers.

Examining how women's aspirational views of motherhood and their strategic deployment of comparisons aligns with and departs from their child-centered discussions of motherhood underscores how fluid this identity is for formerly incarcerated women. One might view this no differently than how many mothers construe parenting: she rationalizes her mistakes and hopes to improve in the future. This is precisely the point. Women's ex-offender status places them along the margin of motherhood but does not strip them of their ability to want what is best for their children. If these women, at their core, want what so many other mothers want for themselves and their children, then it calls into question the manner in which we as a society other-ize formerly incarcerated mothers.

The experiences and sentiments that women shared about their goals for their children also illustrated one of the most important reasons for approaching formerly incarcerated mothers' identity as a dynamically lived experience, rather than a moment-defined life event: A woman's framing of motherhood is context-specific. For example, I found that when asking women to describe their experiences as mothers, they spoke in the past, present, and future tense depending on their experiences up to that point. There was the idea of motherhood as an identity to be attained, when the women's vision of motherhood was based on normative markers of success they had not yet achieved. When women compared themselves to other mothers, they often invoked past experiences as a way to demonstrate that another person's past actions warranted critique when juxtaposed against their own experiences. And, when explaining their identity as mothers vis-à-vis their children, women spoke both about their present interactions and their future aspirations for their children. In this way, women might feel excluded from or frustrated with one area of motherhood, while simultaneously creating space for themselves to exist and thrive in another area of that role.

AIN'T I A MOTHER?: DUALITY AND INTERSECTIONAL MOTHERHOOD

Born an enslaved woman in the nineteenth century, Isabella Baumfree was given the promise of freedom by her captor only to have him later renege on that promise. Undeterred, she emancipated herself, believing that freedom was hers whether or not a man or the law stated so. Not long after she walked to freedom, she changed her name to Sojourner Truth to mark the genesis of a new life. That name, in more ways than one, served as a testament to the activism that defined her life's work. In one of her most notable speeches, Sojourner Truth addressed the Ohio Women's Rights Convention of 1851, providing an incisive critique of sexist chauvinism pervasive in mid-nineteenth-century United States.[38] The speech not only addressed the insidious ways in which sexism impeded women's social and political rights, it also underscored how the political sisterhood which would later be known as suffragettes and the architects of the nineteenth amendment, reproduced the type of exclusivity they sought to ameliorate. In their fight for the most basic of political expressions, they relegated Black women to marginal actors in the fight for the vote.

On that day in Ohio, Sojourner Truth spoke truth to power, with words that elevated the intersectionality of her womanhood, race, and freedom status in antebellum society. Pointing out her marginal status and that of other Black women, she posed the now-famous question to her audience: "Ain't I a woman?"[39] Since then, this question has echoed across classrooms and boardrooms, picket lines and picket-fenced suburbs. It is a question for the past and one for this present moment. In examining the experiences of formerly incarcerated mothers, I pose a similar question, one that interrogates how the intersecting identities of race, gender, class, and freedom-status inform how women make sense of their roles as mothers and how scholars can thoughtfully engage with women's experiences using nuanced and holistic frameworks.[40]

Over the course of the year when I interviewed women, with the exception of a few, there was almost no discussion about how race shaped their relationship with the criminal justice system. However, I would argue that race nevertheless structured their experiences in other substantial ways. One of the reasons why the freedom status of women must be included in intersectional analyses of mothers who have been surveilled and incarcerated by the state is that those experiences change how women speak (or don't speak) about their other identities. The toll of a criminal record is felt acutely by all formerly incarcerated women seeking work, but on Black and Brown ex-offender women the impact is particularly devastating. Black and Latina women enter prison with lower levels of education than white women and therefore have a more difficult time acquiring employment after prison.[41] Moreover, because many of the occupations from which ex-offenders are barred are disproportionately held by women, escaping poverty is an uphill battle they must climb from the first day they leave prison. For example, jobs that require state licensure, such as child care work and cosmetology, are unavailable to women with criminal records. As a consequence, the reduced economic options for minority mothers means that their children are less likely to be with their mothers and end up in foster care, a well-documented site along the carceral continuum.[42] So, when examining how women like Cadence, Aaliyah, or Elise frame their postincarceration hopes and expectations, it is important to understand how race structures their experiences in both subtle and explicit ways.

While a hypothetical, counterfactual view based on a "what if a white woman from an upper-class neighborhood were arrested" line of reasoning is rhetorically provocative, it isn't needed to illustrate the very real impact of race on criminalization. One need look no further than empirical data to see that social context does in fact inform how race and class influence respondents' freedom status. In her audit study of formerly incarcerated women, Ortiz finds that while a criminal record only marginally impacted the employment prospects of female job candidates, race proved to significantly influence prospective employers' decisions. Black women without a criminal record were less likely to be hired than both white and Hispanic women.[43] Specifically, Black women had a 37 percent lower chance of being called back for a job interview than their white counterparts. One of the reasons for this is that even without a criminal record minority woman are subjected to negative stereotypes, such as the "welfare queen" trope, that prejudges their work ethic.[44] Furthermore, minoritized women are more vulnerable to victimization, less likely to receive resources from social services, and more likely to be treated harshly by the criminal justice system. Indeed, it is the marginalizations *within* marginalizations that results in the heaviest consequences born by society's most vulnerable mothers.[45]

CHAPTER 5

The Project of Rehabilitation

The Duality of Place and People

At the entrance of the sunlit room where Mother's Love held workshops and classes was a collage of photographs. Looking at the photographs, I paused on one that featured an immediately recognizable face. Standing next to smiling program participants was a well-known actor, most known for his roles as a leading man in popular romantic films in the 1980s and 1990s. In other photos, Mother's Love's executive director stood alongside women dressed in formal attire at what appeared to be gala events. Eva, a former client and current staff member, smiled in some of these photos. She was proud of her role in helping to raise awareness about the challenges formerly incarcerated women faced. Doing so was important, not just for the purpose of raising awareness, but also for the pragmatic purpose of fundraising.

Like Mother's Love, Helping Hands, Inc., and Restoration House were nonprofit organizations and were regularly involved in efforts to raise money. As is the case for many nonprofits, a key element of fundraising is convincingly demonstrating prior success in previous initiatives. For transitional organizations, success hinges upon the rehabilitation of women. In conversations with women it became clear that what rehabilitation looks like extends beyond recidivism rates. Rehabilitation is defined and understood in ways that differ from woman to woman and is measured by intangible metrics not always captured by annual reports.

Overwhelmingly, women appreciated the services that they received from transitional organizations. This was especially true for women at Helping Hands and Restoration House. At Helping Hands women attended workshops from once to a few times per week. When not at Helping Hands some women resided at shelters, others were in between housing and stayed with relatives or friends, while other women were trying to secure subsidized housing options that did not discriminate against applicants with criminal records. Therefore, weekly visits to Helping Hands was a change of pace from their daily routine. There, women were able to catch up with other formerly incarcerated mothers, speak with staff about ongoing challenges, and learn about new opportunities for employment. At Restoration House, women were not only a part of a residential program but one with an organizing religious philosophy that permeated almost every aspect of the organizational model. This, as I discuss later, created a challenge in ascertaining women's genuine feelings about staff and the organization.

Most women at Mother's Love also spoke favorably about their organization. They received housing and training for work, and even had assistance with child care, which did much to help their transition from incarceration. Yet, there was greater nuance in the sentiments that they shared compared to women at the two other organizations. What they revealed and what other scholars who have investigated postincarceration rehabilitation services have substantiated is that a woman can appreciate the services they receive from a transitional organization, while still feeling that the enduring weight of carceral surveillance is reinforced by that organization.[1]

Although women have little flexibility to defy the rules and expectations of transitional organizations, they asserted their agency by challenging organizational expectations even if *in practice* they remain compliant. You see, to exist as a marginal member of society does not mean that one is unable to offer a counter response that challenges the very systems that mete out rewards or consequences based on one's ability to follow the rules. To the contrary, duality at the margins means that one is capable of recognizing both the structural and legal exclusion embedded within carceral and carceral-adjacent institutions, while navigating the precarious space between conformity and resistance.[2]

When women at Mother's Love critiqued the organization, it became clear that the duality that existed at the individual and the structural levels was further reinforced at the level of the institution. One of the reasons that this occurred was because there was a type of duality that was reproduced within the organizations themselves. Not only are transitional organizations tasked with meeting the needs of women, but they must also comply with the expectations set by correctional institutions because some clients are on probation or parole. Even for clients who were no longer under the surveillance of correctional institutions, the requirements for curfew, employment, and limitations on who could visit women in housing, echoed some of the restrictions that they experienced while incarcerated. Thus, for some women the carceral gaze didn't cease when they arrived at transitional organizations, but instead changed in scope and kind.

A SUCCESS STORY

As far as Mother's Love's leadership was concerned, Eva was the embodiment of postincarceration success. She was only thirty at the time of our conversation, but by that point she had lived several lives. She was a U.S. citizen but spent the majority of her childhood and adolescence in Mexico with her close-knit family. After high school she moved to California, where she began coursework to learn English. Not long after completing classes she returned to Mexico where she learned that she was pregnant. At that point, her life seemed unsteady, as she faced the possibility of being a single mother. So, when the husband of one of her girlfriends asked if she would transport diamonds in exchange for cash, she saw it as an opportunity to make easy money. Because of the strength of the U.S. dollar relative to the Mexican peso, she could sell diamonds in the United States for several times more than their original price, garnering a significant profit. With her share of the proceeds she planned to start a new life for her and her son in California.

Her plan, however, was a grave miscalculation. She never examined the contents of the suitcase her friend's husband gave her to carry, and it wasn't until she was arrested by custom agents that she learned that it didn't contain diamonds at all. In the small room in the airport where detainees were held, Eva learned that instead of diamonds her suitcase contained five kilos of heroin. That room was also where the arresting officer told her that she would likely never see her son again. Recalling that moment, Eva felt with certainty that life, as she knew it, was over. As she compared that time in her life with her present position as an employee and a working mom, she remained in awe at just how much her journey evolved over the years.

And I was Mrs. O'Malley's administrative assistant for five years. And, as a supervisor, she's the best. She'll work with you, show you. And I was very dedicated to my job. And next thing you know, she encouraged me to go to school. Six months later, I got my own apartment, which is beautiful. They gave us five thousand dollars to get a designer to design our own apartment. My first laptop I ever had she gave me my first year here, my first year here . . . I was promoted and I was overseeing the house with the employees and doing some financials in the financial department. Then I was promoted.

Considering the narrative arc of Eva's story, it's not surprising that her experience at Mother's Love is framed in uniformly positive terms. The organization didn't just help her to identify available resources, they provided her with a job, one of the most important needs for ex-offenders during reintegration. By all accounts, Eva beat the odds of recidivism and defied stereotypes of formerly incarcerated mothers. She was living proof of what organizations like Mother's Love advertised in their promotional materials: With hard work and determination women could begin new lives and reach their full potential.

Glossy pamphlets and neatly packaged five-minute videos created by transitional organizations may make for effective marketing, but they do not fully capture the realities of formerly incarcerated women. For every story like Eva's, there is a woman who faces the revolving door of rejected job applications, unstable housing, denied welfare benefits, and seemingly unending legal battles for child reunification. To navigate the challenges of motherhood, women with criminal records develop their own understanding of successful reintegration, even while they manage the competing demands of the institutions to which they belong and the criminal justice system to which both women and transitional organizations are beholden.[3]

Some of the women, like Eva, embraced the message of personal responsibility and individual work ethic espoused within institutional settings. But for others, that messaging wasn't solely about the ability to pull oneself up by her bootstraps. Nor was it a wholesale dismissal of systemic and institutionalized structures that perpetuate inequality. Even when drawing upon principles of personal responsibility to frame some aspects of postincarceration success, women exerted agency in what principles they critiqued and how they embraced an individualized version of success that met their needs. The ability to flat out reject services of a transitional organization based on a program's shortcomings is a type of privilege that formerly incarcerated women simply do not possess. Women understand the role that transitional organizations play in helping them meet their postincarceration requirements, but they also recognize that their personal goals and those of organizations do not always align.

THE REHABILITATIVE PARADOX

I pondered Sandra Minor's comments for a moment before responding. After weeks of back and forth, I was finally granted permission to interview women at Restoration House. During our first face-to-face meeting, Restoration House's supervisor seemed interested in my project and was willing to share information with residents. There was, however, a catch: Ms. Minor informed me that she would select the women she thought best met the study's requirements. While I knew that she might simply screen participants who met the study's core requirement of being a formerly incarcerated mother, I sensed that Ms. Minor's comments were not only in reference to identifying prospective respondents based on parental status. She would select, she said, the women who she believed would be most receptive to the study. Wanting more time to contemplate her comments, I told her I'd return the following week.

I went on to interview only two women at Restoration House and found that by and large their challenges and experiences were similar to women I interviewed at other organizations. There was, however, one noticeable difference. When I asked women at Mother's Love and Helping Hands to discuss their experiences with staff members and share their opinions of the organization, women shared a range of feelings, mostly positive and some negative, rooted in their personal interactions. At Restoration House, however, women not only described their residential experiences based on personal relationships and interactions, but also as an extension of the organization's therapeutic ideology infused with religious teachings. While the two women I interviewed both described their experiences as overwhelmingly positive, their discussion of the organization included their compliance of and belief in the religious tenets of the recovery process central to Restoration House's programming. In this way, any critique of Restoration House might also be a criticism about the overarching philosophy guiding the organization's principles. Considering how this might influence the women Ms. Minor selected to participate in the study (i.e., choosing women most likely to describe the organization in positive terms), I ultimately decided to conclude interviews after the second interview.[4]

While my time at Restoration House was brief, it did underscore a dynamic I witnessed at the other organizations. In that first meeting, Ms. Minor spent time showing me promotional materials that highlighted data emphasizing the impact of the organization's faith-based methods on clients' low recidivism rates. Women were successful, she implied, because the organizational model was successful. What became clear in the course of interviewing women and staff members across the other organizations was that the relationship between women and transitional organizations was both transactional and personal. Transactional because the success of women impacted the viability and longevity of the organization. Women's outcomes validated the methods implemented by organizations, which provided a justification for their funding from private and public donors. The personal relationship exists because some women and staff members become friends and these relationships sometimes outlast the tenure of women's formal participation in programs.[5] Both types of relationships can and often do exist simultaneously because women and organizations exist within the broader context of the other relationships that they inhabit. In particular, the criminal justice system surveilles women meeting their postincarceration requirements, while partnering with organizations that provide reintegration programming for women. In other words, transitional organizations are reliant on referrals from courts, district attorneys, and correctional officers, and women rely on the favorable report of transitional organizations who report to these state actors and agencies.[6]

The number of individuals who are reincarcerated within three years of their release from jail or prison is used by both critics and advocates of criminal justice reform to support competing policy agendas. Over the last decade the recidivism rate for women has remained relatively high, with 60 percent of women being rearrested. Of the women who return to their community from prison, 38 percent will be reconvicted and 30 percent to 45 percent will be incarcerated within three years.[7] For formerly incarcerated mothers, the rate of recidivism is influenced by a variety of factors including the frequency with which they are able to visit their children. Women who do not have visitation rights have recidivism rates that approximate the recidivism rates of women without children, while those who do maintain visitation rights have significantly lower rates.[8] Even after women regain custody of their children, they continue to grapple with the competing demands of reintegration and parenting. Just as pregnancy-related vulnerabilities can exacerbate existing challenges for women in unstable relationships, parenting while attempting to meet the expectations of reentry and correctional institutions can add stress and tenuity to a woman's life.[9]

One might view the durability of such high recidivism rates as evidence of the fact that the social and economic costs of incarceration are only further compounded by ineffective rehabilitation. On the surface, this may appear to be a failure of correctional institutions, but in reality it highlights a troubling paradox: while a woman's failure to meet rehabilitation requirements may result in her reincarceration, it can also prove to be profitable to correctional institutions. This creates a type of *rehabilitative paradox* which means that effective rehabilitation, which results in low recidivism, can also negatively impact the economics of incarceration.[10] Consider Grace's discussion of her probation obligations and her feeling that her goals were at odds with the expectations she was required to meet:

> *Geniece:* And so, you feel like, if you didn't have to fulfill all those obligations, with probation . . . you could actually . . .
>
> *Grace:* Focus on what really is gonna get me somewhere! You know what I mean? 'Cause the . . . my probation obligation ends August. . . . I'm not in trouble, so that I don't end up going to jail. But then, at the same time, like, that's not getting me nowhere in life. . . . It's ridiculous . . . I have to, like, squeeze [probation requirements] into my schedule. You know what I mean? Like, it's just awful. It's awful.

Grace describes a common frustration held by individuals returning home from prison: the desire to begin one's life on one hand, but the need to follow through with check-ins, comply with curfews and attend workshops that can overwhelm one's schedule, on the other. The reality is that while correctional institutions may be described in pseudotherapeutic terms by some, at their core they are businesses reliant on the economic gain that comes from the warehousing of human beings. If those individuals are released from prison, but are then rearrested and sentenced again, there is the mixed result of ineffective rehabilitation at one level and economic profitability at another. This dynamic is at the root of what justice scholars call the prison-industrial complex.[11] From a business standpoint, the latter of these results is a net positive for those who own, operate, and benefit from the growth of jails and prisons, even as the social and economic costs to the public remains high.[12] To address the former of these issues, institutional ineffectiveness is framed not as a failure of correctional organizations, but rather as a failure of the individual. If personal responsibility operates as the de facto method of explaining recidivism, then it becomes easier to overlook the sociohistorical, economic, and systemic factors that yield consistently poor outcomes for marginalized members of society. The veneer of effectiveness can remain intact if the cause and solution for recidivism lies primarily at the feet of the presently and formerly incarcerated.

The rehabilitative paradox exposes the counterproductive logic that stymies the transition of individuals returning home from jails and prisons. A system that profits from the reincarceration of formerly incarcerated individuals and then blames those very people for failing to attain success in a society that awaits with closed doors and few opportunities, is one in which failure isn't an accident, but an expectation.[13] Furthermore, when women arrive at transitional organizations they may share the experience of incarceration but this does not mean that their experience as marginal members of society are the same. Race and economic status, for example, can exacerbate existing challenges.[14] There are other factors, particularly those that influence securing housing and employment, that also shape how women address their most pressing concerns after incarceration.

"THEY WANT TO HELP YOU" VS. "THEY DON'T CARE"

Not long after we began speaking, it became clear to me that Diana's outlook on life had changed since the last time we spoke. She was now upbeat and optimistic about her future, and even considering enrolling in school. This was a striking contrast to our first interview six months earlier.[15] At the time of our first interview her experience in prison continued to shape how she defined herself. When I asked her about the changes that occurred over the previous six months she spoke less about her new job and more about a renewed sense of self-confidence.

> I guess I'm sort of getting that prison stink off of me, you know the mentality that you have. I thought that when I first got out it was gone, the stink when you first step out. At least that's what I thought. The moment I stepped out I'm free. I was physically but not mentally. So like I feel, that maybe those chains are breaking in my mind, you know.

At forty-eight years of age, Diana was entering into a place of self-acceptance and personal freedom. The woman I first interviewed recounted the rejection she experienced from her father, her significant other, friends, and siblings. When she began embezzling money from the law firm where she was employed, it was less about the money and more about showing her family just how alone and unloved she felt. She never wanted to go to prison, but she also knew that the crime would inevitably be discovered, that she would be arrested and that her family would be forced to finally acknowledge her pain. It took years before she realized that her actions were rooted in depression and by then she had lost so much, particularly time with her daughter.

The first time Diana went before the parole board her request was denied. By the second time the board met, she had been in communication with Mother's Love and viewed that relationship as pivotal in the board's decision to grant her parole. Like Eva, who viewed Mother's Love's intervention as key to her successful transition, Diana describes her experience with the organization as overwhelmingly positive:

> And they [merit board] were like "Well, who's gonna hire you?" I said here at Mother's Love that's what I'm looking for, to be with them. So I had plans and they knew it. . . . Places like this, [Mother's Love] This is what's up! See, you have to have a place. I got out March 15th, I was here March 19th with them, ready to start the program. Some people don't care. You know they don't care. But those that do care they need to come to places like this where they take you with open arms. They want to help you. They want you to learn. You know, like to be able to get a job. No matter where the job is at least get you started. You need clothes. The place is just great and there's not enough of them.

The positive testimonials like those of Diana's and Eva's were crucial in the marketing of Mother's Love. However, when women arrived with similar expectations that were not met, the criticism was sharp.

When I first met Trisha, she had been out of prison for three months. She was eager to retell her story of arrest and conviction to almost anyone who would listen because she felt compelled to share her experience with LGBTQ discrimination within the criminal justice system. In our first meeting she described writing Susan O'Malley, the executive director of Mother's Love, while still in prison. Once she was granted permission to stay at Mother's Love everything seemed to change for the better and, in her words, she had "been happy ever since." A year after that first interview, however, her feelings about Mother's Love soured. When I reminded her about her initial comments about the organization she explained that since our first interview her outlook had changed significantly.

> *Geniece:* Do you think your perspective of the program has changed . . . over the course of the year you've been here?

> *Trisha:* It's dramatically changed. Like I can't stand it. I can't stand it! I love some of the people, some of the staff, but a lot of them like Susan, she's like the main vessel. . . . We're basically like stool pigeons. They use us in their working women program; they pay us three dollars and some change a hour. You're only allowed to make up to two hundred forty dollars a week, doesn't matter if you have two or three kids. You know, they beast you to go to welfare so that they can get their rent money. If you have to go and work there on your own for something else they don't support you. When you're losing hours . . . and they'll pay you as part of working program to go to welfare to set up the rent and stuff. But after that if the welfare mess up your appointments or whatever, she said you have to go up there on your own. That's affecting you. They're already getting their rent money. They don't care.

In our first interview Trisha referenced the three-dollars-per-hour wage and criticized other women in the program who complained, citing that Mother's Love was providing them with housing. By the following year, what Trisha once saw as a reasonable payment structure, she now described as an unethical claim on women's welfare benefits. While the organization provided housing and employment assistance, they also expected to be subsidized by federal programs such as WIC (Women, Infant, Mother's program).[16] The sentiment underlying Trisha's comments was that what she once believed was an organizational mission to help women like her, was actually a transactional relationship.

Krystal, a Black twenty-four-year-old mother from New York, leveled similar criticisms against Mother's Love. When I followed up with her a year after our first interview she described Mother's Love as "unhelpful" and "money hungry." Krystal drew upon an incident involving her daughter to illustrate her point:

> Okay for example, money hungry: When it's time to go down to your welfare appointments there was an incident when I got custody of my daughter she wasn't added onto to my case right away. And it took like about . . . four months, they'd call me down to the office . . . so then I need to go down to welfare office or I was gonna get kicked out [of Mother's Love], and it was only like a extra twenty-five dollars they'd pay for the kid. So, it's like really money hungry. They're all about publicity. The more people you get here the more welfare pays you rent or whatever. How many kids you have in your budget. So, it wasn't really like—they gave you a place to stay but you have rules and stuff like that. I mean, they're money hungry.

The youngest woman I interviewed, eighteen-year-old Jordyn, a white mother from New York, was also critical of Mother's Love's payment structure. Although she worked at the program she, like Krystal, was frustrated that expulsion from the program was used to force her into compliance.

> *Jordyn:* And it's like I really bust my ass. I bust my ass and I don't so much as get a thank you. . . . Plus, we're making—I don't know if you know this—We get a stipend. We get a stipend, I have a ten-month-old son, okay? I'm trying to save so that I can get out of this program. Two hundred and forty dollars isn't going to do nothing.
>
> *Geniece:* Every week or—?
>
> *Jordyn:* Every two weeks. Plus, they've been screwing me over on my paycheck. I've been working twenty-six hours, thirty-six hours, forty hours, and I haven't gotten paid for them. I know that this program lost a lot of its funding, but if you guys can't afford to pay me, then just let me know. You know what I mean?
>
> I don't mind working. I love working. I love my job. I like just doing what I gotta do. But it's just too many headaches. I'm struggling with money. . . . My son doesn't make it any easier on me. But he's who I'm doing all this for. Because if it wasn't for my son, I would have left a long time ago. And I probably would be back in Bedford [correctional institution] maxing out.
>
> But it's just the whole . . . I have a problem with being told what to do. All my life I was told what to do—when to do it, when to eat, when to shower. It's like Eva, she sent one of the directors an email about me, my counselor, saying that we have a workshop tomorrow, which we're not supposed to have. And if I don't show up or if I show up with an attitude, then she's kicking me out of the program. So I'm just going to put in a transfer to Syracuse and go back, because it's . . . really, I've been here for eight months and I've tried to compromise, and I've tried to . . . they know I'm a hard worker. And I've worked for them, I've done this for them. I just can't do it anymore. At this point, I quit.

While the criticisms that women outlined were directed at one organization, they are not unique. In fact, the challenges formerly incarcerated mothers face when interacting with the welfare system complicate an already difficult period of social adjustment.[17] For Trisha and Krystal these challenges are further compounded by embedded biases. Both Black, each woman's discussion of her experiences underscores the broader challenges of applying for welfare as a marginalized woman. Even for Black mothers without a criminal record, securing social welfare benefits has historically been fraught with stereotypes of fraud and laziness.[18] The now notorious epithet "welfare queen" illustrates the extent to which public policy and public opinion casts entire groups of people as unworthy and innately criminal for simply seeking governmental support.[19] For women who actually possess a criminal record, applying for and receiving welfare benefits is unsurprisingly even more challenging and rife with stigmatizing assumptions. Despite this, women like Krystal and Trisha felt that leadership within the organization downplayed those hurdles leaving them to feel both frustrated and abandoned.[20]

Diana's and Eva's description of their experiences at Mother's Love contrasts sharply with those of Trisha, Krystal, and Jordyn. Why is that? How can participants in the same program have such different experiences? Is it possible that women were receiving different messages from program staff? One of the key factors that seems to be at play is the organization's role in demarginalizing some women by employing them and giving them decision-making power. Although both Eva and Diana were once subject to the same payment structure that frustrated other women, they were now employed in positions that offered more than the small stipend given to other mothers in the program. Eva, for example, was in a supervisory position and was responsible for regulating women's participation in programs. As illustrated by Jordyn's experience, she saw Eva not as a fellow mother in the program, but as a staff member with the authority to expel her. In this sense, their shared experience of being formerly incarcerated mothers was of minimal relevance. To Jordyn, Mother's Love, and by association Eva, felt like an extension of the constraints that she experienced while incarcerated.

When examining organizational philosophies that ascribe women's individual success to personal responsibility, it is important to recognize that the labor required to achieve institutionally lauded "success" often entails the kind of hidden labor Trisha, Jordyn, and Krystal describe. While women expect and hope to be gainfully employed, the interim between joblessness and employment may necessitate that they jump through bureaucratic hoops that leave them feeling frustrated and ultimately questioning the mission of the transitional organization. If women feel that the effort required to meet organizational demands, such as securing welfare benefits, are disproportionate to the tangible and intangible benefits that they receive from the program, their patience can grow thin and that in turn can color their view of the organization. What this means is that whether intentionally or unintentionally, transitional organizations can be a site of further marginalization for the women that they serve. They differ from correctional institutions because they provide services that women readily recognize as improving their quality of life and, for some women, the benefits are life-altering. Other women, however, are reminded of their marginalized status and thus find themselves, yet again, negotiating the outsider status that many have grappled with over the course of their lives.

Some in the general public might find it perplexing that anyone with a criminal record would criticize an organization that offers formerly incarcerated individuals resources. Such a sentiment, however, fails to recognize how rehabilitation labor, born disproportionately by women and their families, is sometimes exacerbated by these very organizations. According to sociologist Susila Gurusami, after prison women are not only penalized for not acquiring a job, but they are also expected to secure specific types of jobs.[21] The work that they secure should be reliable, meaning it has a specified schedule of days and times to which the employee must participate; recognizable, in that it meets the standards of legitimacy of state actors; and finally redemptive, such that it diminishes the stigma of incarceration. While Gurusami focuses on state-imposed requirements, women's critiques illustrate that rehabilitation labor is also reproduced within transitional organizations.[22] Because women are required to secure benefits as a condition of remaining in subsidized housing at places like Mother's Love, they are not only tasked with finding a job and reestablishing relationships with children, but also with navigating the bureaucratic maze of red tape needed to find and claim welfare benefits. For Trisha and Krystal, the challenge of identifying those benefits became a source of stress and soon outweighed the positive aspects of the organization.[23]

What struck me most about the critiques women leveled against Mother's Love was that they were rooted in a deep-seated sense of betrayal. Critiques were not universal (e.g., this is and has always been a bad organization), but rather personal and specific (the organization used to value me but now they treat me poorly). Part of this had to do with the fact that women initially thought of transitional organizations as separate and distinct from the correctional institutions they just left. While they knew that staff were expected to report law-violating behavior to probation officers and parole boards, the relationships that were formed, especially during the early days after release, provided a sense of familial closeness. When that relationship became more formal and expectations were coupled with potential consequences, some women found it disorienting.

While at some level it may be apparent that transitional organizations are extensions of correctional institutions because they surveil women and report violations, the experience of living among staff and other women can muddle boundaries and create a sense of intimacy. Women were not surprised to be stigmatized by would-be employers and social acquaintances. At some level, they even anticipated it and concealed information and structured relationships to minimize ostracization. In transitional organizations, however, staff knew about their past and listened to them recount the intimate details of fractured relationships and broken childhoods. In that space it was not their ex-offender status that marginalized them, rather it was their perceived inability to be economically useful that struck some women as hurtful.

In speaking with women, I came to see that the perception of an organization was shaped by how their own lives were impacted, not just in the short term but in ways that supported their longer-term goals for their future. That praise and critique of the same organization exists simultaneously illustrates that the approaches used by an organization may resonate with some women, while alienating others. Moreover, those who do not conform to the expectations of success can endanger their place within the organization which can impact their ability to meet their postincarceration goals. So, even while women criticize policies, they still do the work required of them and meet necessary expectations, knowing that failure to do so may result not only in their removal from the program, but possibly sanctioning from correctional institutions.

"RESPONDING FROM THE MARGINS"

One of the challenges of living on society's margins is the constant need to readjust to the context-specific ways that marginalization occurs across different spaces. Marginalization means one thing when negotiating one's role as a mother, another when applying for a job or housing, and yet another within transitional organizations.[24] What it means to satisfy expectations for one entity may not work in other settings and it is this iterative negotiation of one's place along society's moral outskirts that makes the transition to life after incarceration particularly daunting. For formerly incarcerated women, this means defining postincarceration progress in ways that differ from traditional rehabilitation measures. These agency-driven narratives are not necessarily radical. In fact, they may even draw upon framing similar to rehabilitation messaging. What distinguishes these narratives, however, is that women center their marginality as well as their agency, in order to challenge notions of how success is attained and what success means to them.

Policy and institutional practices premised upon an ideology of personal responsibility often overlooks the broader systemic problems that contribute to mass incarceration and high rates of recidivism.[25] As problematic as this rhetoric is in obscuring underlying issues of social inequality and injustice, its pervasiveness can also make it tempting to critique, without nuance, the coping methods women deploy that center themselves and their personal beliefs. What sometimes makes separating the ideology of personal responsibility from one's personal beliefs difficult is that any individual-focused solutions advanced by marginalized populations may appear to be ideological extensions of the very systems that wield decision-making power over their lives. For example, in Haney's analysis of rehabilitative programming within prisons, the language and philosophy of personal responsibility discourages women's reliance on social welfare assistance.[26] Likewise, Sered and Norton-Hawk's research examines how the limitations of personal-responsibility rhetoric can shape how formerly incarcerated women downplay well-documented contributing factors of inequality but elevate individual factors.[27]

Criticism of policies that ignore the impact of entrenched inequality is needed, but so too is an acknowledgment that one's embrace of individual focused methods of navigating inequality can also be a valid and rational response, not necessarily tethered to institutional messaging. Even while in transitional organizations, women conceptualize their postincarceration journeys through frameworks that they believe speak to their distinct experiences. The generic models in correctional institutions and transitional organizations used to structure classes for all women don't necessarily meet their individual needs and in response women draw upon belief systems that provide them with the tools to process the ongoing challenges they encounter in daily life. I argue that recognizing structural inequity and injustice does not and should not negate the legitimacy of narratives of self-empowerment and other cultural frames through which women view themselves as central to changing their trajectory. In particular, respondents' framing of their religious faith and self-help solutions reflects an ability to exert agency, not just in lieu of other options but in response to the limitedness of organizations to address their unmet needs.

"IT'S YOUR FAITH"

After being arrested for parental kidnapping, Sage was despondent when she learned that it was her husband who devised the plan to strip her of parental rights. When I asked her to share how she was managing the separation from her young son, she explained how narratives of loss and resilience in biblical scripture offered a source of comfort. In particular, a gender-informed reading of scripture helped her to better identify with the struggles of marginalized women in the Bible. Sage explained:

> It's your faith. It is your faith, when I tell you, because for me to have gone through something so traumatic and not have lost my mind, because I know somebody else that was going through something similar, but not to the magnitude that I was, and she lost her mind. . . . So I would have to say I've really been blessed in all of that, and I can't give anybody glory other than God. . . . It's like, "God, why do I have to hurt so bad?"
>
> Yeah, I know the story of Job, but Job wasn't a woman. It's like different when you read in the Bible and you see the challenges that Job went through, that Daniel went through, that David went through, that Joseph went through. And you're like, "OK, but I'm more sorta like Naomi," like I went out full with everything and I came back empty into my homeland with nothing—no children, no husband. Nothing. So I can understand when she says, "Mara," which means "the Lord had dealt bitterly with me." Because I did feel scorned. But in all that, God had a purpose, because while I was there, he wanted me to work with them [other inmates]. He wanted me to pray for them. He wanted me to minister with them. I have to say, it's been great. I mean I'm still in contact with a good fifty of them, that I write to them regularly. They're probably getting on me right now because I haven't written as frequent.

Similar to Sage, Cynthia, a white mother from Restoration House also connects her journey to a broader, divine purpose:

Geniece: What are some of the things that make you hopeful now?

Cynthia: Changes that I've already seen in myself and just little things that are part of the restoration process with my kids, I see that happening and I know that there's a plan, I know that God has a plan, a purpose and I didn't just go through all that and make what was terrible. . . . I know that there was a bigger picture somewhere in there.

Geniece: Do you have a sense of what that bigger picture might be?

Cynthia: It looks a lot like me helping other girls who were on the street. I'm not really sure exactly how or when but I know that I know the things that they're going through, the things that they're feeling, the emptiness and the things that they're running from and I can help.

For Sage and Cynthia, the ability to connect their experiences with their faith helped them to place their personal obstacles within a broader context and see themselves as a part of a larger purpose. Not only did they view their religious faith as a way to cope with the separation from their families, but also as a way to help counsel and support other women they met during and after prison.

Felicia, a resident at Restoration House, arrived at a similar realization after many years of substance abuse. Sobriety was a long-fought battle that Felicia spent many years fighting. According to her, her initial efforts to abstain from drugs were unsuccessful because she relied on her "own strength." Highlighting the difference between how she approached sobriety before her faith in God and after, she stated:

> In my own strength, like I tried to stay clean, I tried doing all the right things. But something was missing, something—I wasn't able to keep myself together, like, I could not do it. Like, I held everything together for so long, like, I did. I was working. I started NA [Narcotics Anonymous] in my community. Like, the kids were great. They were—I was going to church. Like, everything was good. But like, I didn't have God in my life.

What stands out about Felicia's comments is that she felt that the very behaviors and practices that would make her an exemplar of personal responsibility—working, caring for her children, attending Narcotics Anonymous—were ultimately not enough to help her maintain her sobriety. Faith, because it is so personal and draws upon an individual's beliefs to enact change, can in some ways seem to affirm aspects of a personal responsibility rhetoric. Yet neither Felicia nor Sage frames it that way. Faith for them provides a way to acknowledge their perceived vulnerabilities and strengths, even if that strength is rooted in a higher being.

In describing how she tried to abstain from drugs, Felicia explains that despite previous efforts she ultimately relapsed and fell deeper into her drug addiction. Although she was involved in church, the fact that she didn't have a personal faith meant that she was relying on practices rooted in personal responsibility rather than faith. She saw the language of rehabilitation as a list of dos and don'ts that didn't translate into prolonged sobriety. Like other respondents who drew upon their religious ideology to frame their responses to postincarceration marginality, Felicia identified the limitedness of formulaic approaches in helping her meet her personal goals. Religious faith, then, is not solely about the spiritual elements of lived experiences, but a way that some women harness an alternate ideology that helps them to accomplish something that they believe rehabilitative framing of correctional and transitional organizations do not: to exist apart from their marginalized status, while bringing the fullness of who they are to the world around them.

When invoking the role of religious faith women reference the temporary nature of their difficult circumstances. They view themselves as evolving and view each life experience as opportunities to become better versions of themselves. Like Sage and Felicia, Olive viewed her life through this perspective. The most difficult times, she argued, were temporary and would ultimately pass:

> You don't have to subject yourself to a person having control over you. The only person that's got control over you is God. That's it because he gave you life. . . . You know what, if you're having it hard okay. It's not that it's okay but that's just a phase; it's just a season. You're going through something. It's alright. You'll come out of it. You'll come out of it in due time. . . . But don't forget to pray always because only prayers are powerful things. You pray and you believe and you have faith. It may not be today or tomorrow but you'll come out of it. . . . God gives you what you need.

The recurrent theme of a life before and one after hardship captures much of the thematic arch found in the Judeo-Christian narratives with which women identified. Moreover, the subtext of temporality and transformation point to a time before and after loss. For example, Sage compares herself to the Old Testament story of Naomi, who readers are introduced to after the sudden and devastating loss of her husband and son.[28] There is a "before time"—marriage, children, a household—followed by an after time—widowhood, loss, and homelessness. In Felicia's case, she describes how she struggled to maintain sobriety until *after* she established her faith in God. And then there's Olive, who describes the inevitability of eventually "coming out" of difficult circumstances.

For many women, being marginalized from the very earliest stages of life means that prison wasn't the only defining stigmatizing event in their lives. As a result, some women weren't necessarily trying to return to the life they had before prison, but to a new life, something they had yet to experience. Personal responsibility as a guiding framework offered women steps and actions to take ownership of their past, but for these women their faith offered them something different. Not only did they find a type of reprieve from the scrutinizing eyes of the world around them, such as correctional agencies, staff members at transitional organizations, or employers, but a means by which they might see themselves unfiltered through the views of others. This is central to how duality at the margins shapes women's responses to outside institutions. Viewing the world through the lenses of others, while trying to center one's own identity is the core idea of Du Bois's double-consciousness. The way that women engage with the two-ness they inhabit is through developing ways in which seeing themselves, as others would see them, becomes less prominent in their lives.

Stringer's analysis of the role of religion in the lives of incarcerated women finds that the intersection across race, culture, and gender holds meaningful implications for how women understand their role as mothers.[29] The study, based on interviews with incarcerated African-American mothers, reveals that in the absence of an institutionalized religious setting women integrate personal religious faith with African-American cultural traditions to help craft a motherhood identity that challenges negative assumptions about their ability to parent. In describing the role of faith in their lives, the women with whom I spoke also wedded their view of God with their lived experience and relationships. In reuniting with their children, seeking housing, and finding a job, they believed that God would work on their behalf, not only to help them meet their goals, but also to guide them through disappointment.[30]

Finding sources of positive affirmation can be scarce when the primary identity through which the world views an individual is one that assumes untrustworthiness and law violation. Identification with a system of beliefs, specifically reading and applying that system of beliefs in a personalized manner that affirms one's humanity and dignity, can provide a useful internalized counterframe to external realities.[31] Indeed, one of the most important roles that religious faith played in the lives of some women was that it offered a counternarrative to the stigmatizing identity of the ex-offender status. For these women God was not an aloof deity but a God-of-the-oppressed, one aligned with and empathetic to society's most marginalized.[32]

"IT'S JUST ME": SELF-WORK AND PERSONAL RESPONSIBILITY

While there are similarities between narratives of personal responsibility and the religious framing some women used, key differences illustrate how women's religious beliefs are distinct from institutional or public policy messages. By contrast, the self-empowerment and self-help framing that some women articulate shares more in common with a personal-responsibility philosophy. In this way, one can see the overlapping programmatic goals that women share with transitional organizations. There were distinctions, however, in the way that woman discussed their ability to address the challenges they faced through individual-level strategies. In discussing self-help as a strategy for change most women didn't view it as the sole means of achieving their goals. Depending upon the problem they faced, a self-help framing of situations might serve to address some challenges, but it wasn't necessarily a universal solution to all of the issues women faced after incarceration. In fact, even when describing an outlook that might be categorized as self-help, women would also emphasize their ability to identify other resources or people that might help them meet their needs. Some women, rather than describing their experiences using the language of self-help, focused on the pragmatic steps they took when institutions were unable to meet their stated goals. To distinguish self-help from this action-oriented form of self-empowerment, I use the term *self-work*.

Krystal's discussion of her reintegration process illustrates the nuanced differences between personal responsibility and self-work. On one hand, she was critical of Mother's Love because of their expectation that she secure welfare benefits as a condition of her residence at the organization. On the other hand, she was adamant that it was through her own individual efforts that she secured any semblance of normalcy after leaving prison. It might seem odd that she would attribute an essential necessity like housing to the very transitional organization she criticized, while claiming that she was responsible for retaining housing. However, Krystal didn't view residential provision as a benevolent act. While she didn't pay rent for housing, she also didn't feel that her residence was cost-free. She invested time and effort contacting and traveling to social services offices, while being reminded of the consequences for failing to meet expectations. Within the broader context of her life, she had come to expect that nothing was freely given. She might receive help, but even then that help was often conditional. Just as was the case in her preincarceration experiences, she felt that she needed to be her own advocate and saw those efforts as the reason for any success she achieved.

Geniece: So last time you were talking about your upbringing, your parents' things like that. So, what would you say in the past . . . have been—some of the most helpful, positive relationships for you in your life?

Krystal: Meaning like family life?

Geniece: Just in general. Just positive, like good relationships? People who have been supportive and helpful to you in life?

Krystal: I don't find anything, it's just me. I was determined to get out there and find a job. They don't—my family is—I was adopted. . . . Whenever

I need something from my sister I could reach out and she'll talk to me if she had it she'll give it or whatever. Mainly, I just always had to work, I always had to come up with a solution to get money.

Lucille's framing of self-work was more common among women, even those who didn't attribute their short-term success to themselves. Unlike the help Lucille received from others, she could only rely on the intangible resources in her possession to maintain her postincarceration success.

> *Geniece:* So, what has life been like to you since you left the correctional facility?
>
> *Lucille:* I wouldn't say easy, but I would say it's a day-to-day struggle. Just staying focus, motivating yourself, not letting people get in the way of you, making the best possible decisions for yourself or doing the right thing, or being influenced the wrong way. So, I do a lot of self-talk or self-empowering, and it's very hard when you don't have that pat on your back. It's not that you get it so much when you get older but I think a pat on your back, oh, good job is required for all. You're doing something right, so I do that a lot and I think—it's hard . . . but it gets easier in time.

Like Lucille, Trina emphasized focus and discipline as a way to accomplish her goals:

> *Geniece:* What are some goals that you want to accomplish for yourself?
>
> *Trina:* My main goal is to keep focus. I finish parole in December, which is four months away, December 1st. So, my main goal is to stay focused and be more of a parent to Mia. . . . Where I'm at right now this is really helping me to move forward. So my main goal is to stay focused on being a parent and change my way of thinking and to get a job and to show dedication.

All of the women I interviewed mentioned self-initiative or the importance of taking responsibility for their actions in varying degrees but many also acknowledged the social and structural odds stacked against them. The "self-talk" and "self-empowerment" that Lucille references underscores the belief among some respondents that the primary source of support throughout the reintegration process lies within the individual. Respondents like Lucille do not dismiss systemic obstacles, but she also views her own journey to recovery as a result of individual choices. Similarly, Vickie, an employee at Mother's Love, explains how her newfound sense of self-determination and purpose enabled her to be successful following her last stint in prison. Vickie also explained that those who were unable to successfully make the transition from prison were hobbled by an unwillingness to put in the work necessary to achieve personal goals.

> When I'm done with something, I'm done. When I said I'm done with Linda's father after struggling for five years, I was done. You know, when I said I was done using drugs, I was done. You know, I don't say I'm done with shit and then not be done with it. When I say I'm done I'm done. And after that I was like an adult and I knew it. Because I know inside of me, I can't imagine what could possibly cause me to lose my life, that could cause me to do that. I can't—I can't even fathom it, you know what I'm saying? I can't, I can't imagine it. So why am I any different from the next? You're struggling with it because deep down inside of you, you still want to get high. And sooner or later, you've got to give in. It's just a matter of time. You know and that always causes some issues with me.

Vickie didn't push back against the narrative of personal responsibility as a deterministic prerequisite for success. By contrast, she uses it to explain why other women failed where she succeeded.

The reader may view Vickie's opinion of women who continued to struggle with addiction after prison as unsympathetic, but within the context of her postincarceration journey it underscores important aspects of marginality and identity. Like Eva, Vickie worked at Mother's Love and spent time both as a client and an advisor to other mothers. Her apartment, where we met to conduct the interview, was subsidized by the organization. It offered a marked contrast to the communal residential housing where I conducted interviews with other women. A stone's throw from Mother's Love, it was a modest living situation but she had a personal phone line, her own living spaces and, most significantly, the apartment afforded her a level of privacy absent in the communal residence. Because of the decision-making authority related to her job title, she also held something rare among the small universe of women at Mother's Love: privilege. Even with her criminal background and the stigma that came with it, she was a success story among her peers.

The nuanced ways in which Vickie and other women articulate their experiences in transitional programs reveals how competing frameworks of postincarceration reintegration are framed by formerly incarcerated women. For them, personal responsibility is not simply about urging others to be better people and make better choices. It is, at its core, a perspective that claims people can achieve success so long as their actions and beliefs align with the standards of those assessing character and progress. Those in charge of evaluating success may be known entities but the assessment itself is subjective, meaning that women are regularly adjusting what they do and what they say to meet the standards of others. Moreover, women reveal that they too view themselves as a part of the assessment process even if their self-evaluations are not included in the equation that determines the resources, opportunities and plaudits that they receive.

When considering if and how women reject or embrace the language of personal responsibility in transitional organizations, it's important to acknowledge the interplay between marginality and context specific privilege. A woman may be well acquainted with the marginalization associated with the ex-offender status, but time and distance from that position can influence how she views the decision-making practices of those still grappling with the daily challenges of transition. While the overwhelming majority of women I spoke to described their criminal involvement in the past tense, it was only staff who were also formerly incarcerated mothers, who spoke of the transitional period and the related hurdles as obstacles they overcame successfully. Most women were still thinking about the next step in transition, whether it was housing, employment, or child reunification. As such, personal responsibility or the ability to change one's fortunes through self-determination was an insufficient framework in and of itself. Self-work and religious framing offered a more useful way to think about how personal motivation in conjunction with social support helped women approach future goals.

In chapter 3 I argued that the rationalization most women provided of their arrests and incarceration centered upon redefining the crime and their role in the act rather than diverting responsibility or culpability. In this same way, women who framed their success as a result of self-initiative do so in part to convey ownership and agency over their carceral and postcarceral narratives. The self-work narrative that some respondents used to frame their postincarceration experiences illustrates what women perceived as the limitedness of external support in maintaining lasting success. Women were in no way dismissive of the help that they received from family or friends, but they believed that such help would not necessarily translate into success over the long term if they were not personally invested in succeeding. The self-work narrative also challenges the stigma that comes not only with their ex-offender status, but also from the perception that women were either fully dependent upon others and unwilling to take ownership of their journeys.

THE UNFREEDOM OF POSTINCARCERATION

In her groundbreaking work *Golden Gulag*, geographer and prison abolitionist Ruth Wilson Gilmore, explains that one cannot fully understand the goals of rehabilitation without understanding its relationship to other key elements of prison philosophy: retribution, deterrence, and incapacitation.[33] As such, rehabilitation isn't simply preparation for a life beyond prison, but "an occasion for the acquisition of sobriety and skills, so that, on release, formerly incarcerated people can live lives away from the criminal dragnet."[34] A key challenge arises when the very institutions that profit from the deprivation of human liberty are also tasked with preparing women to live freely beyond the walls of prisons. Postincarceration rehabilitation programs are not as encumbered by the economic objectives which are premised upon the dehumanizing punitiveness that exists within carceral structures, but they do act as both formal and informal intermediaries between women and the criminal justice system.

Every woman I spoke to wanted to secure housing or to be reunited with their children. However, the path they took to attain those goals and the time table they set for themselves did not always align with those of transitional organizations. In a broad sense, transitional organizations may be helpful in meeting the tangible needs of women but this did not mean that all women viewed them above reproach. Like other carceral adjacent institutions, some women found that while organizations might support some areas of their lives, they also reminded them that to wider society their position was tenuous and subject to scrutiny. In such instances, women drew upon internalized frameworks, such as religious faith and self-work, believing that while they couldn't immediately change structural obstacles, they could find ways to navigate the smaller, daily hurdles that shaped their lives. In this way, women illustrate how life on the margins calls for resilience and adaptation. Given their limited material and social resources, resilience isn't merely a virtue and adaptation isn't a skill of choice. Each are born out of a need to survive, and exacts an emotional cost in women's lives that often goes unmeasured.

Conclusion

The Unasked Question

On my way home after interviewing women, as I waited on a crowded subway platform or boarded a noisy bus, I would reflect on the intimate details women had shared with me that day. During conversations in vacant conference rooms, coffee shops, and small living rooms, there were moments of levity, in which women and I both laughed. There were also moments of candor and raw honesty, in which women cried and I, despite my best efforts, joined them in tears. As much as I empathized with their stories, however, I was an outsider trying to connect their realities to theories. I rehearsed this fact to myself constantly, in the hopes that I would avoid the trap of the well-intentioned researcher who views herself in pseudo-heroic terms, swooping in to "give voice" to the forgotten. True, many of these women were forgotten by society, but they were not voiceless and their stories were their own. Years after conducting the last interview, as I sat in my living room one evening, I was reminded yet again, that no one can better convey the lived realities of formerly incarcerated women than they can. Watching my television, I recognized the face on the screen instantly: it was one of the last women I interviewed.[1]

During interviews, I didn't ask women why they were willing to speak with me. Some volunteered that they found interviews cathartic, while others saw academic research as one way to share their story with a wider audience. The woman featured in the documentary I saw that evening fell into the latter category. In fact, the last time we spoke she shared that it was her dream to one day make a film based on her experiences within the criminal justice system. In her words,

> There are other ways I'm fighting [discrimination] because I do a lot of speaking. We're doing a documentary. It's just like the civil rights movement. It took a while for somebody to come up with that and come up with laws to protect us as African-American people and any other people, so it's the same thing we going to do.

That evening, as I watched this woman narrate her life, I thought about the other women I met years earlier. I thought about how they too had fought to be seen, to be heard and to prove themselves to systems and arbiters of morality that judged their humanity and found them wanting.

Justice involved women know that prisons and jails are not just places on maps. They know that one does not enter or exit carceral institutions in the way that one leaves most physical settings. Incarceration takes place in the past, with painful unfolding events that occur before a sentence is ever rendered. Incarceration also extends beyond the date of one's release, into relationships, denied opportunities and facial expressions that ask: "How does it feel to be a problem?"

CARCERALITY AND MOTHERHOOD

In one of his most well-known works, Du Bois describes the sense of anticipatory judgment one experiences in their daily interactions as the "unasked question." He explains how Black Americans, navigating postbellum society, faced the question: "How does it feel to be a problem?"[2] This question focused on how racism problematized Black lives, but it can also be applied to how other groups grapple with occupying a marginal identity. Listening to formerly incarcerated women describe the balancing act of conforming to expectations, while preserving their sense of self, it was clear that they too felt the weight of this question in both subtle and explicit ways. Where they could live, the loss of parental rights, the box on a job application—these were all reminders that society saw them as flawed, as undeserving, and as problems.[3] Like so many who have faced the stigma of social exclusion, women often faced scrutiny even after completing their sentences. How women responded to the unasked question of their presumed inferiority offers important answers for the ways society has handled and mishandled approaches to criminal justice.

If the unasked question that formerly incarcerated women face is "How does it feel to be a problem?" then one should interrogate, as Du Bois did, the legitimacy of the question itself. Asking that question takes for granted that people are problems, rather than the systems and structures that reinforce inequality and disparate outcomes. For example, one might look at the high proportion of women in jails unable to post bail as an unfortunate but deserved consequence of their poor decisions and criminal behavior. Construed this way, these women are readily written off as "a problem." Yet, when the layers of inequality are peeled back, it becomes clearer that marginality does not result from a single moment or act, but rather it results from interconnected narratives and systems. Even before arrest and prison the majority of incarcerated individuals are in an economically precarious position. The median income for incarcerated women in 2015 prior to incarceration was $13,890, approximately 41 percent less than the median income for nonincarcerated women.[4] Given that approximately 80 percent of women are mothers at the time of incarceration, parenting was already a formidable economic burden for a significant number of women.[5] It is then no wonder that many women cannot afford bail fees as they wait in legal limbo.

One of the continuing challenges researchers face in gauging the changes within women's prisons and postprison experiences is that data collection focusing on women lags behind the data collected on male populations.[6] The data that do exist underscore the unique challenges incarcerated women face. When examining the total incarcerated population, approximately twice as many individuals are in state prisons compared to jails. For women, however, the picture of incarceration looks different. Most incarcerated women are in jails, not state prisons, a fact that points to two realities: First, women are mostly incarcerated for less serious offenses, and second, many are detained while still awaiting trial. Regarding the latter issue, roughly 60 percent of women who are in jail have yet to be convicted of a crime. What this means is that reasons, such as the inability to pay bail fees, are at the root of increasing jail populations among women. That women are separated from families without trial or criminal conviction due to their lack of economic resources underscores how broader systemic inequities structure disadvantage within the U.S. criminal justice system.[7]

Economic marginality, like other factors underlying women's fragile social position, help to explain why women develop certain relationships with the institutions in their lives. Inhabiting a space of marginality requires fluency in the language of compliance, so that women can abide by institutional expectations, while selectively subverting expectations to preserve their agency.[8] One of the great challenges of inhabiting a marginal status is that the legitimacy of one's very existence is subject to the judgments and decisions of powerful actors. In this way the ex-offender status extends a type of pseudo unfreedom, the ongoing and lingering experience of prisonlike constraints that persists outside of prison. The ability to vote, live in a particular building, acquire employment—these are realities that are decided in rooms where formerly incarcerated persons are not allowed. Living on the margins means making choices not based solely on freedom of will, but on the permissible options chosen by others. I argue that duality at the margins of society is a response to these untenable choices. It is recognizing the spaces in which resistance and challenge are possible, while also recognizing where conformity and deference are necessary.[9]

In *Unequal City,* Carla Shedd elucidates the concept the "carceral continuum" to show the degree to which young people are sanctioned and stigmatized in ways that place them within proximity to the criminal justice system.[10] The women I interviewed also reveal how carcerality is a spectrum, not limited to a prison sentence or formal surveillance. While academics discuss the impact of early childhood experiences of criminal activity, the reality is that outside of juvenile courts, early life risk factors are viewed as empty excuses rather than a basis for empathic and informed policy. For example, women like Kishana and Aaliyah wanted to escape the abusive environment of their homes but they were children with no resources and little familial support. When they did leave home, they had to navigate the world as young, single mothers already carrying the weight of a dysfunctional home environment and socioeconomic limitations. Their later involvement in crime can be traced to their economic needs: an assault charge against a financially stable but physically abusive partner for Kishana, and a petty larceny charge while homeless for Aaliyah.

The preincarceration experiences of women figure prominently in how they thought about their roles as mothers and the reasons they engaged in law-violating behavior. In the earliest, most vulnerable stages of life, women experienced marginalization through circumstances beyond their control and made decisions as adults based on circumstances born out of need. To understand why and how criminal offenses occurred, marginality must also be understood as resulting from a confluence of factors, rather than isolated or linear events. When understood this way, incarceration can be seen as one in a series of experiences that concretized women's already marginal status.

The systems that do exist to identify at-risk young adults often employ what might be called a soft punitive approach, that exacerbates the existing fear that young people in precarious situations already feel. Aaliyah for example, found that telling social workers about her sexual abuse didn't lead to immediate intervention, which meant that she had to remain in the same home as the adults who ignored her abuse and coerced her into lying about the circumstances of her pregnancy. In other instances, status offenses such as running away from home may not hold the same consequences as criminal activity, but they nevertheless result in police contact and the formal intervention of the criminal justice system.[11] It is no wonder, then, that when facing the choice between what young women perceived as punitive intervention or remaining in volatile homes, they created a third option that sometimes resulted in criminal activity.

BRICK BY BRICK

Looking out into a sea of tiny American flags, where people usually stood, Joseph R. Biden delivered his inauguration-day speech, highlighting the events that shaped the previous year. There was a global pandemic, the police murder of George Perry Floyd, which sparked worldwide racial justice protests, and a recent siege of the U.S. Capitol building which exposed the fragility of democracy itself. On that January morning, the new president declared, "A cry for racial justice some four hundred years in the making moves us. The dream of justice for all will be deferred no longer."[12] Days after those words were spoken, Andrea James, the executive director of the National Council for Incarcerated and Formerly Incarcerated Women and Girls, called upon the president to demonstrate the "administration's commitment to long-overdue justice system reform" by granting clemency to a hundred women within the first hundred days of his term.[13] Four months later, as the Biden administration marked its hundredth day in office, only one of the hundred women submitted by the National Council was no longer on the list. Her name was Martha Evanoff and she died in prison on April 12, 2021.

To begin the difficult work of addressing this country's incarceration crisis, a two-pronged approach that changes both how women are treated when arrested and dismantles the very procedures and systems that lead to arrest and incarceration are needed. At first glance these two goals appear to be in conflict with one another. Why ameliorate the conditions of incarceration if the goal is to interrogate the legitimacy of carceral institutions? In what can be called a brick-by-brick approach, I acknowledge the harmful impact of incarceration on marginalized people, while also recognizing the constraints of policy driven social change.[14]

One example of an area ripe with potential for significant policy changes is to answer the call of the National Council and grant clemency to incarcerated women. According to the lead counsel for the National Council, Catherine Sevceko, the power to grant clemency and pardons is one power of the presidency that can be used to address this nation's history of systemic injustice. To hold fast to the presidential tradition of waiting until the twilight of one's tenure in office to consider clemency means that women like Martha Evanoff will die before they see their loved ones outside of prison.[15]

Another area in need of considerable overhaul is the treatment of incarcerated pregnant women. To date, there is no federal standard of care for pregnant incarcerated mothers, which means that the care that they receive varies based on the state in which they are imprisoned.[16] According to the Prison Policy Institute, twelve states do not even have detailed guidelines for prenatal care. The most recently available data underscores this vacuum in care. For example, only 54 percent of expectant mothers reported that they received prenatal care while incarcerated.[17] Because incarcerated pregnant people are more likely to experience high-risk pregnancies, due to higher rates of poverty, greater likelihood of sexually transmitted diseases, and poor nutrition, the lack of prenatal care can increase the possibility of poor health outcomes for both parent and child. One option for addressing these issues is to develop models of care that allow women to receive access to on-site obstetric and midwifery services that resembles the timeline for scheduled visits nonincarcerated women receive. Developing these on-site services, however, would be costly given the lack of existing resources and from a practical point garnering political will to support such initiatives will likely be difficult.[18] Given the uneven health care for incarcerated pregnant people and the impact that it has both on them and their unborn child, a more holistic approach is needed.

Once the mother gives birth there are challenges that remain, namely how long she should remain out of prison and where her baby will be placed if she is incarcerated. In a 2018 study, only eleven states had nurseries within prisons, meaning that the majority of mothers are separated from their infants.[19] For both mother and child, the impact of this separation is devastating.[20] Research on the impact of child-mother separation during imprisonment shows that infants who remain with their mothers during the first year of her imprisonment fair better in their social, emotional, and educational outcomes during preschool. Additionally, mothers who are able to care for their children while imprisoned have lower rates of recidivism, while those who are separated from their children report higher rates of mental and emotional distress.[21] The most comprehensive way to address this issue is by investing in nurseries at all correctional institutions, at the local, state, and federal levels.

Kishana's experience provides an insightful example. She had her son at Bedford Hills, the women's prison that houses the nation's oldest prison nursery.[22] Although she was able to give birth to her child while at Bedford Hills, she wasn't able to keep him with her for the duration of her sentence. Describing her experience, Kishana stated:

> When I found out that I couldn't keep the child with me at the nursery in Bedford Hills he [her ex-boyfriend] came to pick the child up. . . . It was either that or put my child in foster care. I was not putting my child in foster care. He came and brought my child up every weekend so that I could see my child.

For Kishana this was an especially difficult decision because although she was certain she did not want her child to enter the foster care system, the only other available option was to place her child in the custody of the man who physically abused her and whom she blamed for her incarceration.

Other women who were in correctional institutions with prison nurseries describe only being able to keep their babies with them for a year or two. This means that the length of one's sentence determines the difference between being able to care for a child for the duration of one's sentence or undergoing a painful separation. One way to address this problem is to move away from the incarceration of pregnant mothers and mothers of young children. In Minnesota, for example, the Healthy Start Act, signed in 2021, ends the separation of mothers from their newborns.[23]

Focusing on clemency for incarcerated women and changing how pregnant mothers and mothers of newborns are treated are significant steps, but these recommendations do not represent the ceiling of what is possible. They are bricks to be removed from the criminal justice system in the hopes that one day the edifice itself can no longer stand under its own weight. In their mission, the National Council for Incarcerated and Formerly Incarcerated Women and Girls illustrates that even while lobbying for the clemency of a hundred incarcerated women, they do so with a broader goal of "abolishing incarceration for women and girls," because "the prison experience increases trauma in women, and, if they are mothers, to the children they are separated from . . . the current criminal legal system has failed and needs to be dismantled." Similarly, an approach that addresses immediate steps to reduce harm, while working toward ending the source of that harm is not only possible but necessary. To focus solely on decarceration, or the reduction of the number of people incarcerated, implies that there is some acceptable threshold of incarcerated people. In my view, this places a limit on the possibility of transformative change and does not solve the very real possibility that a disproportionate number of society's most marginalized will still be incarcerated, even if at lower levels. Fewer Black, Latina, or poor women in prison is an improvement, to be sure, but there is so much more that can and should be done to address systemic injustice.

One of the most significant challenges to transformative justice is rejecting the belief that some people are disposable and thus lacking in social value.[24] Even for those who might empathize with sixty-three-year-old Ana, whose conviction was based on her relationship with a violent offender, they might see Dani, who assaulted her boyfriend's new girlfriend, as deserving of separation from society. When such dichotomies are drawn between the redeemed and the irredeemable, it becomes easier and easier to justify the maltreatment of many because, after all, "those people" are out of the collective sight and mind of society writ large. Using the criminal offenses of some to justify maintaining or expanding the current system overlooks a central claim of transformative justice: Reducing harm is not just reactionary, or changing how society responds to crime. Rather, transformative justice not only seeks to abolish the penal system in its current form, but also seeks to address the root causes of system-wide inequality.[25]

For those who recognize the ills of mass incarceration and policing but are uneasy with the idea of across the board transformation, I encourage you to focus on dismantling each harmful element piece by piece. For you that may be abolishing the incarceration of pregnant mothers within your state or abolishing the imprisonment of nonviolent drug offenders. By focusing on your area of radical trans-formation, whatever that might be, you set a goal that drives forward movement, rather than an arbitrary benchmark that might foster com-placency. When aspects of the system are considered individually, how they harm marginalized communities in very concrete ways, the idea of transformative justice becomes less implausibly radical and comes to represent a pragmatic approach to a system that has revealed its obsolescence.[26]

BEGINNING A NEW CHAPTER

Often the rhetoric used to describe life after prison emphasizes inclusion through redemption. Words like reentry, reintegration, and rehabilita-tion describe a process whereby formerly incarcerated people can expect a return to normalcy so long as they prove their social and moral worth. What is often missing from institutional framing of these processes, however, is that there is often no "normal" in which to return. If reentry is meant to connote full acceptance and integration into society, then it is a mirage that formerly incarcerated women realize soon after their release. Leaving the confines of prison, many encounter a gentler cage, one in which poverty and unaddressed trauma are enhanced by their ex-offender label. To address the toll of incarceration on women it is far more beneficial to center recovery-oriented policies that address the fac-tors at the root of social inequality and criminalization, rather than to pretend that leaving prison eliminates existing marginality.

There is a misconception that rehabilitation requires paternalistic oversight of individuals by the state. However, if reentry efforts are to lead to durable change, women should be equipped with tools that sup-port self-actualization. The legitimacy of the type of work women do has often been regulated by transitional organizations and correctional institutions, which in turn limits the opportunities available to women.[27] By expanding the possibilities for postincarceration work, women can wed their individual experiences with work that supports other women.[28] Research shows that such an approach to gender-informed reintegration positively impacts both recidivism rates and postincarcer-ation satisfaction.[29] For example, art-centered programs that allow women to share their stories with the general public give women an opportunity to engage in purposeful work. Integrating these programs with more traditional income-generating labor can allow women to exert agency over the future direction of their postprison lives. There is also promising research on care-centered work that allows formerly incarcerated women to support other marginalized women.

Monica McLemore and Zakeya Hand find in their research that doula work in particular uniquely situates some formerly incarcerated women to advocate for expectant mothers. The authors found that this line of work was particularly beneficial to formerly incarcerated women of color who served other women of color, who are historically at higher risk for poor maternal health outcomes.[30] In addition to care-centered work, formerly incarcerated women would greatly benefit from a change to existing laws that ban them from professions that require state licensure. Because roughly one in five jobs require occupational licensure, the inability to secure licenses in fields such as education, healthcare, transportation, and cosmetology, greatly limit the possibility of securing employment after incarceration.[31] These bans are particularly devastating for women of color, who enter prison with lower levels of education and thus have more opportunities closed off to them.

The range of possibilities for formerly incarcerated women has for far too long been confined to work that meets a standard of acceptability delineated by institutional actors. The perception, spoken and unspoken, is that for certain woman self-actualization is an undeserved luxury, rather than a necessary consideration. Discussions of prisoner reentry usually focus on rehabilitation policies and programs a woman participates in after she completes her sentence. When women spoke about their transitional experiences, they shared that educational and training opportunities were limited while in prison, requiring them to balance postincarceration employee training with their other obligations. This experience is not unique to the women I spoke to, since many encounter the hurdles of reintegration, while striving to meet the benchmarks required of them.[32] For a system that touts the importance of low recidivism, it is counterintuitive that women should return to society with the textbook list of risk factors associated with reincarceration.

Even in considering the opportunities described, it is important that the methods and strategies for postimprisonment reintegration come from and center the work and activism of formerly incarcerated women. For scholars of justice studies, even those engaged in radical and abolitionist scholarship, the reality is that there are blind spots to the daily needs of justice involved individuals. As Joy James notes, the connection of academics to institutions that have historically upheld the needs of the privileged, constrains the kind of work and activism that academics pursue.[33] In disseminating information with wider audiences, scholars should defer to justice involved people whose lived realities provides a level of expertise needed for transformative justice.

THIS IS WHO WE ARE

The image of the United States as a global beacon of justice is all at once aspirational and an enduring myth. Though political leaders deny the insidious ways in which systemic racism and poverty-by-design economic structures perpetuate injustice, the fact remains that many have and many will be harmed by carceral institutions.[34] The knee-jerk retort "This is not who we are!" weakly masks the reality that this *is* who we are, and the narratives of women like those whose stories fill this book attest to the falsehood of national inculpability.[35]

Throughout this book I have referred to the institutions that punish, adjudicate, and surveill those charged with and convicted of criminal offenses as the "criminal justice system." For the sake of clarity this term is a useful one in that many readers will share this broad definition. In the literal sense, however, the term reflects a reality that is often absent in legal, correctional, and judicial settings. From the barriers placed before formerly incarcerated people, to the Constitution which enshrines the subhumanity of incarcerated individuals within the Thirteenth Amendment, these United States have long embraced a version of justice that have harmed much of its citizenry.[36] Indeed, if the criminal justice system itself were to stand trial by the those most harmed by it, it would be found guilty of wrongs that have caused incalculable damage.

In considering how the spectrum of carcerality impacts a woman over the course of her life and how motherhood can exacerbate existing areas of vulnerability, I argue that standard approaches of reform-oriented policies fall short of creating the systemic changes needed to rectify longstanding inequities. The fact that women are the fastest-growing group within the incarcerated population and that women of color are disproportionately impacted is a crisis of generational proportions.[37] In many ways the generational component of the incarceration crisis is echoed in the stories women shared about their lives. For example, when I think about thirty-nine-year-old LaToya, who lost custody of her children while battling drug addiction, I cannot help but think about her mother, whose own addiction made her unable to care for LaToya and her siblings. And when I think about LaToya's mother, it is difficult not to think about Trisha's mother, whose addiction resulted in imprisonment and left her young daughter in unsafe situations. Then there is Aaliyah, whose home was raided by drug enforcement agents when she was a child, as they searched for evidence to connect her father with drug dealing. When I think about all of these women, it is impossible not to consider how their lives are connected by the policies of the War on Drugs, which overwhelmingly impacted people from their communities.[38]

This work offers insight into how formerly incarcerated mothers engage with the complexities of life after imprisonment, yet in many ways it is only a page in a massive tome documenting the interwoven legacies and consequences of harmful policy decisions. The politics of prisoner reentry focuses on quantifiable outcomes so often that the stories of women are sometimes lost and their humanity obscured. The women featured in this book have all faced marginalization as a result of their criminal records, but they are also contending with structural and social disadvantages to varying degrees. They grapple with life at the margins, acknowledging their status as social outsiders, while fighting to tell their own stories, with their own words, in their own way. By centering the life histories and experiences of mothers, my goal in writing this book has been to demonstrate how policy discussions around reintegration and rehabilitation must attend to the lived realities of women, rather than detached state and institutional policy objectives. If policies that address the defining challenges of this time are to effect lasting and consequential change, they must first and foremost be human-centered.

Appendix

Research Methods and Respondent Characteristics

Between 2010 and 2011 I conducted taped interviews with seventy-one formerly incarcerated mothers while I was graduate student in the department of sociology at Harvard University. Interviews and observations were only conducted after I received approval from Harvard's institutional review board, which reviews studies involving human subjects. Due to sound-quality issues of two interviews, initially sixty-nine interviews were a part of the study. Using editing software that enabled me to decrease background noise (window unit air conditioners in both cases), I was able to later include one of those interviews, for a total of seventy interviews, which are featured in this book (see appendix table 1). Additionally, I conducted seven taped interviews with staff members (see appendix table 2). Three of the women categorized as formerly incarcerated mothers were also employed by a transitional organization, however I did not include these women in both groups but categorized them as formerly incarcerated mothers. Because their experience working at organizations was relatively brief compared to the preincarceration and incarceration period of their lives, much of their experiences and narratives focused on the salience of criminal involvement and reintegration.

One woman with a criminal background, Ms. Sandra Minor, was categorized as a staff member. Because she was a program director at the time we spoke and held considerable authority in determining program participants' access to resources, scheduling, and whether I could interview women, I determined that her status as a staff member was more germane to this research. Related to this point, only two formerly incarcerated women at Restoration House, where Ms. Minor was the program director, were interviewed. While all materials advertising the study emphasized the voluntarily nature of interviews, I was not comfortable that Ms. Minor, a person in a position of authority, would select the women who could participate (as per her request). The possibility that women might feel coerced into participating in interviews ultimately dissuaded me from continuing interviews at that research site. Interviews with the three other staff members at transitional organizations were brief, not exceeding thirty minutes. These interviews were focused on learning about the organization, the services provided and how staff members felt about the organization. Analysis of those interviews were useful in detailing the organizational context but quotes and narratives from staff members (who were not also formerly incarcerated mothers) were not featured in the book.

Women were recruited using a flyer posted in visible areas of each organization and by word-of-mouth. At Helping Hands, for example, the receptionist would inform mothers upon entry to review the materials advertising the study. If interested, women would provide their contact information on a sign-up sheet which I would collect each day. Once interviewed, respondents received twenty dollars in cash. Because of Restoration House's guidelines, which discouraged participants receiving cash, participants were given gift cards with a value of twenty dollars. I did not receive outside funding for the study. Rather, I compensated women from the proceeds of my graduate stipend.

The results of this study are based primarily on in-depth qualitative life-history interviews. Interviews focused on women's formative childhood years, pregnancy, motherhood, criminal involvement, relationships, and postincarceration experiences. At every stage of the research process, all measures were taken to comply with Harvard's Institutional Review Board regulations. Respondents' were never coerced during data collection and confidentiality was maintained at all times. Interviews were usually conducted at one of the transitional organizations in a private room. At a woman's request or convenience interviews were also conducted in other locations, such as her residence or a coffee shop. Upon receiving participants' permission, I used a digital recorder to record interviews, which lasted between one to two hours in length. When traveling to and from the research site I secured the recorder in small metal security box that was stored in a backpack that never left me. After interviews were completed they were transcribed and analyzed for recurring themes. I used the analytical software program ATLAS.ti to organize and code interviews so that shared themes could be readily identified.

In addition to interviews, I spent approximately a hundred hours at Helping Hands, organizing and updating contact information for one of their programs and creating a monthly newsletter updating clients and prospective funders about new developments. These activities, at the request of the executive director, helped to support one of their community programs, while allowing me to spend time informally conversing with staff members and clients throughout the day. At Mother's Love I spent approximately three hundred hours engaged in observation of workshops and informally speaking with clients, staff, and community members with ties to the organization. Thus, while interviews overwhelmingly inform the findings of this book, my framing of women's experiences in organizations is also shaped by observations.

A NOTE ON INTERVIEWING ON TRAUMA

I made the decision to not include questions that explicitly asked women to discuss childhood abuse. Respondents' descriptions of childhood abuse usually emerged when describing their overall childhood experiences. In instances when women detailed abuse, I was careful to listen quietly, rather than probe intrusively. If there was a part of their narrative that was unclear or vague I might ask them to clarify a term or phrase. This allowed women to respond with as much or as little detail as they felt was appropriate. When women responded with brief or curt responses I changed the line of questioning to another topic, taking that as a cue that they didn't feel comfortable discussing the issue any further.

One of the reasons I believed that it was important to tread carefully when respondents discussed traumatic histories was that the mere act of discussing those experiences can be retraumatizing.[1] While some women received professional counseling and therapy, it was not possible for me to know the extent to which the interview might cause emotional distress. As such, it was important for me to balance the questions that I asked against the risk of causing undue harm to women. For the most part, I employed the same strategy when intimate-partner victimization was discussed. There were no direct questions about relational abuse, but all women were asked about their relationships with the father(s) of their children. While I did ask direct questions about the level of a father's parental involvement, I did not ask women to elaborate on abusive incidents or their rationale for staying with an abusive partner.

SAMPLE CHARACTERISTICS

In determining who I would interview I established two main criteria. First, I wanted all respondents to be mothers. Second, respondents had to have been arrested, incarcerated, or under the supervision of correctional entities. At the time of interviews some women had been out of jail or prison for less than three months, while other women had been released for up to four years. This difference in the time outside of correctional institutions no doubt impacted how far along a woman was on her reintegration journey.

While seventy interviews comprise the study, the book focuses on the narratives of a much smaller subset of women, adding the voices of other women to substantiate a concept in each chapter. The reason particular women are repeatedly referenced throughout the text is to provide the reader with narrative continuity, so that they can follow the experiences and journeys of certain women who illustrate broader themes reflective of the book's overarching ideas.

To gauge respondents' changing views over time, I endeavored to reinterview women six months to a year after their initial interview. Follow up interviews with women proved to be difficult, which was not unexpected given the transient nature of formerly incarcerated women as they find new housing arrangements and acquire new telephone numbers. I was able to reinterview seven women, the findings of which proved valuable in examining how their views about transitional organizations evolved.

Pseudonym	Age	Race/Ethnicity	Criminal Offense	Age of First Pregnancy	Number of Children
Aaliyah	20	Black	Petty Theft	13	2
Alyssa	46	Black	Selling Drug	15	4
Ana	63	Puerto Rican1	Accessory to Homicide	19	3
April	25	White	Assault; Statutory Rape	/	2
Amara	36	Black	Drug Trafficking; Assault	17	2
Ariana	29	Hispanic	Assault with a Weapon	20	1
Audrey	25	Black	Selling Drugs	21	5
Becky	32	White	Selling Drugs	21	/
Breanna	47	Black	Drug Use	22	1
Bridgette	58	White	Assault on Police Officer	17	3
Brittany	36	White	Drug Use; Drug Trafficking	21	2
Cadence	28	Mixed (Black and Hispanic)	Larceny	19	2
Carissa	36	Black	Selling Drugs	13	6
Carlita	46	Hispanic	Drug Use	17	1
Cassandra	33	Black	Forgery; Assault; Larceny	19	2
Chelsea	28	White	Prostitution; Sale of Drugs	24	/
Cheryl	39	White	Drug Use	25	2
Collette	45	Black	Prostitution, Drug Use, Sale of Drugs	18	5
Cynthia	36	White	Drug Use	18	2
Dani	29	Black	First Degree Assault	18	1
Diana (was also staff)	48	White	Embezzlement	25	1
Elise	28	Black	Assault	17	6
Emily	45	White	Child Abuse	31	1
Eva (was also staff)	30	Hispanic	Drug Trafficking	18	2
Faith	25	Black	Second Degree Manslaughter	18	1
Felicia	38	White	Drug Use	23	2
Gabrielle	33	Black	Drug Use	20	1
Grace	20	Mixed	Assault	18	2
Graciela	33	Hispanic	Drug and weapon possession	29	1
Hannah	45	White	Drug Use	18	3
Isabelle	31	Black	Drug Use48	14	3

Jackie	35	Black	Drug Selling, Assault	20	1
Jane	48	White	Drug Use/Sale of Drugs	20	3
Jasmine	37	Black	Drug Use, Prostitution	20	1
Joanne	46	White	Prostitution, Drug use, Robbery	15	5
Jordyn	18	White	Burglary (as a juvenile); Violation of Protective Order (as an adult)	16	1
Juanita	44	Hispanic	Drug sales, Prostitution, Larceny	16	4
Judy	37	Black	Drug Use, Prostitution	16	7
Khloe	28	White	Drug Use	19	3
Kiana	35	Mixed Race (Black and Hispanic)	Armed Robbery	18	3
Kim	23	Mixed Race (Black and Hispanic)	DUI	15	2
Kishana	25	Black	Assault	14	2
Krystal	24	Black	Robbery	16	1
LaToya	39	Black	Drug Possession, Use	17	4
Lucille	35	Black	Drug sale, DWI	17	5
Lynn	36	Mixed Race (Asian, White)	Drug Possession	19	4
Marcia	49	Black	Drug Use	18	6
Margie	42	White	Drug Use	29	2
Meghan	21	White	Sale of Drugs	18	3
Monica	23	White	Prostitution, Burglary	25	2
Nadiege	31	Black	Sale of Drugs	26	2
Nicole	44	White	Fraud	37	1
Nina	47	Hispanic	Sale of Drugs, Identity Theft	18	542
Olive	49	Black	Drug Use	19	4
Penelope	39	Hispanic	Third Degree Robbery	17	3
Rashida	36	Black	Assault	15	3
Rita	52	Hispanic	Drug Use	17	1
Rose	51	Black	Assault	23	5
Sage	41	Black	Kidnapping of Her Child	32	2
Summer	26	White	Sale of Drugs	18	2
Tammy	37	Mixed Race (White, Puerto Rican)	DUI, Drug Possession	17	9
Tanya	40	Black	Armed Robbery	18	3
Tiffany	47	Black	Sale of Drugs	21	5
Trina	22	Black	Sale of Drugs	19	1
Trisha	28	Black	Assault	20	1

(continued)

Pseudonym	Age	Race/Ethnicity	Criminal Offense	Age of First Pregnancy	Number of Children
Valerie	41	White	Forgery, Burglary, Drug Use	25	2
Vickie (was also staff)	36	White	Drug Use	17	2
Wanda	62	Black	Assault, Theft	17	1
Wendy	28	Black	Gun Possession, Drug Possession, Assault	20	1
Yvette	36	Black	Assault	20	2

1. If the respondent emphasized her ethnicity or national origin when answering demographic questions, I included that identifier. This was true for Ana and Inez.

APPENDIX TABLE 2   PROFILE OF STAFF*

Pseudonym	Position	Race/Ethnicity	Transitional Organization
Inez	Day care teacher and foster mother	Dominican	Mother's Love
Jaimie	Social Worker Intern	White	Helping Hands
Keisha	Receptionist	Black	Helping Hands
Kaitlin	Social Worker Intern	White	Helping Hands
Pilar	Day care worker	Hispanic	Mother's Love
Susan O'Malley	Director of Mother's Love	White	Mother's Love
Sandra Minor	Program Director	Biracial	Restoration House

*While I did have several conversations with the director of Helping Hands, Ms. Brown, we did not have a formal interview.

Notes

INTRODUCTION

1. Johnson et. al (2019). To gain a sense of the tense climate surrounding the protest, watching a brief video may prove insightful to the reader. The hyperlink citation is provided in the references but for the reader's convenience, searching "Activists in support and opposed to President Donald Trump protest outside Benedict College" on YouTube will find a video of the event described.

2. Motsinger (2020).

3. N. James (2019); Department of Justice (2019).

4. McCorkel's study of incarcerated women provides a rich accounting of how the War on Drugs has impacted women, particularly those from marginalized backgrounds.

5. Throughout the book I use the term *criminal justice system* to refer to the set of systems, such as the judicial, correctional, law enforcement, and legislative systems, that regulate and punish behavior. Literally, however, I recognize that "justice" or the fair treatment of all and respect for humanity, is often denied to some, particularly society's most marginalized.

6. Hobson and Rosenblum (2019).

7. See Kessler (2019) for political framing of the Fair Sentencing Act and First Step Act in the 2020 presidential election. In the months prior to the 2020 presidential election there was ongoing debate as to the extent to which the Fair Sentencing Act and by extension the Obama administration contributed to the decriminalization of non-violent drug crimes specified in the First Step Act. See First Sentencing Act (2010: Sec. 404) which directly cites the Fair Sentencing Act of 2010 provision to eliminate mandatory sentencing and changed sentencing guidelines, each of which contributed to early releases for inmates like Tanesha Bannister.

8. News 19 WLTX (2019).

9. My emphasis on nonviolent offenders does not reflect my personal scholarly position that there is a fixed hierarchy of worthiness among incarcerated and formerly incarcerated persons. The emphasis is meant to highlight how policy advocates, particularly elected officials, often frame reform.

10. Interviews with seventy formerly incarcerated women form the basis of this study, however I interviewed seventy-one formerly incarcerated women. Due to sound quality issues, two interviews were initially not included. While those issues were resolved with audio software for one of those interviews (increasing the sample size from sixty-nine to seventy), one interview beyond repair. Details on how audio issues were remedied are included in the appendix.

11. Miller (2021).

12. Sawyer (2019).

13. See Shedd (2011, 2015) for examination of how carcerality exists on a spectrum. The "carceral continuum" is not a binary concept, rather it underscores that are varying levels and in varying degrees the lives of individuals who have been formally sanctioned by the criminal justice system are surveilled and judged in ways that structure opportunity and shape experiences.

14. In order to anonymize the third research site it is important not to mention the state or city. It is a smaller state in New England and may thus be easy to identify based on the description of the residential program.

15. See Leverentz (2014) and Miller (2021) for discussion of postincarceration as an extension of challenges that existed prior to and during incarceration.

16. This is a framing of motherhood that is racialized and classed based, often in reference to white upper-income women. See Roberts (1993) and Dow (2016).

17. In hooks's (1989) analysis of marginalization she highlights the importance of viewing marginality, particularly for Black women, not solely as a site of oppression, but as a space of resistance.

18. See Avery and Lu (2020) for a timeline of the year states adopted a version of the Ban the Box measure.

19. Alexander (2010).

20. See Pfaff (2017). While Pfaff is critical of criminal justice policies he argues against the ideas that the ballooning prison rate was due to drug offenses. Rather, he says violent crime offenses drove increasing prison rates.

21. Mangual (2019).

22. Kajstura (2019). As of 2019 the Unites States incarcerates more women than Russia, China, and Thailand combined.

23. Jails are operated at the local, usually county level. Women are incarcerated in jails prior to trial, if they are unable to bond out or to serves sentences, typically not in excess of two years. Prisons operate at the state and federal level and women are incarcerated in prison upon convictions for lengthier sentences, typically longer than one or two years.

24. Sawyer (2018).

25. Bonczar (2003).

26. Bonczar (2003).

27. Monk (2015).

28. Monk (2019).

29. Miller (2021). See Curtis (2019) for an analysis that examines how fathers negotiate their roles as parents while imprisoned.

30. Du Bois (1909).

31. See hooks (1989).

32. Morris (2015).

33. Rabaka (2010), Gilkes cited in Morris (2015:220).

34. See Balfour (2005) and Simpson (2015) for examples of how Du Bois sometimes presented Black women's role in society in problematic ways. Balfor, in particular, notes how his essay "The Damnation of Women" valorized the resistance of Black enslaved women and economic ingenuity of freedwoman, while there remains a masculinist tenor to how he writes about social change.

35. Elder (1994).

36. Elder (1985).

37. Laub and Sampson (1993).

38. Edin, Nelson, and Paranal (2004).

39. The research on the impact of motherhood on women's postincarceration research is diverse. Leverentz (2014) highlights the strain that motherhood adds to the postincarceration transition period. While Michalsen (2011) has found that motherhood can both lessen the likelihood of reoffending even while adding stress to women's lives. Others, such as Uggen and Kruttschnitt (1998), find that motherhood is associated with a decrease in offending.

40. Richie (2001); Western (2006); Pager (2007).

41. Sawyer and Bertram (2018).

42. Clifford and Silver-Greenberg (2017).

43. Hanlon, Carswell, and Rose (2007) discuss the role that grandmothers play in caretaking, particularly when their daughter is incarcerated. For Black mothers, once she is incarcerated the majority of children live not with their fathers, but with grandmothers or other relatives.

44. Flores (2016).

45. Gabbidon (2001, 2016); Rios, Carney, and Kelekay (2017); Clair (2021).

46. Neil and Sampson (2021).

47. Pink and Morgan (2013).

48. Sawyer (2019).

49. Detailed information about how I gained access to each research site and how I collected and analyze data is described in the appendix.

50. Cannata (2017).

51. Cannata (2017).

52. Staley (2008).

53. U.S. Department of Health and Human Services (2009).

54. Because I am anonymizing this city, I am unable to provide the exact percentage because it would be readily identified in the National Survey on Drug and Use Health data.

55. The use of the racial descriptors *Hispanic* and *Latina* are a result of respondents' self-identification during interviews. When using the terms, unless referring to how a woman described herself, I will usually use the term Latina, which refers to region (originating from Latin America) from which the respondent or her family is from. It should be noted that at the time of data collection

there was much less public discourse surrounding the nomenclatural differences and the term *Latinx* was not a term used in public discourse, so no respondent used that term. See Noe-Bustamante, Luis, and Lopez (2020).

56. When I conducted interviews I was in my mid-twenties. Regarding social class, I didn't reference my class background but it is possible that some respondents may have inferred assumptions about my class background based on my level of education.

57. This is a quote from an interview Trisha, a respondent whose experiences are chronicled throughout the book.

58. Edin and Kefalas (2005).

CHAPTER 1. MARGINALIZED FROM THE BEGINNING

1. Before interviews I always made it clear to women that I was a researcher, unaffiliated with transitional organizations or correctional institutions.

2. Outside of the organization's facilities I would encounter staff/volunteers like Pablo at local eateries and convenience stores. While we had several exchanges of this nature I never felt unsafe nor did I behave in a way that compromised by stated goals as a researcher.

3. In this description, I focus on Mother's Love, the New York site, to draw parallels between my upbringing in New York and some of the descriptions of women's childhood experiences. I do not draw similar parallels with other research sites. Moreover, while I mention geographic regions, large cities, states, and neighboring communities, I do not specify the location of organizations.

4. The specific section of St. Albans where notable jazz musicians, athletes, and Black intelligentsia like Du Bois lived is Addisleigh Park, is now a recognized historical district. My home was not located in Addisleigh Park but adjacent to it, sharing the same zip code. Distinguished by Tudor-style homes, the once all-white neighborhood experienced a demographic shifted in the mid-twentieth century and has been predominately African American and Afro-Caribbean since the 1980s. See Noonan (2011); Gregor (2014).

5. An example of a mural like the one I describe is located on Linden Boulevard in St. Albans in Queens, New York. Designed by Joe Stephenson, the mural depicts musicians, such as Billie Holiday, Fats Waller, James Brown, and Lena Horne. See Walsh (2013).

6. My reference here is to Whitney Houston, Mariah Carey, and Michael Jackson. In the mid-1990s I was either in elementary school or middle school, a time in which the musicians mentioned were widely popular and R&B female groups like SWV and Total and male groups like Boyz II Men had crossover pop music success.

7. Potter (2006) emphasized the importance if distinguishing women's criminal acts from their overall identity as women.

8. Filipas and Ullman (2006); Horwitz et al. (2001); Davenport, Browne, and Palmer (1994); Beitchman et al. (1991).

9. Laub, Nagin, and Sampson (1998); Laub and Sampson (1993).

10. Brazelton (2015).

11. Brazelton (2015). Silencing exists both within the family and in the broader local community. Brazelton's respondents feared retribution much like the kind experienced by Aaliyah. Moreover, repeated disclosure created the threat of revictimization by family members and acquaintances who exploited that information to the detriment of victims.

12. Stone (2007) cited in Brazelton (2015); Abney and Priest (1995);

13. Goffman's distinction between discredited and discreditable persons offers insight into the difference between visible and invisible sources of stigma. A discredited person bears an identifying characteristic that is visibly and easily recognizable as stigmatizing. For example, being a person with a visible disability or a member of a racial minority in a society with a history of treating members of that group poorly. A discreditable person is one who has a stigmatizing characteristic that can be concealed from the wider public. See Goffman (1963).

14. There are many online services that offer background checks to the general public, typically for a fee. Other databases, like state sex-offender registries are offered by the state governments.

15. The agreement between Kiana and her daughter's biological father was verbal and informal in nature. They did not sign a contract.

16. Self-blame is common among childhood victims of sexual abuse. See Feiring and Cleland (2007); Filipas and Ullman (2006); Beitchman et.al. (1991).

17. Sharp and Marcus-Mendoza (2001).

18. Within the juvenile justice system there is more willingness to consider how underlying sources of trauma lead to delinquent behavior and those experiences are often used during the adjudication process. For adults, by contrast, childhood experiences may be used to frame documented mental illness, which can be a legitimate criminal excuse, but traumatic experiences during childhood apart from a clinical diagnosis present during the commission of the crime are not the basis for a criminal defense.

19. During interviews I was careful not to make causal arguments about a respondent's childhood abuse and later criminality. While many victims of childhood abuse may commit crime, many other do not.

20. See Werth (2013), for an examination of offenders as beholden to a punitive ideology that frames rehabilitation as the offender's responsibility, as well as subject to correctional staff's methods of punitive regulation.

21. I differentiated instances of physical abuse from what respondents considered typical strict parenting. Spanking, for example, may be viewed a normal act of discipline by some and abusive behavior by others. If respondents spoke about spanking as associated with positive parenting I used their descriptions to determine if it was abusive or not. See the appendix for details on coding methods.

22. I make this distinction because respondents didn't always expect that the victimization they experienced would result in intervention by the criminal justice system but they did expect social repercussions.

23. I provide more details about Trisha's case in chapter 5.

24. Hoffmann and Dufur (2018); Hirschi (1969). See also Fader (2013) for an ethnographic accounting of how social support impact reintegration after detention.

25. I use this anecdotal example, not to generalize an experience, but rather to highlight how, as an outsider, I saw the daily difficulties of a child who had an ill mother. While this experience took place many years ago, because of the frequency of those interactions I still recall the details well. There is no embellishment.

26. When Trisha's mother was incarcerated Trisha and her brother lived with their grandmother, not their stepfather.

27. Craig et al. (2017); Longshore, Chang, and Messina (2005); Hirschi and Gottfredson (1983).

28. Craig et al. (2017).

29. Michalsen (2019); Bachman et al. (2016).

30. Brown and Bloom (2009).

31. Pager (2007).

32. Luster and Small (1997).

33. Fantuzzo and Mohr (1999).

34. McLaughlin et al. (2016).

35. Trina's description of her mother's addiction and her own incarceration experience is very similar to that of another respondent, Trisha. Because of the similarity in this part of their story it is important to underscore that they are two different women.

36. Alameda et al., (2015); Banyard (1997); Follette et al. (1996).

37. Jipguep and Sanders-Phillips (2003); Fantuzzo and Mohr (1999); Groves (1997); Davenport, Browne, and Palmer (1994).

38. Du Bois (1909:1).

39. Carlson and Shafer (2010) find that that nationally 11 percent to 36 percent of women have been victims of physical abuse as children. Women in prison report rates between 26 percent to as high as 73 percent for physical abuse. The data on childhood sexual abuse among incarcerated women also varies widely, ranging between 11 percent to 80 percent; McDaniels-Wilson and Joanne Belknap (2008) found in their study of nearly 400 female inmates that approximately 30 percent of their respondents were victimized by three or more individuals, illustrating this population's susceptibility to multiple instances of victimization.

40. Horwitz et al. (2001).

CHAPTER 2. LOVE, BABY, AND CHAOS

1. Tomei (2010).

2. Cahn (1999); Davis (1998); Stitt (1988) describes how and why some crimes are defined as victimless and the implications of that definition on policy and practice.

3. McLean and Pratt (2006). Examine the impact of identity status and related narratives on shaping turning points for young adults. The role of identity status changes and turning points is particular relevant for pregnancy and the impending shift toward motherhood.

4. Edin and Nelson (2013); Edin and Kefalas (2005).

5. McMurtry and Lie (1992).

6. Van Brown (2019) discusses the progression of domestic violence. The initial stages of relationships are often marked by relative calm. Moreover, Gary's deflection of Kishana's concerns by blaming his ex-wives is not uncommon within relationships marked by domestic violence.

7. Hayes and Jeffries (2016).

8. Morash et al. (2015 discuss how women under the supervision of a probation or a parole officer fear the potential repercussions that may come with police contact. This fear can regulate behavior that is perceived as law violating.

9. The term *golden handcuffs* stems from behavioral economics, which describes the social and psychological costs of remaining in an unfulfilling high-paying career. The use of the term here is solely to describe the perceived economic benefit that pales in light of intimate partner victimization. The metaphor in no way is meant to imply that the what domestic abuse survivors face is comparable to working an unfulfilling jog. See Nissley and Hartigan (2001). For a description of the economic use of the term.

10. Sufrin (2017).

11. Edin and Nelson (2013).

12. Gibson-Davis (2014); Edin and Kefalas (2005).

13. Keene, Smoyer, and Blankenship (2018).

14. Leverentz (2011).

15. Bell et al. (2018) discuss the factors that influence young adults' decision-making processes to contraception and the possibility of pregnancy.

16. Most of the women who specifically stated their opposition against abortion cited either their own religious beliefs or the religious beliefs of their family. Larger studies demonstrate that religiosity shapes views on abortion. See Wilcox (1990) and Hess and Rueb (2005).

17. At the age of fourteen Kishana would have needed parental consent to have an abortion in the state where she resided. See Anon (2016).

18. I am specifically revering to individuals reliant on parental consent for abortion.

19. Herring (2020); also see Toscano (2005) for examination of how pregnant women who are addicted to drugs are criminalized.

20. The discussion around pathologizing single motherhood, namely Black single motherhood, became widely debated in the wake of the Moynihan Report of 1965. The Moynihan Report, written by Daniel Moynihan, analyzed the "Negro Family"—highlighted sources of poverty, which honed in community-level aspects of poverty such as the high rate of single-mother households. The perception that marriage provides a salvo to issues of economic displacement became widely embraced in the twentieth century in sociology and more commonly challenged in the last two decades. Still, pathologizing single mothers across race still exists, hold particularly damaging consequences for Black and Latina(x) women. See Lenhardt (2016) and Hamilton (2004) for further analysis of the implications of the Moynihan Report.

21. Dow (2011).

22. Clone and DeHart (2014); Leverentz (2011).

23. Day et al. (2018).

24. Rettinger and Andrews (2010); Bonta, Pang, and Wallace-Capretta (1995).

25. Dani explained that her first-degree assault charge and conviction was due to the disfigurement of the victim.

26. Postpartum depression can have a negative implications on both mother and infant. Left untreated, it can contribute to women engaging in uncharacteristic and harmful behavior. See Patel et al. (2012) for a review of the contributing factors and consequences of postpartum depression.

27. McLanahan (2009).

28. Greenfield and Snell (1999).

29. McDonald et.al. (2011) find that for some women, child birth related post-traumatic stress may impact parenting in the short term.

30. Greenfield and Snell (1999).

31. Badu (1997).

32. Ortiz and Briggs (2003); Logan (1999).

33. While most media reports focusing on the intersection of race and the opioid addiction crisis emphasize addiction among white Americans, it should be noted that deaths among minorities from opioid overdoses has increased in recent years. In 2015 78 percent of fatal deaths were white Americans, Black Americans comprised 12 percent of deaths and 8 percent of fatal overdoses. Between 1999–2015 Indigenous groups experienced the largest increased of opioid deaths when compared to other racial groups. Further discussion of statistical change can be found in Shihipar (2019); Yankah (2016); and Netherland and Hansen (2016). See also Danquah-Brobby (2017) for a discussion of the legalization of marijuana in some states and the continued incarceration of minorities incarcerated for drug offenses.

34. Elliott, Powell, and Brenton (2015); Edin and Kefalas (2005).

35. McLanahan (2009).

36. For an examination of how the state conflates marriage policy see Hamilton (2003).

CHAPTER 3. CRIME, AGENCY, AND POSTCARCERAL NARRATIVES

1. At the time of the robbery attempt Kiana was in her late twenties. During the interview she was thirty-five years old.

2. Bandura (2002).

3. Foster (2012); Crewe (2011); McBride (2010).

4. Kiana was referring to a felony kidnapping charge. In criminal cases, if a co-conspirator in one crime commits another crime during the commission of the original crime other members of the party are held liable. Known as the Pinkerton liability rule, this principle is colloquially known as the "what one did, they all did" rule. See Pauley (2005).

5. Maeve (1999).

6. Wyse, Harding, and Morenoff (2014); Zoutewelle-Terovan et al. (2014).

7. Wyse, Harding, and Morenoff (2014).

8. Cooper-Sadlo et al. (2019); Bachman et al.(2016); Broussard, Joseph, and Thompson (2012); O'Brien and Young (2006).

9. English was Ana's second language, so some of her speaking did not conform to normative English sentence structure.

10. Rossi et al. (1974).

11. Blum-West (1985).

12. Thompson (2017); Danquah-Brobby (2016).

13. Stylianou (2003).

14. See Sallmann (2010) for an analysis of how women manage stigma by reframing their interactions with the criminal justice systems and social relationships.

15. Victimless crimes are crimes that do not typically cause direct harm to other individuals. Drug use, for example, falls under this category. It is important to note than "harm" in this context does not include the emotional and psychological harm that family members experience when a loved one is struggling with drug addiction. See Abrams and Della-Fave (1976).

16. See Husak (2004); DeVille and Kopelman (1998).

17. Maruna (2000).

18. I use the term *good* to describe how women describe morality. In this context, I am not attributing a moral interpretation of respondent's actions but rather using the language that they use to frame morality vis-à-vis their criminal pasts.

19. Potter (2006).

20. In an effort to protect the identity of this respondent, I removed references to her specific prison sentence and the details of her plea deal.

21. Discrimination against lesbian women within the criminal justice system, though underresearched, is certainly not without precedent. One of the most well-known examples in the last decade is the wrongful conviction of four Latinx queer women, referred to as the "San Antonio Four." Legal analysis of the case and court proceedings indicate that discrimination as a result of their sexual identity led to a violation of their legal rights. See Grappo (2020) and Nadal et al. (2015).

22. Although the acronym LGBTQ is an acronym for lesbian, gay, bisexual, transgender, and queer individuals, Nadal et al. (2015) did not include transgender youth in their analysis.

23. Legal cynicism describes the situational nature of trust expressed by marginalized mothers when interacting with law enforcement. See Bell (2016).

24. Weare (2013).

25. Redmond et al. (2020); Frank et al. (2014).

26. See Shedd (2011) for analysis of the carceral continuum which examines how social institutions exacerbate the criminalization of young people over their life course.

CHAPTER 4. THE DUALITY OF MARGINALIZED MOTHERHOOD

1. Pew Research Center (2007).

2. Douglas and Michaels (2005) examine how the idealization of motherhood has impacted how mothers are evaluated and judged across society.

3. Roberts (1993).

4. Garcia (2016); Dow (2011, 2016); Hill-Collins (1994).

5. Collins (1994); Potter (2013).

6. Brown and Bloom (2009).

7. The term *good mother* is commonly used in scholarship to reflect how mothers project and interpret morality vis-à-vis societal expectations of motherhood. See May (2008).

8. Rios, Carney, and Kelekay (2017); Du Bois (2016).

9. Trautner and Collett (2010); Stringer (2020).

10. Heidemann, Cederbaum, and Martinez (2016). discuss the value respondents placed on having a "normal life" and persevering as markers as success. These subjective measures of success underscore that women don't rely solely on the objective measures of success used in evaluations by institutions and organizations.

11. O'Brien (2001). See also Gurusami (2019) for an examination of how formerly incarcerated mothers engage in strategic motherhood as a means of managing the restrictions placed upon them by state actors.

12. In this description I am referring to idealized version of heterosexual, cis women. See Douglas and Michaels (2005).

13. Collins (1994).

14. Alignment with moral behavior is a way to diminish stigma/regain moral self-worth. See Sachdeva, Iliev, and Medin (2009).

15. Abrams, Hill, and Maxwell (2019).

16. According to Shih (2004) stigmatized individuals deploy three methods to minimize assaults on their character: compensation, strategic interpretations, and multiple identities. The first of these three methods, compensation, can be used to assert one's character strengths or disconfirm a negative stereotype. This aligns with women's identification with ideal types of motherhood.

17. Sherman (2005).

18. Dow (2011).

19. Williams, Spencer, and Wilson (2021).

20. I apply this observation to Bridgette, who draws upon her perception of Black mothers, recognizing the marginalized status that Black motherhood has with social discourse. It is important to note that Bridgette specifically focuses on disciplinary practices she attributes to Black mothers, not "Black motherhood" in the broader sense.

21. Crocker and Major (1989).

22. DCF is an acronym for Department of Children and Family in Massachusetts.

23. Sered and Norton-Hawk (2014).

24. Elliot, Powell, and Brenton (2015) define how "good motherhood" has been defined, particularly for marginalized mothers.

25. LaToya's other child was in the custody of a relative.

26. See Barnes and Stringer (2014) and Stringer (2020) for another examination of how mothers negotiate their roles as parental figures and caregivers.

27. Leverentz (2011).

28. Gurusami (2017) notes that what counts as acceptable employment must meet criteria of reliablilty, recognizeable and redemptive. Work that does not

meet that criteria is invalidated and holds negative implications for how women are evaluated by state actors.

29. Aiello and McQueeny (2016).

30. Ross and Buehler (2001).

31. Jones's (2009) analysis of how marginalized Black girls experience and respond to neighborhood-level crime and the systemic forces impinging on the social interactions underscores the precarceral experiences that marginalized women discuss and how such experiences may shape their postincarceration worldview.

32. Brown and Bloom (2009).

33. Myers et al.(1999).

34. Nesmith and Ruhland (2008); Dallaire (2007).

35. Pettit and Western (2004) discuss the significance of contextual factors surrounding incarceration at the community level. Findings from their study showed that in some neighborhoods young men were more likely to have a criminal record than complete college.

36. Dallaire (2007).

37. Myers et al. (1999).

38. Truth (2020).

39. Brah and Phoenix (2004).

40. In this section I am not making a direct comparison between the institution of chattel slavery and imprisonment. The description of Truth's emancipation is used to provide context for her speech, which provides rhetorical inspiration for the question "Ain't I a Mother?"

41. Hong (2017).

42. Shedd (2015); Hong (2017); Clifford and Jessica Silver-Greenberg (2017);

43. Ortiz (2014).

44. Ortiz and Briggs (2003).

45. I credit disability activist and film maker Jennifer Brea for the expression "marginalizations within marginalizations." Jennifer Brea's Twitter page, https://twitter.com/jenbrea?ref_src=twsrc%5Egoogle%7Ctwcamp%5Eserp%7Ctwgr%5Eauthor (retrieved August 13, 2020).

CHAPTER 5. THE PROJECT OF REHABILITATION

1. Gurusami (2017).

2. hooks (1984, 1990) discusses the importance of viewing marginalization as a potential site of resistance, not solely as a site of oppression.

3. Cobbina (2010) examines how postincarceration success is interpreted and defined by women during the reintegration period.

4. I was also reluctant to continue interviews because of concerns that women might feel pressured into participating in the interview if they were approached directly by someone occupying a position of power.

5. Gilmore (2017) discusses how funding needs of nonprofit organizations influences their objectives.

6. Thompson (2007).

7. Goshin, Byrne, and Henninger (2014).

8. Laughlin et al (2008).

9. Michalsen (2011).

10. Scholarship on the prison industrial complex examines and critiques economic factors driving and sustaining mass incarceration and correctional institutions more broadly. See Fulcher (2012); Scholosser (1998); Davis (1998).

11. Danquah-Brobby (2016).

12. Gilmore (2007). While private prisons and private contracts that work with both private and public prisons may profit from the high rate of incarceration, taxes are used to pay for the costs of incarcerating individuals and pay for the salaries of correctional staff.

13. This echoes the in-prison concept of punitive ideology examined by Werth (2013).

14. I speak more extensively about the intersection of race and gender as it relates to social exclusion in chapter 4.

15. Cobbina and Bender (2012) discuss the factors that shape women's postincarceration optimism about the future, even as they balance the challenges awaiting them.

16. WIC is the federally subsidized Women, Infant and Mothers program that provides families with subsidies for food, infant formula, and other essential items.

17. Allard (2002).

18. Jarrett (1996). See also Roberts (1999) for an analysis of how the restructuring of welfare negatively harms poor mothers.

19. Dow (2015).

20. See Cammett (2016) and Williams, Spencer, and Wilson (2021) for an analysis of the challenges facing Black mothers in relation to welfare and criminalization.

21. Gurusami (2017).

22. Gurusami (2017).

23. Arditti and Few 2006, 2008.

24. Sykes (2011).

25. Sered and Norton-Hawk (2014).

26. Haney (2010).

27. Sered and Norton-Hawk (2014).

28. New International Version Bible (2011).

29. Stringer (2009).

30. It is important to note that in their describing their faith women either referenced a monotheistic belief system, using the name "God" or specifically referenced attributes of Christianity. How women of other faiths describe the relationship between their faith and their ex-offender marginalized status may bear similarities but there may also be meaningful differences.

31. Frederick's (2003) analysis of Black Christian women illustrates how they integrate their religious beliefs and identity throughout their daily lives.

32. For an examination of how theology engages specifically with the marginalized see Cone (2010).

33. Gilmore (2007)
34. Gilmore (2007:14).

CONCLUSION

1. Given this specificity of this detail, I have chosen not to mention the respondent's pseudoynm because previously mention details may compromise anonymity.
2. Du Bois (1903).
3. At the time of interviews prospective job applicants were required to indicate if they had a criminal record in New York and Rhode Island, not Massachusetts. Ban the Box laws now exist in all three states. See Avery and Lu (2020).
4. Rabuy and Kopf (2015).
5. Sawyer and Bertram (2018).
6. Sawyer (2018).
7. Kajstura (2019).
8. Opsal (2011).
9. hooks (1989); and Kruttschnitt, Gartner, and Miller (2000).
10. Shedd (2015); Foucault (1977).
11. Shedd (2011).
12. The White House (2021).
13. National Council for Incarcerated and Formerly Incarcerated Women and Girls (2021).
14. The term "brick-by-brick" in reference to prison and criminal justice transformation is not original to this book. Numerous scholars have used this metaphor to reference the strategic and methodical dismantling of punitive legal systems.
15. Tucker (2021).
16. Daniel (2019).
17. Bureau of Justice Statistics (2004).
18. The Black Maternal Health Momnibus Act of 2020, brought the House floor by Rep. Lauren Underwood (D-Illinois), has garnered congressional support for addressing the disproportionately poor health outcomes of black mothers. As a model, it illustrates that prenatal and maternal healthcare legislation has the potential for consensus. Applying similar legislation for incarcerated mothers and focusing on the impact of maternal mortality and poor infant health outcomes is one way to attract bipartisan congressional support. See Underwood (2020).
19. Caniglia (2018).
20. Chuck (2018).
21. Goshin, Byrne, and Blanchard-Lewis (2014); Barnes and Stringer (2014).
22. Chuck (2018).
23. Gray (2021).
24. I use the term *disposable* similarly to Giroux's (2006) explanation of the "biopolitics of disposability" which focuses on the maltreatment of poor, black citizens during the United States' catastrophic response to Hurricane Katrina in

2005. See also Vitale (2017) who discusses social resistance against of transformation within the criminal justice system.

25. Kaba (2021).

26. Kaba (2021); Davis (2011).

27. Gurusami (2017).

28. This is a recommendation that acknowledges that not all women will want to engage in this type of work.

29. Carlton and Segrave (2016); Wright et al. (2012).

30. McLemore and Warner Hand (2017).

31. Kight (2021).

32. Michalsen (2011).

33. J. James (2019).

34. Cameron (2021); Brown (2021); Novelly (2021).

35. McDonald (2021).

36. The Thirteenth Amendment abolishes slavery within the United States. However, the amendment makes an exception for the ban on slavery for those being punished for criminal activity. See U.S. Constitution, Article 4, Section 1.

37. Kajstura (2019).

38. According to Neil and Sampson (2021), macrohistorical factors like the War on Drugs, play a greater role in shaping cohort arrest differences than individual factors like self-control and community-level factors such as neighborhood income level and family social and economic status.

APPENDIX

1. Brazelton (2015).

References

Abney, Veronica, and Ronnie Priest. 1995. "African Americans and Sexual Child Abuse." In *Sexual Abuse in Nine North American Cultures: Treatment and Prevention,* edited by L. Fontes, pp. 11–30. Thousand Oaks, CA: Sage Publications.

Abrams, Jasmine A., Ashley Hill, and Morgan Maxwell. 2019. "Underneath the Mask of the Strong Black Woman Schema: Disentangling Influences of Strength and Self-Silencing on Depressive Symptoms among U.S. Black Women." *Sex Roles* 80(9):517–26.

Abrams, Keith, and Richard Della-Fave. 1976. "Authoritarianism, Religiosity, and Legalization of Victimless Crimes." *Sociology and Social Research* 61 (1):68–82.

Aiello, Brittnie, and Krista McQueeny. 2016. "'How Can You Live without Your Kids?': Distancing from and Embracing the Stigma of 'Incarcerated Mother.'" *Journal of Prison Education and Reentry* 3(1):32–49.

Alameda, Louis., et al. 2015. "Childhood Sexual and Physical Abuse: Age at Exposure Modulates Impact on Functional Outcome in Early Psychosis Patients." *Psychological Medicine* 45(13):2727–36.

Alexander, Michelle. 2010. *The New Jim Crow: Mass Incarceration in the Age of Colorblindness.* New York: New Press.

Allard, Patricia. 2002. *Life Sentences: Denying Welfare Benefits to Women Convicted of Drug Offenses.* Sentencing Project. www.prisonpolicy.org /scans/sp/lifesentences.pdf (retrieved August 31, 2021).

Angermeyer, Matthias C., Beate Schulze, and Sandra Dietrich. 2003. "Courtesy Stigma." *Social Psychiatry and Psychiatric Epidemiology* 38(10):593–602.

Anon. 2016. "Parental Involvement in Minors' Abortions." Guttmacher Institute, www.guttmacher.org/state-policy/explore/parental-involvement-minors-abortions (retrieved June 30, 2021).

Arditti, Joyce, and April Few. 2006. "Mothers' Reentry into Family Life Following Incarceration." *Criminal Justice Policy Review* 17(1): 103–26.

———. 2008. "Maternal Distress and Women's Reentry into Family and Community Life." *Family Process* 47(3):303–21.

Avery, Beth, and Han Lu. 2020. "Ban the Box: U.S. Cities, Counties, and States Adopt Fair Hiring Policies." *National Employment Law Project,* http://stage.nelp.org/publication/ban-the-box-fair-chance-hiring-state-and-local-guide (retrieved December 15, 2020).

Bachman, Ronet, et al. 2016. "The Complex Relationship between Motherhood and Desistance." *Women and Criminal Justice* 26(3):212–31.

Bade, Rachael, and Erica Werner. 2020. "Centrist House Democrats Lash Out at Liberal Colleagues, Blame Far-Left Views for Costing the Party Seats." *Washington Post*, November 5.

Badu, Erykah. 1997. "Otherside of the Game." Kedar Records, compact disc.

Balfour, Lawrie. 2005. "Representative Women: Slavery, Citizenship, and Feminist Theory in Du Bois's 'Damnation of Women.'" *Hypatia* 20(3):127–48.

Bandura, Albert. 2002. "Selective Moral Disengagement in the Exercise of Moral Agency." *Journal of Moral Education* 31(2):101–19.

Banyard, Victoria L. 1997. "The Impact of Childhood Sexual Abuse and Family Functioning on Four Dimensions of Women's Later Parenting." *Child Abuse and Neglect* 21(11):1095–1107.

Barnes, Sandra L., and Ebonie Cunningham Stringer. 2014. "Is Motherhood Important? Imprisoned Women's Maternal Experiences before and during Confinement and Their Postrelease Expectations." *Feminist Criminology* 9(1):3–23.

Beitchman, Joseph H., et al. 1991. "A Review of the Short-Term Effects of Child Sexual Abuse." *Child Abuse and Neglect* 15(4):537–56.

Bell, Monica C. 2016. "Situational Trust: How Disadvantaged Mothers Reconceive Legal Cynicism." *Law and Society Review* 50(2):314–47.

Bell, Monica C., et al. 2018. "Relationship Repertoires, the Price of Parenthood, and the Costs of Contraception." *Social Service Review* 92(3):313–48.

Benson, Mark J. 2004. "After the Adolescent Pregnancy: Parents, Teens, and Families." *Child and Adolescent Social Work Journal* 21(5):435–55.

Bloom, Barbara, Meda Chesney Lind, and Barbara Owen. 1994. *Women in California Prisons: Hidden Victims of the War on Drugs.* San Francisco: Center on Juvenile and Criminal Justice.

Blum-West, Stephen R. 1985. "The Seriousness of Crime: A Study of Popular Morality." *Deviant Behavior* 6(1):83–98.

Bonczar, Thomas P. 2003. *Prevalence of Imprisonment in the U.S. Population, 1974–2001.* Bureau of Justice Statistics. Washington, DC: U.S. Department of Justice.

Bonta, James, Bessie Pang, and Suzanne Wallace-Capretta. 1995. "Predictors of Recidivism among Incarcerated Female Offenders." *Prison Journal* 75(3):277–94.

Brah, Avtar, and Phoenix, Ann. 2004. "Ain't I a Woman: Revisiting Intersectionality." *Journal of International Women's Studies* 5(3):75–86.

Brazelton, Jewell. 2015. "The Secret Storm: Exploring the Disclosure Process of African American Women Survivors of Child Sexual Abuse across the Life Course." *Traumaulogy* 21(3):181–87.

Broussard, C. Anne, Alfred L. Joseph, and Marco Thompson. 2012. "Stressors and Coping Strategies Used by Single Mothers Living in Poverty." *Affilia* 27(2):190–204.

Brown, Marilyn, and Barbara Bloom. 2009. "Reentry and Renegotiating Motherhood: Maternal Identity and Success on Parole." *Crime and Delinquency* 55(2):313–36.

Brown, Matthew. 2021. "Kamala Harris Responds to Tim Scott Saying America Not Racist Country." *USA Today*, April 29.

Bureau of Justice Statistics. 2004. *Medical Services Received by Female Prison Inmates*. Washington, DC: U.S. Department of Justice.

Bursik, Robert J. 1988. "Social Disorganization and Theories of Crime and Delinquency: Problems and Prospects*." *Criminology* 26(4):519–52.

Cahn, Naomi. 1999. "Policing Women: Moral Arguments and the Dilemmas of Criminalization Symposium: Bridging Divides: A Challenge to Unify Anti-Subordination Theories." *DePaul Law Review* 49(3):817–30.

Cameron, Chis. 2021. "In a Speech to a New Hampshire G.O.P. Group, Pence Calls Systemic Racism a 'Left-Wing Myth.'" *New York Times*, June 4.

Cammett, Ann. 2016. "Welfare Queens Redux: Criminalizing Black Mothers in the Age of Neoliberalism Symposium on Reframing the Welfare Queen." *Southern California Interdisciplinary Law Journal* 25(2):363–94.

Caniglia, John. 2018. "Growing Up behind Bars: How States Handle Prison Nurseries." Cleveland.com, March 18, www.cleveland.com/metro/2018/03/growing_up_behind_bars_how_sta.html (retrieved November 23, 2020).

Cannata, Nicholas C. 2017. "Prison Population Trends." Massachusetts Department of Correction. Concord, MA: Research and Planning Division.

Carlson, Bonnie, and Michael Shafer. 2010. "Traumatic Histories and Stressful Life Events of Incarcerated Parents: Childhood and Adult Trauma Histories." *Prison Journal* 90(4):475–93.

Carlton, Bree, and Marie Segrave. 2016. "Rethinking Women's Post-Release Reintegration and 'Success.'" *Australian and New Zealand Journal of Criminology* 49(2):281–99.

Chuck, Elizabeth. 2018. "Prison Nurseries Give Incarcerated Mothers a Chance to Raise Their Babies—Behind Bars." NBC News, www.nbcnews.com/news/us-news/prison-nurseries-give-incarcerated-mothers-chance-raise-their-babies-behind-n894171 (retrieved November 23, 2020).

Clair, Matthew. 2021. "Criminalized Subjectivity: Du Boisian Sociology and Visions for Legal Change." *Du Bois Review Social Science Research on Race* 18 (2): 289–319.

Clifford, Stephanie, and Jessica Silver-Greenberg. 2017. "Foster Care as Punishment: The New Reality of 'Jane Crow.'" *New York Times,* July 21.

Clone, Stephanie, and Dana DeHart. 2014. "Social Support Networks of Incarcerated Women: Types of Support, Sources of Support, and Implications for Reentry." *Journal of Offender Rehabilitation* 53(7):503–21.

Cobbina, Jennifer E. 2010. "Reintegration Success and Failure: Factors Impacting Reintegration Among Incarcerated and Formerly Incarcerated Women." *Journal of Offender Rehabilitation* 49(3):210–32.

Cobbina, Jennifer E., and Kimberly A. Bender. 2012. "Predicting the Future: Incarcerated Women's Views of Reentry Success." *Journal of Offender Rehabilitation* 51(5):275–94.

Collins, Patricia Hil. 1994. "Shifting the Center: Race, Class, and Feminist Theorizing About Motherhood." In *Mothering: Ideology, Experience, and Agency,* edited by E. N. Glenn, G. Chang, and L. R. Forcey, pp. 45–66. New York: Routledge.

Collins, Sean. 2020. "Trump Did Make Small Gains with Black Voters: Here's Why." *Vox,* www.vox.com/2020/11/4/21537966/trump-black-voters-exit-polls (retrieved November 23, 2020).

Cone, James H. 2010. *A Black Theology of Liberation.* New York: Orbis Books.

Cooper-Sadlo, Shannon, et al. 2019. "Mothers Talk Back: Exploring the Experiences of Formerly Incarcerated Mothers." *Contemporary Family Therapy* 41(1):92–101.

Craig, Jessica M., et al. 2017. "Do Social Bonds Buffer the Impact of Adverse Childhood Experiences on Reoffending?" *Youth Violence and Juvenile Justice* 15(1):3–20.

Crewe, Ben. 2011. "Depth, Weight, Tightness: Revisiting the Pains of Imprisonment." *Punishment and Society* 13(5):509–29.

Crocker, Jennifer, and Brenda Major. 1989. "Social Stigma and Self-Esteem: The Self-Protective Properties of Stigma." *Psychological Review* 96(4):608–30.

Curtis, Anna. 2019. *Dangerous Masculinity: Fatherhood, Race, and Security Inside America's Prisons.* New Brunswick, NJ: Rutgers University Press.

Dallaire, Danielle H. 2007. "Incarcerated Mothers and Fathers: A Comparison of Risks for Children and Families." *Family Relations* 56(5):440–53.

Daniel, Roxanne. 2019. "Prisons Neglect Pregnant Women in Their Healthcare Policies." Prison Policy Initiative, www.prisonpolicy.org/blog/2019/12/05/pregnancy (retrieved November 20, 2020).

Danquah-Brobby, Elizabeth. 2016. "Prison for You, Profit for Me: Systemic Racism Effectively Bars Blacks from Participation in Newly-Legal Marijuana Industry Comments." *University of Baltimore Law Review* 46(3):523–46.

Davenport, Clare, Kevin Browne, and Robert Palmer. 1994. "Opinions on the Traumatizing Effects of Child Sexual Abuse: Evidence for Consensus." *Child Abuse and Neglect* 18(9):725–38.

Davis, Angela. 1998. "Race and Criminalization: Black Americans and the Punishment Industry." In *The House That Race Built,* edited by W. Lubiano, pp. 264–78. New York: Vintage Books.

———. 2011. *Are Prisons Obsolete?* New York: Seven Stories Press.

Day, Andrew, et al. 2018. "The Views of Women in Prison about Help-Seeking for Intimate Partner Violence: At the Intersection of Survivor and Offender." *Victims and Offenders* 13(7):974–94.

Department of Justice. 2019. "Department of Justice Announces the Release of 3,100 Inmates under First Step Act, Publishes Risk and Needs Assessment

System." U.S. Department of Justice, www.justice.gov/opa/pr/department-justice-announces-release-3100-inmates-under-first-step-act-publishes-risk-and (retrieved December 7, 2020).

DeVille, Kenneth A., and Loretta M. Kopelman. 1998. "Moral and Social Issues Regarding Pregnant Woment Who Use and Abuse Drugs." *Obstetrics and Gynecology Clinics of North America* 25(1):237–54.

Dodge, Mary, and Mark R. Pogrebin. 2001. "Collateral Costs of Imprisonment for Women: Complications of Reintegration." *Prison Journal* 81(1):42–54.

Douglas, Susan, and Meredith Michaels. 2005. *The Mommy Myth: The Idealization of Motherhood and How It Has Undermined All Women.* New York: Simon and Schuster.

Dow, Dawn. 2011. "Black Moms and 'White Motherhood Society': African-American Middle-Class Mothers' Perspectives on Work, Family and Identity." Institute for the Study of Social Change, Working Paper Series, 2010–11.54.

———. 2016. "Integrated Motherhood: Beyond Hegemonic Ideologies of Motherhood." *Journal of Marriage and Family* 78(1):180–96.

———. 2019. *Mothering While Black: Boundaries and Burdens of Middle-Class Parenthood.* Berkeley: University of California Press.

Dowden, Craig, and D. A. Andrews. 1999. "What Works for Female Offenders: A Meta-Analytic Review." *Crime and Delinquency* 45(4):438–52.

Du Bois, W. E. B. 1909. *The Souls of Black Folk: Essays and Sketches.* 8th ed. Chicago: A. C. McClurg.

———. 2016. *The Souls of Black Folk.* Minneapolis: Learner Publishing Group.

Earp, Brian D., et al. 2019. "Addiction, Identity, Morality." *AJOB Empirical Bioethics* 10(2):136–53.

Edin, Kathryn, and Maria Kefalas. 2005. *Promises I Can Keep.* Berkeley: University of California Press.

Edin, Kathryn, and Timothy J. Nelson. 2013. *Doing the Best I Can: Fatherhood in the Inner City.* Berkeley: University of California Press.

Edin, Kathryn, Timothy J. Nelson, and Rechelle Paranal. 2004. "Fatherhood and Incarceration As Potential Turning Points in the Criminal Careers of Unskilled Men." National Responsible Fatherhood Clearinghouse, www.fatherhood.gov/sites/default/files/resource_files/e000001251.pdf (retrieved December 6, 2020).

Edleson, Jeffrey L. 1999. "Problems Associated with Children's Witnessing of Domestic Violence." Center for Disease and Prevention. Atlanta: Applied Research Forum.

Elder, Glen H. 1985. *Life Course Dynamics: Trajectories and Transitions, 1968–1980.* Ithaca, NY: Cornell University Press.

———. 1994. "Time, Human Agency, and Social Change: Perspectives on the Life Course." *Social Psychology Quarterly* 57(1):4–15.

Eliason, Michele J., Janette Y. Taylor, and Stephan Arndt. 2005. "Assessing Intimate Partner Violence in Incarcerated Women." *Journal of Forensic Nursing* 1(3):106–10.

Elliott, Sinikka, Rachel Powell, and Joslyn Brenton. 2015. "Being a Good Mom: Low-Income, Black Single Mothers Negotiate Intensive Mothering." *Journal of Family Issues* 36(3):351–70.

Fader, Jamie J. 2013. *Falling Back: Incarceration and Transitions to Adulthood among Urban Youth*. New Brunswick, NJ: Rutgers University Press.

Fantuzzo, John W., and Wanda K. Mohr. 1999. "Prevalence and Effects of Child Exposure to Domestic Violence." *Future of Children* 9(3):21–32.

Farr, Brittany. 2016. "The Question That Silences Women: An Interview with Gina Clayton, Founder and Executive Director of the Essie Justice Group." *Souls* 18(2–4):459–62.

Feiring, Candice, and Charles Cleland. 2007. "Childhood Sexual Abuse and Abuse-Specific Attributions of Blame over Six Years Following Discovery." *Child Abuse and Neglect* 31(11–12):1169–86.

Filipas, Henrietta H., and Sarah E. Ullman. 2006. "Child Sexual Abuse, Coping Responses, Self-Blame, Posttraumatic Stress Disorder, and Adult Sexual Revictimization." *Journal of Interpersonal Violence* 652–72.

Flores, Jerry. 2016. *Caught Up: Girls, Surveillance, and Wraparound Incarceration*. Berkeley, CA: University of California Press.

Follette, Victoria M., et al. 1996. "Cumulative Trauma: The Impact of Child Sexual Abuse, Adult Sexual Assault, and Spouse Abuse." *Journal of Traumatic Stress* 9(1):25–35.

Foster, Holly. 2012. "The Strains of Maternal Imprisonment: Importation and Deprivation Stressors for Women and Children." *Journal of Criminal Justice* 40(3):221–29.

Foucault, Michel. 1977. *Discipline and Punish: The Birth of the Prison*. New York: Vintage Books.

Frank, Joseph W., et al. 2014. "Discrimination Based on Criminal Record and Healthcare Utilization among Men Recently Released from Prison: A Descriptive Study." *Health and Justice* 2(1):6.

Frederick, Marla. 2003. *Between Sundays: Black Women and Everyday Struggles of Faith*. Berkeley: University of California Press.

Fulcher, Patrice A. 2012. "Hustle and Flow: Prison Privatization Fueling the Prison Industrial Complex." *Washburn Law Journal* 51:589–617.

Gabbidon, Shaun L. 2001. "W. E. B. Du Bois: Pioneering American Criminologist." *Journal of Black Studies* 31(5):581–99.

———. 2016. *W. E. B. Du Bois on Crime and Justice: Laying the Foundations of Sociological Criminology*. New York: Routledge.

Garcia, Janet. 2016. "Understanding the Lives of Mothers after Incarceration: Moving Beyond Socially Constructed Definitions of Motherhood." *Sociology Compass* 10(1):3–11.

Gibson-Davis, Christina. 2014. "Magic Moment? Maternal Marriage for Children Born out of Wedlock." *Demography* 51(4):1345–56.

Gilkes, Cheryl Townsend. 1996. "The Margin as the Center of a Theory of History." In *W.E.B Du Bois on Race and Culture: Philosophy, Politics and Poetics*, edited by B. Bell, E. Grosholz, and J. Stewart, pp. 111–39. New York: Routledge.

Gilmore, Ruth Wilson. 2007. *Golden Gulag: Prisons, Surplus, Crisis, and Opposition in Globalizing California*. Berkeley: University of California Press.

———. 2017. "In the Shadow of the Shadow State." In *The Revolution Will Not Be Funded: Beyond the Non-Profit Industrial Complex*, edited by

INCITE! Women of Color Against Violence, pp. 41–52. Durham, NC: Duke University Press.

Giroux, Henry A. 2006. "Reading Hurricane Katrina: Race, Class, and the Biopolitics of Disposability." *College Literature* 33(3):171–96.

Goffman, Erving. 1963. *Stigma: Notes on the Management of Spoiled Identity*. New York: Simon and Schuster.

Goshin, Lorie S., Mary W. Byrne, and Barbara Blanchard-Lewis. 2014. "Preschool Outcomes of Children Who Lived as Infants in a Prison Nursery." *Prison Journal* 94(2):139–58.

Goshin, Lorie S., Mary W. Byrne, and Alana M. Henninger. 2014. "Recidivism after Release from a Prison Nursery Program." *Public Health Nursing* 31(2):109–17.

Grappo, Laura Ramos. 2020. "'Four Lives Lost': Criminalization and Innocence in the Case of the San Antonio Four." *Latino Studies* 18(1):3–26.

Greenfield, Lawrence, and Tracy Snell. 1999. *Women Offenders*. Washington, DC: U.S.: Bureau of Justice Statistics.

Gregor, Alison. 2014. "Bragging Rights for St. Albans, Queens." *New York Times,* March 4.

Groves, Betsy McAlister. 1997. "Growing Up in a Violent World: The Impact of Family and Community Violence on Young Children and Their Families." *Topics in Early Childhood Special Education* 17(1):74–102.

Gurusami, Susila. 2017. "Working for Redemption: Formerly Incarcerated Black Women and Punishment in the Labor Market." *Gender and Society* 31(4):433–56.

———. 2019. "Motherwork under the State: The Maternal Labor of Formerly Incarcerated Black Women." *Social Problems* 66(1):128–43.

Hamilton, Vivian. 2004. "Mistaking Marriage for Social Policy." *Virginia Journal of Social Policy and the Law* 11(3):307–71.

Haney, Lynne Allison. 2010. *Offending Women: Power, Punishment, and the Regulation of Desire*. Berkeley: University of California Press.

Hanlon, Thomas E., Steven B. Carswell, and Marc Rose. 2007. "Research on the Caretaking of Children of Incarcerated Parents: Findings and Their Service Delivery Implications." *Children and Youth Services Review* 29(3): 384–62.

Hayes, Sharon, and Samantha Jeffries. 2016. "Romantic Terrorism? An Auto-Ethnographic Analysis of Gendered Psychological and Emotional Tactics in Domestic Violence." *Journal of Research in Gender Studies* 6(2):38–61.

Heidemann, Gretchen, Julie A. Cederbaum, and Sidney Martinez. 2016. "Beyond Recidivism: How Formerly Incarcerated Women Define Success." *Affilia* 31(1):24–40.

Herring, Tiana. 2020. "Since You Asked: What Role Does Drug Enforcement Play in the Rising Incarceration of Women?" *Prison Policy Initiative,* www.prisonpolicy.org/blog/2020/11/10/women-drug-enforcement (retrieved January 3, 2022).

Hess, Jennifer A., and Justin D. Rueb. 2005. "Attitudes toward Abortion, Religion, and Party Affiliation among College Students." *Current Psychology* 24(1):24–42.

Hill, Evan, et al. 2020. "How George Floyd Was Killed in Police Custody." *New York Times,* June 1.

Hirschi, Travis. 1969. *Causes of Delinquency.* Berkeley: University of California Press.

Hirschi, Travis, and Michael Gottfredson. 1983. "Age and the Explanation of Crime." *American Journal of Sociology* 89(3):552–84.

Hobson, Jeremy, and Cassady Rosenblum. 2019."Released from Prison under the First Step Act, Tanesha Bannister Celebrates 1st Christmas with Family in 16 Years." WBUR, www.wbur.org/hereandnow/2019/12/25/first-step-act-inmates-tanesha-bannister (retrieved May 22, 2020).

Hoffmann, John P., and Mikaela J. Dufur. 2018. "Family Social Capital, Family Social Bonds, and Juvenile Delinquency." *American Behavioral Scientist* 62(11):1525–44.

Hong, Stephanie. 2017. "Say Her Name: The Black Woman and Incarceration Notes." *Georgetown Journal of Gender and the Law* 19(3):619–42.

hooks, bell. 1984. *Feminist Theory: From Margin to Center.* London: Pluto Press.

———. 1990. "Marginality as Site of Resistance." In *Out There: Marginalization and Contemporary Cultures,* edited by R. Ferguson, M. Gever, T.T. Minh-ha and C. West, pp. 341–43. Cambridge, MA: MIT Press.

Horwitz, Allan V., et al. 2001. "The Impact of Childhood Abuse and Neglect on Adult Mental Health: A Prospective Study." *Journal of Health and Social Behavior* 42(2):184–201.

Husak, Douglas N. 2004. "The Moral Relevance of Addiction." *Substance Use and Misuse* 39(3):399–436.

James, Joy. 2019. "The Architects of Abolitionism." YouTube, www.youtube.com/watch?v=z9rvRsWKDxo&t=1694s (retrieved August 16, 2021).

James, Lois, David Brody, and Zachary Hamilton. 2013. "Risk Factors for Domestic Violence during Pregnancy: A Meta-Analytic Review." *Violence and Victims* 28(3):359–80.

James, Nathan. 2019. *The First Step Act of 2018: An Overview.* Washington, DC: U.S. Congressional Research Service.

Jarrett, Robin L. 1996. "Welfare Stigma among Low-Income, African-American Single Mothers." *Family Relations* 45(4):368–74.

Jipguep, Marie-Claude, and Kathy Sanders-Phillips. 2003. "The Context of Violence for Children of Color: Violence in the Community and in the Media." *Journal of Negro Education* 72(4):379–95.

Johnson, Elle, et al. 2019. "Protests Erupt as Trump Visits Benedict College." *Carolina News and Reporter,* October 25.

Jones, Nikki. 2009. *Between Good and Ghetto: African American Girls and Inner-City Violence.* New Brunswick, NJ: Rutgers University Press.

Kaba, Mariame. 2021. *We Do This 'Til We Free Us: Abolitionist Organizing and Transforming Justice.* Chicago: Haymarket Books.

Kajstura, Alexs. 2019. "Women's Mass Incarceration: The Whole Pie 2019." Prison Policy Initiative, www.prisonpolicy.org/reports/pie2019women.html (retrieved November 20, 2020).

Keene, Danya E., Amy B. Smoyer, and Kim M. Blankenship. 2018. "Stigma, Housing, and Identity after Prison." *Sociological Review* 66(4):799–815.

Keller, Bill. 2019. "What Do Abolitionists Really Want?" Marshall Project, www.themarshallproject.org/2019/06/13/what-do-abolitionists-really-want (retrieved November 23, 2020).

Kessler, Glenn. 2019. "Biden's Statement That the First Step Act Was an Add-on to a Bill Passed under Obama." *Washington Post,* July 30.

Kight, Stef W. 2021. "The Obstacles to a Second Chance." *Axios,* May 22, www.axios.com/hard-truths-deep-dive-criminal-justice-reentry-recidivism-5b5f4374-964c-48df-96fb-810c47f6f399.html (retrieved June 3, 2021).

Kruttschnitt, Candace, Rosemary Gartner, and Amy Miller. 2000. "Doing Her Own Time? Women's Responses to Prison in the Context of the Old and the New Penology*." *Criminology* 38(3):681–718.

Laub, John H., and Robert J. Sampson. 1993. "Turning Points in the Life Course: Why Change Matters to the Study of Crime*." *Criminology* 31(3):301–25.

Laub, John H., Daniel S. Nagin, and Robert J. Sampson. 1998. "Trajectories of Change in Criminal Offending: Good Marriages and the Desistance Process." *American Sociological Review* 63(2):225–38.

Laughlin, Jade S., et al. 2008. "Incarcerated Mothers and Child Visitation: A Law, Social Science, and Policy Perspective." *Criminal Justice Policy Review* 19(2):215–38.

Lenhardt, Robin. A. 2016. "Black Citizenship through Marriage: Reflections on the Moynihan Report at Fifty Symposium on Reframing the Welfare Queen." *Southern California Interdisciplinary Law Journal* 25(2): 347–62.

Leverentz, Andrea M. 2006. "The Love of a Good Man? Romantic Relationships as a Source of Support or Hindrance for Female Ex-Offenders." *Journal of Research in Crime and Delinquency* 43(4):459–88.

———. 2011. "Being a Good Daughter and Sister: Families of Origin in the Reentry of African American Female Ex-Prisoners." *Feminist Criminology* 6(4):239–67.

———. 2014. *The Ex-Prisoner's Dilemma: How Women Negotiate Competing Narratives of Reentry and Desistance.* New Brunswick, NJ: Rutgers University Press.

Logan, Enid. 1999. "The Wrong Race, Committing Crime, Doing Drugs, and Maladjusted for Motherhood: The Nation's Fury over 'Crack Babies.'" *Social Justice* 26(1):115–38.

Longshore, Douglas, Eunice Chang, and Nena Messina. 2005. "Self-Control and Social Bonds: A Combined Control Perspective on Juvenile Offending." *Journal of Quantitative Criminology* 21(4):419–37.

Luster, Tom, and Stephen A. Small. 1997. "Sexual Abuse History and Problems in Adolescence: Exploring the Effects of Moderating Variables." *Journal of Marriage and Family* 59(1):131–42.

Luther, Kate. 2016. "Stigma Management among Children of Incarcerated Parents." *Deviant Behavior* 37(11):1264–75.

Maeve, M. Katherine. 1999. "Adjudicated Health: Incarcerated Women and the Social Construction of Health | SpringerLink." *Crime, Law, and Social Change* 31:49–71.

Mangual, Rafael. 2019. "Mass Decarceration Will Increase Violent Crime." Manhattan Institute, www.manhattan-institute.org/issues2020-mass-decarceration-will-increase-violent-crime (retrieved May 22, 2020).

Maruna, Shadd. 2000. *Making Good: How Ex-Convicts Reform and Rebuild Their Lives*. Washington, DC: American Psychological Association.

Maruna, Shadd, and Derek Ramsden. 2004. "Living to Tell the Tale: Redemption Narratives, Shame Management, and Offender Rehabilitation." In *Healing Plots: The Narrative Basis of Psychotherapy, the Narrative Study of Lives*, edited by A. Lieblick, D.P. McAdams and R. Josselson, pp. 129–49. Washington, DC: American Psychological Association.

May, Vanessa. 2008. "On Being a 'Good' Mother: The Moral Presentation of Self in Written Life Stories." *Sociology* 42(3):470–86.

McBride, Keally. 2010. "Incarceration and Imprisonment." *Law, Culture, and the Humanities* 6(3):341–53.

McCorkel, Jill A. 2013. *Breaking Women: Gender, Race, and the New Politics of Imprisonment*. New York: New York University Press.

McDaniels-Wilson, Cathy, and Joanne Belknap. 2008. "The Extensive Sexual Violation and Sexual Abuse Histories of Incarcerated Women." *Violence against Women* 14(10):1090–1127.

McDonald, Sarah, et al. 2011. "Post-Traumatic Stress Symptoms, Parenting Stress, and Mother-Child Relationships following Childbirth and at 2 Years Postpartum." *Journal of Psychosomatic Obstetrics and Gynecology* 32(3):141–46.

McDonald, Soraya. 2021. "The Dangerous Magical Thinking of 'This Is Not Who We Are.'" *The Undefeated*, January 14, https://theundefeated.com/features/capitol-attack-trump-the-dangerous-magical-thinking-of-this-is-not-who-we-are (retrieved June 7, 2021).

McLanahan, Sara. 2009. "Fragile Families and the Reproduction of Poverty:" *Annals of the American Academy of Political and Social Science* 621(1): 111–31.

McLaughlin, Katie A., et al. 2016. "Maltreatment Exposure, Brain Structure, and Fear Conditioning in Children and Adolescents." *Neuropsychopharmacology* 41(8):1956–64.

McLean, Kate C., and Michael W. Pratt. 2006. "Life's Little (and Big) Lessons: Identity Statuses and Meaning-Making in the Turning Point Narratives of Emerging Adults." *Developmental Psychology* 42(4):714–22.

McLemore, Monica R., and Zakeya Warner Hand. 2017. "Making the Case for Innovative Reentry Employment Programs: Previously Incarcerated Women as Birth Doulas; A Case Study." *International Journal of Prisoner Health* 13(3–4):219–27.

McMurtry, Steven L., and Gwat-Yong Lie. 1992. "Differential Exit Rates of Minority Children in Foster Care." *Social Work Research and Abstracts* 28(1):42–48.

Michalsen, Venezia. 2011. "Mothering as a Life Course Transition: Do Women Go Straight for Their Children?" *Journal of Offender Rehabilitation* 50(6):349–66.

———. 2019. "A Cell of One's Own? Incarceration and Other Turning Points in Women's Journeys to Desistance." *International Journal of Offender Therapy and Comparative Criminology* 63(6):940–59.

Miller, Keva M. 2006. "The Impact of Parental Incarceration on Children: An Emerging Need for Effective Interventions." *Child and Adolescent Social Work Journal* 23(4):472–86.

Miller, Reuben Jonathan. 2021. *Halfway Home: Race, Punishment, and the Afterlife of Mass Incarceration.* New York: Little, Brown.

Monk, Ellis P. 2015. "The Cost of Color: Skin Color, Discrimination, and Health among African-Americans." *American Journal of Sociology* 121(2):396–444.

———. 2019. "The Color of Punishment: African Americans, Skin Tone, and the Criminal Justice System." *Ethnic and Racial Studies* 42(10):1593–1612.

Morash, Merry, et al. 2015. "The Effects of Probation or Parole Agent Relationship Style and Women Offenders' Criminogenic Needs on Offenders' Responses to Supervision Interactions." *Criminal Justice and Behavior* 42(4):412–34.

Morris, Aldon. 2015. *The Scholar Denied: W. E. B. Du Bois and the Birth of Modern Sociology.* Berkeley: University of California Press.

Motsinger, Carol. 2020. "President Trump Addresses Political Allies as Benedict Students Are Asked to Stay in Dorms." *Greenville News*, October 25, www .greenvilleonline.com/story/news/2019/10/25/president-donald-trump-visit-benedict-college-columbia-sc-hbcu-live-coverage/4083382002 (retrieved May 22, 2020).

Myers, Barbara J., et al. 1999. "Children of Incarcerated Mothers." *Journal of Child and Family Studies* 8(1):11–25.

Nadal, Kevin L., et al. 2015. "Lesbian, Gay, Bisexual, and Queer People's Perceptions of the Criminal Justice System: Implications for Social Services." *Journal of Gay and Lesbian Social Services* 27(4):457–81.

National Council for Incarcerated Women and Girls. 2021. "Calls on Administration to Grant Clemency to 100 Women in First 100 Days." National Council, www.nationalcouncil.us/100days (retrieved August 16, 2021).

Neil, Sampson, and Robert Sampson. 2021. "The Birth Lottery of History: Arrest over the Life Course of Multiple Cohorts Coming of Age, 1995–2018." *American Journal of Sociology* 126(5):1127–78.

Nesmith, Ande, and Ebony Ruhland. 2008. "Children of Incarcerated Parents: Challenges and Resiliency in Their Own Words." *Children and Youth Services Review* 30(10):1119–30.

Netherland, Julie, and Helena B. Hansen. 2016. "The War on Drugs That Wasn't: Wasted Whiteness, 'Dirty Doctors,' and Race in Media Coverage of Prescription Opioid Misuse." *Culture, Medicine, and Psychiatry* 40(4):664–86.

New International Bible. 2011. Bible Gateway, www.biblegateway.com/passage /?search=Ruth%201&version=NIV (retrieved December 7, 2021).

News 19 WLTX. 2019. "President Trump Speaks in Columbia, South Carolina: Full Speech." YouTube, www.youtube.com/watch?v=rarMdpo2rTo&t=1s (retrieved December 28, 2020).

Nissley, Nick, and Rosemary Hartigan. 2001. "When Golden Handcuffs Become More Than a Retention Strategy." *Advances in Developing Human Resources* 3(1):96–99.

Noe-Bustamante, Luis, Lauren Mora, and Mark Lopez. 2020. "About One-in-Four U.S. Hispanics Have Heard of Latinx, but Just 3% Use It." Pew Research Center, www.pewresearch.org/hispanic/2020/08/11/about-one-in-four-u-s-hispanics-have-heard-of-latinx-but-just-3-use-it (retrieved August 18, 2021).

Noonan, Theresa. 2011. *Addisleigh Park Historic District Designation Report*. New York: City Landmarks Preservation Commission.

Novelly, Thomas. 2021. "SC's Sen. Tim Scott Says America 'Not a Racist Country' in President Biden GOP Rebuttal." *Post and Courier*, April 28.

O'Brien, Patricia. 2001. "'Just Like Baking a Cake': Women Describe the Necessary Ingredients for Successful Reentry after Incarceration." *Families in Society* 82(3):287–95.

O'Brien, Patricia, and Diane S. Young. 2006. "Challenges for Formerly Incarcerated Women: A Holistic Approach to Assessment." *Families in Society* 87(3):359–66.

Ocen, Priscilla A. 2012. "Punishing Pregnancy: Race, Incarceration, and the Shackling of Pregnant Prisoners." *California Law Review* 100(5):1239–1311.

Oliver, William, and Creasie Finney Hairston. 2008. "Intimate Partner Violence during the Transition from Prison to the Community: Perspectives of Incarcerated African American Men." *Journal of Aggression, Maltreatment, and Trauma* 16(3):258–76.

Opsal, Tara D. 2011. "Women Disrupting a Marginalized Identity: Subverting the Parolee Identity through Narrative." *Journal of Contemporary Ethnography* 40(2):135–67.

———. 2012. "'Livin' on the Straights': Identity, Desistance, and Work among Women Post-Incarceration." *Sociological Inquiry* 82(3):378–403.

Ortiz, Ana Teresa, and Laura Briggs. 2003. "The Culture of Poverty, Crack Babies, and Welfare Cheats: The Making of the 'Healthy White Baby Crisis.'" *Social Text* 21(3):39–57.

Ortiz, Natalie Rose. 2014. "Race/Ethnicity and Incarceration on Women's Entry-Level Job Prospects." PhD diss., Department of Criminology and Criminal Justice, Arizona State University.

Pager, Devah. 2003. "The Mark of a Criminal Record." *American Journal of Sociology* 108(5):937–75.

———. 2007. "The Use of Field Experiments for Studies of Employment Discrimination: Contributions, Critiques, and Directions for the Future." *Annals of the American Academy of Political and Social Science*. 609(1):104–33.

Pager, Devah, and Lincoln Quillian. 2005. "Walking the Talk? What Employers Say Versus What They Do." *American Sociological Review* 70(3):355–80.

Patel, Milapkumar, et al. 2012. "Postpartum Depression: A Review." *Journal of Health Care for the Poor and Underserved* 23(2):534–42.

Pauley, Matthew A. 2005. "The Pinkerton Doctrine and Murder." *Pierce Law Review* 4(1):1–43.

Paynter, Martha Jane, et al. 2019. "Maternal Health Outcomes for Incarcerated Women: A Scoping Review." *Journal of Clinical Nursing* 28(11–12): 2046–60.

Pettit, Becky, and Bruce Western. 2004. "Mass Imprisonment and the Life Course: Race and Class Inequality in U.S. Incarceration." *American Sociological Review* 69(2):151–69.

Pew Research Center for Social and Demographic Trends. 2007. "Motherhood Today: Tougher Challenges, Less Success." Pew Research Center, May 2, www.pewsocialtrends.org/2007/05/02/motherhood-today-tougher-challenges-less-success (retrieved September 4, 2020).

Pfaff, John. 2017. *Locked In: The True Causes of Mass Incarceration, and How to Achieve Real Reform*. New York: Basic Books.

Phillips, Susan D., and Trevor Gates. 2011. "A Conceptual Framework for Understanding the Stigmatization of Children of Incarcerated Parents." *Journal of Child and Family Studies* 20(3):286–94.

Pink, Sarah, and Jennie Morgan. 2013. "Short-Term Ethnography: Intense Routes to Knowing." *Symbolic Interaction* 36(3):351–61.

Potter, Hillary. 2006. "An Argument for Black Feminist Criminology: Understanding African American Women's Experiences With Intimate Partner Abuse Using an Integrated Approach." *Feminist Criminology* 1(2): 106–24.

———. 2013. "Intersectional Criminology: Interrogating Identity and Power in Criminological Research and Theory." *Critical Criminology* 21(3):305–18.

Rabaka, Reiland. 2010. *Against Epistemic Apartheid: W.E.B. Du Bois and the Disciplinary Decadence of Sociology*. Lanham, MD: Lexington Books.

Rabuy, Bernadette, and Daniel Kopf. 2015. "Prisons of Poverty: Uncovering the Pre-Incarceration Incomes of the Imprisoned." Prison Policy Initiative, www.prisonpolicy.org/reports/income.html (retrieved November 20, 2020).

Redmond, Nicole, et al. 2020. "Perceived Discrimination Based on Criminal Record in Healthcare Settings and Self-Reported Health Status among Formerly Incarcerated Individuals." *Journal of Urban Health* 97(1):105–11.

Renkl, Margaret. 2021. "Lies, Damn Lies, and Georgia." *New York Times*, January 11.

Rettinger, L. Jill, and D.A. Andrews. 2010. "General Risk and Need, Gender Specificity, and the Recidivism of Female Offenders." *Criminal Justice and Behavior* 37(1):29–46.

Richie, Beth E. 2001. "Challenges Incarcerated Women Face as They Return to Their Communities: Findings from Life History Interviews." *Crime and Delinquency* 47(3):368–89.

Richie, Beth E., and C. Johnsen. 1996. "Abuse Histories among Newly Incarcerated Women in a New York City Jail." *Journal of the American Medical Women's Association* (1972) 51(3):111–14, 117.

Rios, Victor M., Nikita Carney, and Jasmine Kelekay. 2017. "Ethnographies of Race, Crime, and Justice: Toward a Sociological Double-Consciousness." *Annual Review of Sociology* 43(1):493–513.

Roberts, Dorothy E. 1993. "Motherhood and Crime." *Iowa Law Review* 79(1):95–142.

———. 1999. "Welfare's Ban on Poor Motherhood." In *Whose Welfare?* edited by Gwendolyn Mink, 152–70. Ithaca, NY: Cornell University Press.

Roberts, Sam. 2016. "Robert Cox, Man behind the 'Just Say No' Antidrug Campaign, Dies at 78." *New York Times*, June 23.

Romans, S. E., et al. 1995. "Factors That Mediate between Child Sexual Abuse and Adult Psychological Outcome." *Psychological Medicine* 25(1):127–42.

Roosa, Mark W., et al. 2005. "Family and Child Characteristics Linking Neighborhood Context and Child Externalizing Behavior." *Journal of Marriage and Family* 67(2):515–29.

Ross, Michael, and Roger Buehler. 2001. "Identity through Time." *Blackwell Handbook of Social Psychology: Intraindividual Processes*: 518–44.

Rossi, Peter H., et al. 1974. "The Seriousness of Crimes: Normative Structure and Individual Differences." *American Sociological Review* 39(2):224–37.

Sachdeva, Sonya, Rumen Iliev, and Douglas L. Medin. 2009. "Sinning Saints and Saintly Sinners: The Paradox of Moral Self-Regulation." *Psychological Science* 20(4):523–28.

Sallmann, Jolanda. 2010. "Living with Stigma: Women's Experiences of Prostitution and Substance Use." *Affilia* 25(2):146–59.

Sampson, Robert J., and John H. Laub. 2003. "Life-Course Desisters? Trajectories of Crime among Delinquent Boys Followed to Age 70." *Criminology* 41(3):555–92.

Sawyer, Wendy. 2018. "The Gender Divide: Tracking Women's State Prison Growth." Prison Policy Initiative, www.prisonpolicy.org/reports/women_overtime.html (retrieved November 20, 2020).

———. 2019. "Who's Helping the 1.9 Million Women Released from Prisons and Jails Each Year?" Prison Policy Institute, July 19, www.prisonpolicy.org/blog/2019/07/19/reentry (retrieved November 20, 2020).

Sawyer, Wendy, and Wanda Bertram. 2018. "Jail Will Separate 2.3 Million Mothers from Their Children This Year." Prison Policy Initiative, www.prisonpolicy.org/blog/2018/05/13/mothers-day-2018 (retrieved June 8, 2021).

Schlosser, Eric. 1998. "The Prison-Industrial Complex." *Atlantic Monthly*, 51–77.

Sered, Susan Starr, and Maureen Norton-Hawk. 2014. *Can't Catch a Break: Gender, Jail, Drugs, and the Limits of Personal Responsibility*. Berkeley: University of California Press.

Sharp, Susan F., and Susan T. Marcus-Mendoza. 2001. "It's a Family Affair: Incarcerated Women and Their Families." *Women and Criminal Justice* 12(4):21–49.

Shedd, Carla. 2011. "Countering the Carceral Continuum: The Legal of Mass Incarceration Special Issue on Mass Incarceration: Mass Imprisonment and Childhood Behavior Problems: Policy Essay." *Criminology and Public Policy* 10(3):865–72.

———. 2015. *Unequal City: Race, Schools, and Perceptions of Injustice*. New York: Russell Sage Foundation.

Sherman, Rachel. 2005. "Producing the Superior Self: Strategic Comparison and Symbolic Boundaries among Luxury Hotel Workers." *Ethnography* 6(2):131–58.

Shih, Margaret. 2004. "Positive Stigma: Examining Resilience and Empowerment in Overcoming Stigma." *Annals of the American Academy of Political and Social Science* 591(1):175–85.

Shihipar, Abdullah. 2019. "The Opioid Crisis Isn't White." *New York Times,* February 26.

Simpson, Celena. 2015. "Du Bois's Dubious Feminism: Evaluating through the Black Flame Trilogy." *Pluralist* 10(1):48–63.

Staley, Michele. 2008. *Female Offenders 2005–2006.* Division of Planning, Research and Evaluation. Albany: New York Department of Corrections.

Stitt, B. Grant. 1988. "Victimless Crime: A Definitional Issue." *Journal of Crime and Justice* 11(2):87–102.

Stone, Robin. 2007. *No Secrets No Lies: How Black Families Can Heal from Sexual Abuse.* New York: Harmony.

Stringer, Ebonie Cunningham. 2009. "'Keeping the Faith': How Incarcerated African American Mothers Use Religion and Spirituality to Cope with Imprisonment." *Journal of African American Studies* 13(3):325–47.

———. 2020. "Managing Motherhood: How Incarcerated Mothers Negotiate Maternal Role-Identities with Their Children's Caregivers." *Women and Criminal Justice* 30(5):336–55.

Stylianou, Stelios. 2003. "Measuring Crime Seriousness Perceptions: What Have We Learned and What Else Do We Want to Know." *Journal of Criminal Justice* 31(1):37–56.

Sufrin, Carolyn. 2017. *Jailcare: Finding the Safety Net for Women behind Bars.* Berkeley: University of California Press.

Sykes, Gresham M. 2007. *The Society of Captives: A Study of a Maximum Security Prison.* Princeton, NJ: Princeton University Press.

Sykes, Jennifer. 2011. "Negotiating Stigma: Understanding Mothers' Responses to Accusations of Child Neglect." *Children and Youth Services Review* 33(3):448–56.

Thompson, Beverly Yuen. 2017. "'Good Moral Characters': How Drug Felons Are Impacted under State Marijuana Legalization Laws." *Contemporary Justice Review* 20(2):211–26.

Tomei, Megan. 2010. "She Just Snapped: Reality Television, Murder, and the Myth of Feminine Evil." Master's thesis, Department of Communication and Multimedia Studies, Florida Atlantic University.

Toscano, Vicki. 2005. "Misguided Retribution: Criminalization of Pregnant Women Who Take Drugs." *Social and Legal Studies* 14(3):359–86.

Trautner, Mary Nell, and Jessica L. Collett. 2010. "Students Who Strip: The Benefits of Alternate Identities for Managing Stigma." *Symbolic Interaction* 33(2):257–79.

Travis, Jeremy. 2005. *But They All Come Back: Facing the Challenges of Prisoner Reentry.* Washington, DC: Urban Institute.

Truth, Sojourner. 2020. *Ain't I A Woman?* London: Penguin Books.

Tucker, Katheryn. 2021. "Lawyer Speaks Up for 100 Forgotten Women in Biden's First 100 Days." Law.com, www.law.com/2021/04/26/lawyer-speaks-up-for-100-forgotten-women-in-bidens-first-100-days (retreived August 16, 2021).

Uggen, Christopher. 2000. "Work as a Turning Point in the Life Course of Criminals: A Duration Model of Age, Employment, and Recidivism." *American Sociological Review* 65(4):529–46.

Uggen, Christopher, and Candace Kruttschnitt. 1998. "Crime in the Breaking: Gender Differences in Desistance." *Law and Society Review* 32(2):339–66.

Underwood, Lauren. 2020. "H.R.6142—116th Congress (2019–2020): Black Maternal Health Momnibus Act of 2020." U.S. Congress, www.congress .gov/bill/116th-congress/house-bill/6142 (retrieved November 20, 2020).

U.S. Department of Health and Human Services. 2009. *Results from the 2008 National Survey on Drug Use and Health: National Findings.* (HHS Publication No. SMA 09–4434). Rockville, MD: Department of Health and Human Services.

Van Brown, Bethany L. 2019. "Battered Woman Syndrome Defense." In *The Encyclopedia of Women and Crime*, edited by F. Bernat et al., pp. 1–2. Hoboken, NJ: John Wiley.

van Olphen, Juliana, et al. 2009. "Nowhere to Go: How Stigma Limits the Options of Female Drug Users after Release from Jail." *Substance Abuse Treatment, Prevention, and Policy* 4(1):10.

Vitale, Alex S. 2017. *The End of Policing.* Brooklyn, NY: Verso Books.

Walsh, Kevin. 2013. "Mural Recalls Jazz Greats Living in Queens." *Brownstoner*, www.brownstoner.com/history/mural-recalls-jazz-greats-living-in-queens (retrieved January 3, 2022).

Weare, Siobhan. 2013. "'The Mad,' 'The Bad,' 'The Victim': Gendered Constructions of Women Who Kill within the Criminal Justice System." *Laws* 2(3):337–61.

Werth, Robert. 2013. "The Construction and Stewardship of Responsible Yet Precarious Subjects: Punitive Ideology, Rehabilitation, and 'Tough Love' among Parole Personnel." *Punishment and Society* 15(3):219–46.

Western, Bruce. 2006. *Punishment and Inequality in America.* New York: Russell Sage Foundation.

The White House. 2021. "Inaugural Address by President Joseph R. Biden, Jr." White House website, www.whitehouse.gov/briefing-room/speeches-remarks /2021/01/20/inaugural-address-by-president-joseph-r-biden-jr (retrieved January 11, 2022).

Wilcox, Clyde. 1990. "Race Differences in Abortion Attitudes: Some Additional Evidence." *Public Opinion Quarterly* 54(2):248–55.

Williams, Jason M., Zoe Spencer, and Sean K. Wilson. 2021. "I Am Not Your Felon: Decoding the Trauma, Resilience, and Recovering Mothering of Formerly Incarcerated Black Women." *Crime and Delinquency* 67(8):1103–36.

Wright, Emily M., et al. 2012. "Gender-Responsive Lessons Learned and Policy Implications for Women in Prison: A Review." *Criminal Justice and Behavior* 39(12):1612–32.

Wyse, Jessica J. B., David J. Harding, and Jeffrey D. Morenoff. 2014. "Romantic Relationships and Criminal Desistance: Pathways and Processes." *Sociological Forum* 29(2):365–85.

Yankah, Ekow. 2016. "There Was No Wave of Compassion When Addicts Were Hooked on Crack." PBS NewsHour, www.pbs.org/newshour/show

/there-was-no-wave-of-compassion-when-addicts-were-hooked-on-crack (retrieved July 30, 2020).

Zoutewelle-Terovan, et al. 2014. "Criminality and Family Formation: Effects of Marriage and Parenthood on Criminal Behavior for Men and Women." *Crime and Delinquency* 60(8):1209–34.

Index

79t; religious framing and, 132–33; strategic comparisons, 101. *See also* marginalization

strategic comparisons, 101–3

Stringer, Ebonie Cunningham, 133

substance use, alcohol, 39, 59–61. *See also* drug addiction

Summer, 40, 109

systemic inequities: contributing to marginalization, 28, 36, 65–67, 140–43; personal responsibility vs., 36, 65–67, 88, 140–43; race and criminalization, 5, 112–14, 170n36; rehabilitative paradox, 18–19, 119–22, 138; systemic moral legitimacy, critiquing, 82–87, 89, 149–50; transformative justice and, 146; the "unasked question," 140–41. *See also* marginalization; personal responsibility; rehabilitation; stigma

Tammy, 107

Tanya, 74–75

transformative justice, 143–47

transitional organizations. *See* Helping Hands, Inc.; Mother's Love; Restoration House

trauma: exacerbated by pregnancy, 44, 64; perpetuated within prison system, 31,

146; resource accessibility, 37–38. *See also* childhood trauma; intimate-partner relationships

Trina, 40, 135

Trisha: access to therapeutic resources, 37–38; criminal involvement, 82–85, 150; experience with Mother's Love, 123–24, 125; preincarceration experiences, 32–36

Trump, Donald, 1

Truth, Sojourner, 112

Tubman, Harriet, 95, 96

turning points, 8, 58–59

"unasked question," the, 140–41

Unequal City (Shedd), 142

Valerie, 54

Vickie, 102–3, 135–36

victimless crimes, 77–78, 165n15

violence: intimate-partner, 47–52, 59–61; witnessing of, 38–39. *See also* childhood trauma; trauma

War on Drugs campaign, 2, 4–5, 9, 150

womanhood, 91, 95–96, 112–14

work. *See* employment

wrongfulness vs. seriousness, 77–78

Founded in 1893,
UNIVERSITY OF CALIFORNIA PRESS
publishes bold, progressive books and journals
on topics in the arts, humanities, social sciences,
and natural sciences—with a focus on social
justice issues—that inspire thought and action
among readers worldwide.

The UC PRESS FOUNDATION
raises funds to uphold the press's vital role
as an independent, nonprofit publisher, and
receives philanthropic support from a wide
range of individuals and institutions—and from
committed readers like you. To learn more, visit
ucpress.edu/supportus.